Beauty, Brains, and Brawn
The Construction of Gender in Children's Literature

EDITED BY SUSAN LEHR

Heinemann
Portsmouth, NH

Heinemann

A division of Reed Elsevier Inc.
361 Hanover Street
Portsmouth, NH 03801-3912
www.heinemann.com

Offices and agents throughout the world

© 2001 by Heinemann

A special thanks to Kristin Lehr for her tireless transcribing.

The author and publisher wish to thank those who have generously given permission to reprint borrowed material:

"Author Profile: Virginia Hamilton" copyright © 2001 by Virginia Hamilton.

"Author Profile: Gary Paulsen" copyright © 2001 by Gary Paulsen. For permission to copy or reprint please contact Flannery Literary, 1140 Wickford Court, Naperville, IL 60563-3300.

"Author Profile: Andrea Pinkney" copyright © 2001 by Andrea Pinkney. For permission to copy or reprint please contact Sheldon Fogelman Agency, Inc., 10 East 40th Street, New York, NY 10016.

"Illustrator Profile: Paul Zelinsky" copyright © 2001 by Paul Zelinsky.

"Author Profile: Pat Mora" copyright © 2001 by Pat Mora.

Excerpts from "Expect the Best From a Girl" are used by permission of the Women's College Coalition. For additional information on the Women's College Coalition please visit www.academic.org.

Library of Congress Cataloging-in-Publication Data

Beauty, brains, and brawn : the construction of gender in children's literature / edited by Susan Lehr.
    p. cm.
  Includes bibliographical references.
  ISBN 0-325-00284-3
    1. Children's stories, American—History and criticism. 2. Gender identity in literature. 3. Literature and society—United States—History—20th century. 4. Sex role in literature. I. Lehr, Susan S.

PS374.C454 B43 2001
810.9'353—dc21
                                                  00-061413

Editor: Danny Miller
Production: Elizabeth Valway
Cover design: Jenny Jensen Greenleaf
Manufacturing: Louise Richardson

Printed in the United States of America on acid-free paper
05 04 03 02 01 RRD 1 2 3 4 5

For Hans
Thirty singular years

and

for Charlotte Huck
An extraordinary role model
for so many of us

Contents

Introduction

Charlotte Huck

When I was growing up my favorite stories were *Little Women* (Alcott 1868) and *The Secret Garden* (Burnett 1910), both stories that portrayed strong female characters. My twin sister's favorite book was *The Little Princess* (Burnett 1905), which I read once and never reread. I didn't like stories where the heroine was a victim even though it ended happily ever after. But sixty years ago few stories had heroines and fewer yet portrayed girls as spunky and determined as Jo in *Little Women* and Mary in *Secret Garden*. Most of the books showed helpless girls who were acted upon as was Sara Crewe, rather than girls who acted on their own initiative and resourcefulness as did Jo and Mary.

Today the raised consciousness level of the children's book world is reflected in the increasing number of books that present positive images of girls and women. We can proudly point to a passing parade of dynamic girl characters, particularly in picture books. Leading that parade would be *Eloise* (Thompson) first published in 1935 and recently reissued. Closely following *Eloise* would be Steig's *Brave Irene* (1986), followed by Kevin Henkes's flamboyant Lilly of *Julius, the Baby of the World* fame (1990), *Mirette on the High Wire* (McCully 1992), *Flossie and the Fox* (McKissack 1986), and *Miss Rumphius* (Cooney 1982). These are all female characters who exhibit spunk, resourcefulness, and self-esteem.

Strong heroines are also found in some chapter books, such as *Julie of the Wolves* (George 1972), *Anastasia Krupnik* (Lowry 1981), Dicey in *Homecoming* (1981) and *Dicey's Song* (1983) (both by Voigt) and Claudia in *From the Mixed-up Files of Mrs. Basil E. Frankweiler* (Konigsburg 1967).

It is important to have books about girls who do things, who make things happen. We have made progress in the past twenty years in producing such books, but there are not enough of them. Ernst (1995) analyzed the titles in children's books and found male names represented nearly twice as often as female names. We still have stories in which the stereotyping is as subtle as in Silverstein's (1964) *The Giving Tree*. Many adults consider this to be a model story of unselfish giving. But why did Silverstein refer to the tree as "She"? The tree gives the man everything he wants, including her life. In the end, the man uses her stump for a seat and "the tree was very happy." Reading that story from the point of view of a woman, it could easily have been titled "The Taking Man"!

Boys, too, are caught in this web of gender stereotyping. They can be and do anything except be a ballet dancer, an artist, or a homemaker. Yet most of us know men today who do all of the cooking in the household, home school their children, and change the diapers of their babies. And increasingly there are more single fathers. Our books need to reflect this changing culture.

Boys are denied another aspect of their development in most literature for children—namely, their feelings. Seldom do we have a story in which a male character exhibits tenderness or compassion. Or if they do, they must do it in secret as does Palmer in Spinelli's (1997) book *Wringer* when he hides his feeding of his pet pigeon from his bully friends. Certainly, he receives little or no support from his parents or the community that sponsors the annual pigeon shooting contest and expects the ten-year-old boys to wring the necks of those who do not die immediately.

Boys may show fear if they overcome it with bravery, but they seldom are allowed to cry or show love. Frequently, destroying that which a boy loves has been portrayed as a rite of passage to manhood. In Rawling's (1938) *The Yearling*, Jody is ordered to shoot his pet deer because it is ruining the family's crops. In Gipson's (1956) *Old Yeller*, after the boy shoots his possibly rabid dog, his father tells him to forget it and go on being a man. And the farmer's son in *A Day No Pigs Would Die* (Peck 1972) must kiss his father's bloody hands after he has butchered his pet pig. Phyllis Naylor's (1991) more recent story *Shiloh* counteracts these tales of cruelty as Marty works hard to rescue a mistreated dog from his abusive owner.

Teachers can limit or expand the possibilities for boys and girls to explore a whole range of experiences and feelings by the selection of books they choose to read aloud in class or provide for children to read. For many years the recommended practice in selecting a book to read to a group was to choose a book that was exciting, that would hold the interest of boys, because girls would listen to anything. Teachers need to be more aware of gender stereotyping, then, in the books they select to share with their students.

In an article on gender issues Mem Fox (1993) maintains:

> Everything we read, from sexist advertisements and women's magazines to romance novels and children's books, constructs us, makes us who we are, by presenting our image of ourselves as girls and women, as boys and men. We who write children's books, and we who teach through literature, need to be sure we are opening doors to full human potential, not closing them. (84)

How then do we choose the books that will help children reach their full potential? While we must be aware of gender bias in books, we still need to select well-written stories that meet literary criteria. We do not have to write social tracts, didactic tales, or "made to order" stories that are overburdened with their message. Children are quick to reject a preaching book, no matter how fine the theme.

It is also important to select books that are true to the nature of both genders. We can't simply substitute girl characters for adventuring boy characters, nor do we want to produce unisex characters. We still have to capture the essence of femininity and masculinity, or children will have a difficult time identifying with the character. Boys and girls are innately different. Boys are more action oriented and do demand more excitement than girls. Girls seem to be more in touch with their feminine side, openly showing their feelings, seeking love and belonging. I maintain that in Avi's (1990) story *The True Confessions of Charlotte Doyle*, Charlotte is really a boy masquerading as a girl. Nothing that she does, including climbing the ship's riggings or leaving the safety of her family for further adventures on the high seas, rings true to her Victorian upbringing or feminine characteristics. The fact that this is a favorite story of boys, not girls, gives further proof to such an exchange of roles. We need stories of adventuresome girls, but they should reveal some of the caring, responsible aspects that make them a girl in the first place. We do not want to substitute one stereotype for another.

Besides being true to the feminine aspect of the character, stories should be authentic to their culture and historical time period. Feminists applauded the publication of *William's Doll* by Charlotte Zolotow (1972). It contained the right message for developing loving, compassionate boys, but it was too far removed from the culture to receive much popularity. By way of contrast, Bernard Waber's (1972) *Ira Sleeps Over*, published in the same year as *William's Doll*, portrays two boys who want their teddy bears as comfort objects before they can go to sleep at night. The popularity of the book would suggest that teddy bears are more acceptable for boys in today's world than are baby dolls.

Writing fine historical fiction that is authentic to its time period and culture is particularly challenging. The novel *Caddie Woodlawn* (1935) by Carol Ryrie Brink has been criticized by some because in the end Caddie has to give up her free tomboy ways and become a lady. I maintain she had no other choice in the 1860s. I am certain she became a different kind of woman because of her time of running wild and free in the Wisconsin woods, but to be accepted in that society, she had to learn the ways of a lady. In writing fine historical fiction, it is essential to be true to historical facts and the mores of the culture.

Honoring authenticity in retelling folktales is even more complex than in writing historical fiction, for the folktale by its very nature is filled with stereotypes. We even have a different name for them—archetypes. We immediately recognize the roles of the evil stepmother, the beautiful princess, the wise woman, the fairy godmother. These are not well-rounded figures, but easily recognized symbols of good and evil that foretell the ways in which these characters will act. When we retell these tales and change these symbolic roles, we destroy the very nature of the folktale.

Three avenues of approach are open to those who would retell folktales that are more gender equitable. First, authors can search for those tales that do portray strong women and compassionate men. They do exist. In researching Cinderella tales, I found the story of *Princess Furball* (Huck 1989) who gets herself to the king's three balls without the help of a fairy godmother. Furball is a spunky character who uses her own ingenuity to win the heart of the king. *Tam Lin* retold by Jane Yolen (1990) is another tale of a strong girl who outwits the fairies in order to save her brother.

And Ed Young (1989) has retold a scary Red Riding Hood story from China titled *Lon Po Po*. In the tale Sheng, the eldest of three sisters, tricks the wolf and scares them all in an ingenious way.

Another approach is to create a modern story in fairy-tale style. This is difficult to do and still capture the sound of the oral telling of the old tales. Yet both Katherine Paterson's (1992) *The King's Equal* and Jane Yolen's (1974) *The Girl Who Cried Flowers* have been successful in providing intelligent heroines who make their own destinies.

Other authors have chosen to write what amounts to a spoof on an original tale, such as Jon Scieszka's (1989) *The True Story of the 3 Little Pigs by A. Wolf,* which shifts the story to the wolf's point of view. Babette Cole's (1987) *Prince Cinders* and Bernice Meyers's (1985) *Sidney Rella and the Glass Sneaker* present boy protagonists in the familiar pattern of the Cinderella story. By comparing these spoofs with the original tales, children can begin to see the implicit bias of the old tales.

Authors, then, must weave their way through the maze of preconceived notions of appropriate female behavior, historical limitations, and literary standards to create fine literature for the twenty-first century. It is not an easy task, for children are going to select role models from their families, friends, movies, TV, and books. The most we can do as teachers and authors is to provide alternative role models that will present well-rounded male and female characters.

How we do this in all genres for children's literature is the subject of these fine essays. Not all of these will be in agreement with what I have written in this introduction, nor will the authors necessarily agree among themselves. But all of them will attest to the significance of adopting more egalitarian gender attitudes and reveal the complexity of the task.

References

ERNST, S. B. 1995. *Gender Issues in Books for Children and Young Adults.* In *Battling Dragons: Issues and Controversy in Children's Literature,* ed. S. Lehr, 67–78. Portsmouth, NH: Heinemann.

FOX, M. 1993. "Men Who Weep, Boys Who Dance: The Gender Agenda Between the Lines in Children's Literature." *Language Arts* 70: 84–88.

Children's Literature

ALCOTT, L. M. [1868] 1968. *Little Women.* Illustrated by J. W. Smith. New York: Little, Brown.

AVI. 1990. *The True Confessions of Charlotte Doyle.* New York: Orchard.

BRINK, C. R. 1935. *Caddie Woodlawn.* New York: Macmillan.

BURNETT, F. H. [1905] 1995. *The Little Princess.* Illustrated by J. Henterly. New York: Grossett.

———. [1910] 1987. *The Secret Garden.* Illustrated by T. Tudor. New York: HarperCollins.

COLE, B. 1987. *Prince Cinders.* New York: Penguin Putnam.

COONEY, B. 1982. *Miss Rumphius*. New York: Viking.

GEORGE, J. C. 1972. *Julie of the Wolves*. Illustrated by J. Schoenherr. New York: HarperCollins.

GIPSON, F. 1956. *Old Yeller*. Illustrated by C. Burger. New York: HarperCollins.

HENKES, K. 1990. *Julius, the Baby of the World*. New York: Greenwillow.

HUCK, C. 1989. *Princess Furball*. Illustrated by A. Lobel. New York: Greenwillow.

KONIGSBURG, E. L. 1967. *From the Mixed-up Files of Mrs. Basil E. Frankweiler*. New York: Atheneum.

LOWRY, L. 1981. *Anastasia Krupnik*. New York: Houghton Mifflin.

McCULLY, E. A. 1992. *Mirette on the High Wire*. New York: Penguin Putnams.

McKISSACK, P. 1986. *Flossie and the Fox*. Illustrated by R. Isadora. New York: Dial.

MEYERS, B. 1985. *Sidney Rella and the Glass Sneaker*. New York: Macmillan.

NAYLOR, P. R. 1991. *Shiloh*. New York: Atheneum.

PATERSON, K. 1992. *The King's Equal*. Illustrated by V. Vagin. New York: HarperCollins.

PECK, R. 1972. *A Day No Pigs Would Die*. New York: Knopf.

RAWLINGS, M. K. 1938. *The Yearling*. Illustrated by E. Shenton. New York: Scribner.

SCIESZKA, J. 1989. *The True Story of the 3 Little Pigs by A. Wolf*. Illustrated by L. Smith. New York: Penguin.

SILVERSTEIN, S. 1964. *The Giving Tree*. New York: HarperCollins.

SPINELLI, J. 1997. *Wringer*. New York: HarperCollins.

STEIG, W. 1986. *Brave Irene*. New York: Farrar, Straus & Giroux.

THOMPSON, K. [1935] 1969. *Eloise*. Illustrated by Hilary Knight. New York: Simon & Schuster.

VOIGT, C. 1981. *Homecoming*. New York: Atheneum.

———. 1983. *Dicey's Song*. New York: Atheneum.

WABER, B. 1972. *Ira Sleeps Over*. New York: Houghton Mifflin.

YOLEN, J. 1974. *The Girl Who Cried Flowers and Other Tales*. Illustrated by D. Palladine. New York: HarperCollins.

———. 1990. *Tam Lin*. Illustrated by C. Mikolaycak. San Diego: Harcourt Brace.

YOUNG, E. 1989. *Lon Po Po*. New York: Philomel.

ZOLOTOW, C. 1972. *William's Doll*. Illustrated by W. P. duBois. New York: HarperCollins.

1

The Hidden Curriculum: Are We Teaching Young Girls to Wait for the Prince?

SUSAN LEHR

Boys are described in popular culture as active, loud, aggressive, unemotional, independent, less mature than girls, strong, handsome, bold, curious, adventurous, tough, and naturally smart. Boys are expected to be rowdy in the elementary classroom and teachers often expect to "control" or "manage" the behaviors of boys. Extremely disruptive boys are labeled and are often medicated to reduce excessive movement. Is this image counterproductive for boys? Does the typical elementary classroom stifle boys by expecting them to be rowdy and quiet in the same instant?

In contrast, girls are described in popular culture as passive, quiet, sweet, nice, emotional, more mature than boys, dependent, hardworking, smart, shy, accommodating, beautiful, pretty, or cute. Females are expected to listen obediently and meekly in the classroom and rarely do females see female experiences as part of the curriculum. Does the typical elementary curriculum set up passive expectations for females by rendering them invisible in the curriculum?

By the age of eight many boys and girls already identify passivity and waiting for the prince as the girl's ultimate role. Many girls consider being beautiful as their main objective, including the eight-year-old girls in one study who wished they could look like a Barbie doll (Wason-Ellam 1997). These girls identified with the beautiful and passive princess in *Tatterhood* (Muller 1984) who was waiting to be rescued by her independent and resourceful sister. In this instance, just reading a book about an active, independent, and resourceful female was not enough; the girls preferred beauty over brains and independence. *Ugly* was not mentioned in the text, yet the girls and boys assigned ugly status to this independent female with messy hair and shabby clothes. Children of both sexes did not connect this independent heroine to the heroes in books about males. In fact, one boy suggested, and was supported by other girls, that when Tatterhood became pretty she got a husband. As Wason-Ellam says, beauty is the standard by which the worth of a character is judged; I would add that getting a man seems to be the ultimate goal.

1

In this chapter I will examine the gendered roles of girls and boys as they relate to the classroom. As my chapter title so flippantly asks, are culturally gendered stereotypes reinforced by classroom life? Society ensures its own continuance within existing social structures that separate and stratify groups based on gender, ethnicity, and economic position. I believe that schools perpetuate and maintain this stratification. These thoughts are hardly new and have been echoed for decades by many researchers across disciplines. Are young girls taught to accept their female status while boys take charge? Before moving to a discussion of the books written for and about the lives of children by the authors and educators writing in this book, I wish to consider the following complex issues within the broader perspective of gender, culture, literacy, and the classroom. I will (1) describe how gender roles are shaped by cultural expectations and social class, which are related to gender status assigned at birth, (2) discuss to what degree teachers reinforce culturally gendered roles for females and males, (3) explore the teacher's role in explicitly challenging inequitable gender roles, (4) describe girls' recent classroom successes and whether they are cause for celebration or perceived as a threat to males' entitled status, (5) characterize the literacies that girls develop oppositionally to establish female identity, (6) illustrate how boys are discouraged from developing a full range of literacy competencies, and (7) finally, offer some final remarks about the potential of feminist literature as part of the curriculum.

Research suggests that girls read resistantly (Gilbert and Gubar 1988), for their own purposes, independent from the typical classroom dynamic that provides males with most of the attention and resources. In contrast, boys' resistance is frequently characterized by a rejection of literacy, which is perceived as being "female." Classroom research has documented that many girls are ignored by teachers for being too smart or too aggressive, but find themselves equally ignored for being too quiet or too passive. Is this simply the natural order? I begin with a biological framework defining *sex* and *gender*. A growing body of research profiles the nature of girls' and boys' classroom interactions through words and play and the resulting power positions assigned to males and females. Since so much media attention has been given to failing boys in countries such as the United States, Great Britain, Australia, and Canada, current research as it relates to the failure of boys and the successes of girls in the classroom will be presented. Through a discussion of girls' and boys' literacies I will examine how girls and boys approach literacy in the classroom and in their private lives to establish gender roles and lifelong reading preferences, prejudices, and patterns.

The Difference Between Biology and Behavior

When we talk about female and male, what is actually biologically based? It is helpful to begin by briefly explaining the difference between the terms *sex* and *gender*. *Sex* refers to the child's assignment at birth as either genetically male (XY) or female (XX), and is considered a biological fact (Paechter 1998). That doctors do this based on physical characteristics has caused difficulties for children born with ambiguous genitalia and unusual chromosome combinations (XO, XXY, XYY, and so on). In rare cases some children have genetically male chromosomes and are unable to react to androgens; these children are born with what appears to be external female and male genitalia, making their external genitalia ambiguous. Some males who are born without penises are typically assigned female status and are raised as females. When menstruation does not occur at the onset of puberty these children experience great distress, because they have developed female identities based on their assigned gender at birth. Recent studies even suggest that some of these children have identified themselves as males although they have been raised as females. These exceptions are rare, but I mention them because they suggest that how children are treated in families and communities helps to determine the development of gender identity (Paechter 1998). Although these cases are anomalies, this data suggests that *gender* is, at least partially, a social construction based on a child's sex, which is assigned at birth. Is gender, therefore, socially defined and determined?

Kindlon and Thompson (1999) describe two biological differences between girls and boys that affect development and behavior. "The first is that girls' verbal abilities, on average, mature faster than boys'" (12). That girls typically talk at an earlier age and are more fluent than boys is documented in research; that boys typically catch up eventually is also documented. "The second difference is that boys tend to be more physically active than girls, moving faster and staying in motion longer" (12). Kindlon and Thompson conclude that beyond these two differences there is very little biological difference between boys and girls. One can even question whether these biological differences are inherent or nurtured from the earliest years of a child's life. In fact, researchers remark again and again that for the vast majority of children there is great overlap and that the differences are largely unremarkable (Walkerdine 1998; Fausto-Sterling 1992; Jacklin 1981). "The ranges between the most and least active boy, and the most and least active girl, are much greater than the statistical difference between all the girls compared with all the boys" (Thorne 1993, 57).

What about testosterone? Media reports suggest that testosterone is a major factor in violent males. Research thus far contradicts popular media and suggests there is as yet no scientific basis for the claims about the association between testosterone and aggressive behavior (Tremblay et al. 1997; Archer 1997; Kindlon and Thompson 1999). What is known so far is that violent boys have testosterone within normal ranges (Constantino et al. 1993), all boys entering adolescence have a testosterone surge but not all boys are aggressive, and children of both sexes have about the same amount of testosterone up until the age of ten. Kindlon and Thompson further report that after males committing aggressive acts were measured for testosterone levels it was found that there was an increase, suggesting that the high levels of testosterone are effects of the aggressive acts rather than causes. There are still a lot of unanswered questions about the relation between testosterone and violence.

Using biological explanations for behavior ultimately promotes social injustice and inequality between males and females as well as between races and doesn't ultimately get at the root of the problem (Bem 1993). When it comes to sex and gender, much of what we label "natural" in Western culture is socially constructed (Paechter 1998). Wearing pink is not biologically natural for girls, nor is long hair, lipstick, cooking, and being obedient. Expecting boys to be fond of trucks as they throw blocks in the block corner is also socially constructed behavior rather than biological fact. Yet, as children grow up these socially gendered expectations take on a life of their own. In the next section I explore how that gender identity is shaped in early childhood.

Shaping Gender Identity in Early Childhood

Children are reinforced in their experiences by each other and by adults, and neuronal connections in the brain are reinforced through repeated experiences (Sacks 1993). These different experiences build different neural connections (Paechter 1998). Environment shapes brain development. Smith and Lloyd (1978) found that children assigned to either female or male roles receive different behavioral messages from their parents from a very early age. Parents and others "modify, from infancy, their behavior and responses to the child according to its perceived sex" (Paechter 1998, 44).

Why then do boys seem to "naturally" choose blocks and girls seem to "naturally" choose the kitchen corner? Children actively socialize each other and are not passive recipients of their gender roles; children resist, rework, create, and influence adults as well as each other (Thorne 1993). Lloyd and Duveen (1992) report that preschool age children identify with "gender-appropriate" toys, that children "police" each other, and that they play with children of their own gender by the age of three.

Whereas boys are encouraged to play with blocks, tools, trucks, and Legos, girls do not typically play with toys that develop large motor coordination, although I would hope that this has begun to change. Since this pattern is reinforced from birth, many girls do not have access to this type of experiential development and play. Conversely, developing small motor skills is a standard part of the curriculum, so that boys access both types of development and play in school from a very young age.

Is it ever too late to challenge confining gender roles? Girls historically have avoided science courses, although research now suggests that even this is beginning to level out. Kenway and Willis (1998) found that girls in high school physics classes were reluctant to "mess about" with unfamiliar tools and materials because the boys usually took over. They found that in small science laboratory groups the males typically took charge while girls watched. The Australian authors describe an alert physics teacher who brought in tools and Legos and allowed the girls to experiment on their own away from the boys, with successful results. This suggests that excellent teaching practice in early childhood should standardize large motor skill development as part of the curriculum for girls as well as for boys. Teachers can actively challenge confining gender roles with something as simple as giving girls structured time in the tool, block, and truck corner. In science activities with older children teachers can experiment with all-female groups so that girls cannot remain passive observers.

Falling Through the Cracks

Quiet girls are "good girls" and often fall through the cracks and receive less educational support than boys, because they are easy to have in the classroom (American Association of University Women 1992, 1995). The AAUW report suggests that being rowdy and disruptive in the classroom, as girls typically are not, pays off and equals more attention, more resource support, thus more money spent on remedying learning disabilities and a host of other problems. Passive females with learning disabilities are easier to maintain, which also means they are easier to miss, which is why they are not diagnosed or given support as frequently as their male counterparts. Do teachers encourage quiet girls to remain quiet because it is easier? Boys speak more in classroom contexts, receive more positive and negative attention from teachers, are referred for special help more frequently than are girls, and ultimately have more tax dollars spent on their educations than do girls (AAUW 1995).

Girls overwhelmingly described ideal selves as "nice, kind, and helpful" and chose other girls in their classes as people they wished they were like (Walkerdine 1998). Most of the boys in Walkerdine's study chose male football sport figures including classmates and famous sports figures. In contrast, teachers often chastise or ignore aggressive girls (Kenway and Willis 1998; Sadker and Sadker 1994). When girls take on "male" traits and strategies in order to be heard and to be successful in the classroom, these same researchers found that girls are pushed back into passive roles. Ironically, Walkerdine found that smart girls are often characterized as hard workers, whereas their male counterparts are described as either naturally smart or not living up to their potential. Walkerdine also found that teachers' perceptions of some boys was characterized by their saying that if the boys only worked harder they would be achieving at a high level. These teachers perceived them as being naturally smart. In contrast, the hard work of many female students was devalued because it was not perceived as being innate intelligence as found in boys. Girls in these classroom studies were also characterized as being encouraged to be classroom nurturers and helpers. These teachers also used girls in elementary and secondary classrooms to tame and civilize the aggressive rowdiness of boys, but at what cost to the girls?

One teacher, having read the AAUW report *Shortchanging Girls, Shortchanging America* (AAUW 1992), discussed Orenstein's (1994) findings with her class and told the children she was going to call on both boys and girls equally. By the second day the boys blew up, complaining that she was being unfair and saying that she was calling on the girls more that the boys. When the teacher showed them this wasn't true they backed down. Other researchers have found the same odd phenomenon, with the same anger and hostility from boys who expect to receive most of the classroom attention. Many girls were often not even aware that they were being ignored and when teachers deliberately tried to even things up in the classroom the boys were angry, indignant, and hurt by the equal attention, which they perceived as unequal. Kenway and Willis (1998) found that many boys and male teachers became even more hostile in situations where female teachers highlighted or celebrated the accomplishments of women. Unfortunately, this issue rarely comes up in most classrooms, and the boys often continue their entitled status while girls remain largely invisible. By the time girls enter high school, they know who counts, who can be heard, and what is expected of them; many choose to remain silent, at least in the classroom.

When Play Becomes Aggression

From an early age many adults encourage and accept the more active behaviors of boys, while encouraging girls to pursue quiet or more sedate pastimes (Cherland 1994; Walkerdine 1998; Orenstein 1994). Thorne's (1993) dynamic studies of children's playground behaviors found that boys typically control the large spaces and are given preference for both the use of space and the use of equipment, whereas girls typically use a tenth of the space that boys do. Yet when given the opportunity in all-female physical education classes, at girls' camps, or when equipment is equitably reserved for girls during free time, Kenway and Willis found that many females will play active sports and even talk enthusiastically about their experiences.

One of the reasons researchers have found that girls avoid active sports at school is because they often get hurt when playing with boys (Cherland 1994; Thorne 1993). Culturally based norms for females from certain ethnic or religious groups also demand that girls behave in a prescribed sedate and proper manner. For example, girls with Islamic or Asian backgrounds often avoided sports and active situations due to cultural conditioning, but when given all-female experiences in physical education classes and at camp, many of the girls in Kenway and Willis's study discovered that they liked physical activity.

Thorne (1993) found that with young children there is a group of boys who seem to specialize in teasing, invading, or disrupting girls' space and play although most boys do not engage in this activity. Some of it is ritualized play that is enjoyable for both girls and boys. But when does it go beyond fun and when is it no longer enjoyable?

Kindlon and Thompson (1999) have written about the emotional illiteracy of young boys and have worked extensively with boys discussing this type of aggressive behavior, which is typically male against female and male against male. They suggest that this "culture of cruelty imposes a code of silence on boys" and requires them to be silent witnesses or to suffer silently (92). Thus one is masculine and strong if one is attacking or if one is silent. Teachers can be complicit in this abuse because they tolerate this type of cruelty and pretend not to see, or they address grievances in superficial ways. "What would it mean for teachers to support various versions of masculinity?" ask Lensmire and Price (1998, 131). What would it mean for teachers and students to speak out against this type of cruelty and bullying, which often escalates into physical abuse? Unfortunately some male teachers perpetuate the dominant male hierarchy overtly in their teaching and in their interactions with students of both sexes, even to the point of using threatening language and body posture (Kenway and

Willis 1998). Popular culture suggests that these aggressive tendencies of males are biological fact, and that reinforcement for this aggression begins at an early age.

When Words Become Weapons

> You're a stupid cunt, Annie (Walkerdine 1998, 63).

Terry, age four, has just attempted unsuccessfully to take a piece of Lego away from Annie, age three, who is adding it to her building. The teacher tells Terry to stop, at which point Terry and Sean, both preschool children, threaten the teacher verbally.

TERRY: Get out of it, knickers Miss Baxter.
SEAN: Get out of it, Miss Baxter the knickers paxter knickers, bum.
TERRY: Knickers, shit, bum.

The teacher replies to these and other verbal assaults by twice interjecting and labeling the boys' behavior as silly. "I think you're being very silly." Ignoring her weak response, they continue and escalate.

SEAN: Miss Baxter, knickers, show your knickers.
TERRY: Miss Baxter, show off your bum.
TERRY: Shit Miss Baxter, shit Miss Baxter.
SEAN: Take all your clothes off, your bra off.
TERRY: Yeah, and take your bum off, take your wee-wee off, take your clothes, your mouth off.

The boys continue and Miss Baxter finally responds: "Sean, go and find something else to do, please" (Walkerdine 1998, 63).

I am profoundly disturbed by the words used to control the teacher in Walkerdine's study and by the teacher's unwillingness to address the violence of the boys' words. I struggled with removing this conversation from this chapter so that I would not offend educators reading this book, but by doing that I would not be addressing one of the most complex issues facing teachers. Ignoring the sexually explicit verbal violence of this problem will not make it disappear.

Language is power and can be used to control women. Valerie Walkerdine suggests that boys learn about power and the power of sexist discourse at an early age. I find I am haunted by the words of Terry as he does verbal violence against Annie. What roles have Terry's and Sean's parents or caretakers played in the boys' use of socially unacceptable, destructive, demeaning, and explicit sexual words?

What role can a teacher play when confronted by behavior so obviously destructive and inappropriate? Where does a teacher learn to respond to situations of this nature? In my years in elementary classrooms I have found that this type of behavior and language is not uncommon, although the ages of the children in this example are extremely young. I have also observed that teachers are woefully unequipped to handle situations like this. Most teachers that I have observed ignore inappropriate sexual behavior or simply tell children that it is not nice and to stop doing it.

By not rejecting the boys' verbal assault, by not showing her own anger or displeasure at their verbal assault, by not labeling the words as unacceptable, this teacher reinforced her social position as inferior. Ms. Baxter gave the boys the right to use threats of defecation and maiming her genitalia as a means of verbal control. There is nothing silly about their words. Rather the whole conversation has the threat and violence of men who are verbally assaulting a woman. It is probably not a coincidence that the boys want to remove her mouth as well. Silencing women is perhaps something they are all too familiar with in their daily lives.

What did Terry and Sean learn that day in preschool? What did Annie learn at the age of three? The lessons were rather big ones about the use of power. The children learned that it is all right for boys to attack a girl with sexual words. It is all right to attack a teacher with words about her genitalia. It is merely silly to do so. Do the boys know what they are saying? It hardly matters, since they have now learned it works to say these words. This type of behavior does not disappear as boys grow older, which is documented in research with certain adolescent males who target females for sexual harassment.

One of my college students shared her story in class about a boy who stalked her in elementary school. He scared her day after day. She was six. The principal's and teacher's solution? They kept her safely locked inside the classroom week after week so that the aggressive behavior of the boy would not continue against her on the playground. The victim was imprisoned.

This type of harassment can include explicit verbal and physical assaults on a daily basis over the course of several years in elementary and secondary schools; it is heavily documented in research (Thorne 1993; Walkerdine 1998; Orenstein 1994; Kenway and Willis 1998; Cherland 1994; Epstein et al. 1998; AAUW 1992; Sadker and Sadker 1994; Kindlon and Thompson 1999). Thorne in particular has studied the effect of boys treating girls as the contaminated gender. Pollution games include something as basic as cootie games in the primary grades that can escalate to contamination labels on certain girls in junior high and high school. Harsh terms like *slut* and *whore* are used in vicious verbal attacks on certain teenage girls, often those who are poor, overweight, or ethnically different. Male against male pollution games also involve explicit verbal assaults about males who act like females. Teachers and principals often dismiss this form of aggression as teasing or the natural behavior of young males; their dismissals are not so very different from Miss Baxter's use of the word *silly*. The violence that erupted in schools in the United States in the 1990s suggests that this type of bullying and aggressive behavior cannot be ignored.

Much has been written about the recent failure and frustration of boys in the classroom as girls begin to succeed in what were once male domains. Extremists blame women's emerging successes and expanding rights as destroying society's morals and making white males the new victims. This rationalizing blames the victim for wanting to remove her subservient status and empowers certain males to act out in violent ways in response. In the next section I will provide a brief consideration of girls' successes and boys' failures in schools.

Impact of Gender, Race, and Class on Achievement

Who exactly is failing today? Overall girls are performing equally to boys in most areas of the curriculum in Great Britain, Australia, Canada, and the United States. But which girls? And which boys? Boys from minorities and lower socioeconomic backgrounds are continuing to drop out of school at alarming rates. In the United States the Latino population reaches dropout rates as high as 50 percent for males and 40 percent for females. There is no cause for celebration and little difference between male and female dropout rates for this group of children. In England white working-class boys are at risk of failure, as are African Caribbean boys. Working-class boys increasingly continue to resist achieving academically; with the decline of many of the historically "masculine" jobs available in England they have been unable to define themselves academically (Walkerdine 1998). Race and poverty often equal academic failure for boys and girls.

Middle-class girls have begun to equal or outperform their male counterparts in many Western countries. For example, all-girl schools have shown higher ratings than all-boy or mixed schools in two British studies examining student success (Arnot et al. 1996). Middle-class girls in Australia are performing at rates equal to their middle-class male peers in math and chemistry (Kenway and Willis 1998). Studies of math performance in Western countries support that overall, girls are outperforming males (Ernest 1998; Smith and Walker 1988; Stockard and Wood 1984; Hanna 1989; Ethington 1990; Brandon and Jordan 1994; Cheung 1989). The research even indicates that if there is a problem, it is peculiar to Anglo-Saxon countries.

The research suggests two profiles of male students. Middle- and upper-class boys who are successful in school go on to be successful in college and in entering good professions. In contrast, failed students are typically white working-class boys and African Caribbean boys in Great Britain (Epstein et al. 1998) and African American and Latino males in the United States. Jackson (1998) suggests that some boys cope with school failure and "humiliating economic and social circumstances" by giving meaning to their lives through a reassertion of "manliness," which is exhibited in violent racism, sexism, xenophobia, and a rejection of school values.

Mac an Ghaill (1994) interviewed boys and their attitudes toward school and found many responses that equated school work with girl's work, not real work, and kids' work. So for many underperforming boys school and working hard in school is not valued. For the urban poor "success in school represents a severe break with the underclass community" (Weis in Epstein et al. 1998, 125).

The issue is compounded for males of color. Even some boys who work hard and want to achieve often cannot get past the combination of their gender and the color of their skin. Some teachers treat them in predictably negative ways and have negative expectations for them, regardless of their hard work and regardless of difficult circumstances they are purposefully trying to override (Sewell 1998).

The work of Kathleen Rockhill (1993) in the United States parallels these findings for Hispanic women who wanted to learn English and get an education but did not have the freedom to leave their homes and go to school. The men in their lives were so threatened by their women becoming "ladies," i.e., educated women who would leave the barrio, that some were beaten and many were threatened. The women in this study were oppressed by a male hierarchy that could not risk the education of a wife or girlfriend, who might eventually leave the family. Literacy was perceived as being so powerful that denying access was seen as the only recourse to save the dominant male family structure.

Success for some seems to be related to class position in society. Middle-class girls are achieving at competitive rates with their male peers. Walkerdine (1998) boldly suggests that middle-class males are barely allowed to fail because too much has been invested in their middle-class status. The media and politicians, rather than celebrating the successes of girls and approaching ways to address the underachievement of boys, have had a tendency to minimize girls' success and act as if this success threatens and keeps boys from succeeding.

If girls are achieving in solid and meaningful ways, this should not be redefined as a deficit for society (Walkerdine 1998). This "deficit" theory suggests that the fabric of society is unraveling because women are taking "male" jobs and are leaving their children with strangers while they go off to work. This polarization of the sexes perpetuates a hierarchy that benefits no one, because the idea of victim and oppressor must be maintained. How are these male and female identities shaped in school? It is time to move to a discussion of girls' and boys' literacies.

Girls' Literacies

What do girls read? How are their book experiences shaped by experiences at home, within the wider community, and in school? How does social class structure these experiences? What are girls' purposes for reading? Does gender identity shape reading identities? Two extensive ethnographic studies in Ontario and Iowa (Cherland 1994; Finders 1997) provide detailed studies of girls' literacies in middle school and junior high school. Additionally, the work of Linda Christian-Smith (1993) with adolescent girls and romance novels provides a provocative picture of lower-middle-class girls who are not typically successful in school settings. After extensive searching I could not find corresponding studies on the literacies of boys, which is disappointing and reveals a gap in literacy research. Notable exceptions include work done in reader response research, which chronicles and profiles classroom reading behaviors, choices, and responses to literature in elementary classrooms but does not focus exclusively on "gender" studies (Hickman 1983; Hepler 1982; Lehr 1991, 1995a; McClure 1990; Enciso 1994; Lehr and Thompson 2000; Hancock 1995).

As I said at the beginning of the chapter, I believe that society ensures its own continuance within existing social structures that separate and stratify groups based on gender, ethnicity, and economic position. I also believe that schools unwittingly perpetuate and maintain this stratification. This stratification is so deeply embedded within our culture that we are often unaware of its existence and therefore rarely examine its underpinnings. The emerging profiles of girls and their literacy practices documented in recent literacy studies suggest, however, that girls' uses of reading and writing are a way of maintaining identity in communities that divide people by gender and give dominance to males. Many girls read in "resistant" ways, outside the male "canon," and for their own purposes. *Resistant* in this sense means that girls often reject imposed gender stratification consciously and unconsciously. Researchers document that many girls are often socialized into helplessness, silence, and deference, and by adolescence are lacking in confidence and unwilling to assert themselves (Gilligan 1982; Cherland 1994; Walkerdine 1998).

Many young adolescent girls read horror stories and watch horror movies, which reinforces this sense of fear, helplessness, and potential victimization (Hall and Coles 1999). Horror movies typically depict girls as victims who are mutilated; these images parallel the female's fragile status in society, in which females are frequently the targets of male violence. As a result, Cherland (1994) suggests that girls who are perceived as potential victims of sex and violence are protected and warned by parents and kept in a lingering childhood that conflicts with messages from popular culture.

This notion of a safe, lingering childhood is juxtaposed against images from popular culture that urge girls to be sexy, provocative, and alluring to men. Cherland also found that mothers in her study who were active readers of fiction encouraged their daughters to read partly because reading kept their daughters safely occupied at home in a worthwhile pursuit, and off the streets and out of trouble. Many of the mothers in Finders' (1997) study recalled grandmothers and mothers reading fiction, so that reading fiction is passed down female to female as a valued and shared event between mothers and daughters.

Boys are equally penalized in that they often view themselves as dominant and identify with violent male characters in books and movies. Analysis of boys' writing in two studies shows that they frequently use sadistic and violent forms of male domination in which girls and weaker boys are blown up, crucified, or killed by firing squads (Gilbert 1989; Hu in Cherland 1994).

Many girls read romances, which reinforce an idea of femininity that includes the goal of beauty as a way of getting and keeping a man (Cherland 1994; Finders 1997; Christian-Smith 1993; Davies 1993). According to these researchers, girls in romances who are intelligent, independent, and assertive don't typically fare well, so girls are being socialized into certain ways of thinking about themselves and their future roles as women. Obtaining a man is still the basic goal of the romance novel. Interestingly, some girls read the series novels and romance books and find the assertive independence of characters in ways that adults would not. For example, in one of the Sweet Valley High books the girls have jobs and earn their own money to buy cosmetics and clothing. Cherland (1994) found that girls interpret these events as females earning their own money sources and becoming independent. In this sense the girls read against the grain and pulled their own meaning from the books. Jennifer Armstrong's chapter on the Sweet Valley High books shows how she purposely included active and independent female characters with a range of choices when she wrote fifty Sweet Valley High and Sweet Valley Twins novels.

Magazines and Series Books

Reading preference surveys and case studies of groups of girls indicate that girls use magazines as the dominant means of learning about who they should be and who they hope to be (Finders 1997; Cherland 1994; Hall and Coles 1999). Hall and Coles surveyed 8,000 English children and found that teen girls buy, read, reread, and share most of the magazines bought by children in Great Britain. Magazines inform girls about every aspect of attracting and keeping a male. How to dress, how to talk, how to kiss, how to go out on a date, how to stay thin, are all topics of passionate discussion in and out of school. Girls also read series books, including the Sweet Valley High books, Sweet Valley Twins, Babysitters Club, *Flowers in the Attic* series, and in England Point Horror books, because they are about girls their own age.

Girls in Hall and Coles' study indicated that they spend their allowances on series books, share books and magazines with each other, discuss, recommend, and exchange books regularly in and out of school. Cherland also found that 75 percent of the girls in her study pursued reading extensively in their free time compared to 33 percent of the boys, who did not receive the same kind of encouragement for reading. Hall and Coles's study corroborates this finding. Girls read more than boys, with a significant decline in fourteen-year-old boys' reading. As a result, teachers often try to "hook" boys on reading by loading up the literature curriculum with books about male protagonists.

The Invisible Curriculum

Female perspectives are all but invisible in the typical language arts classroom curriculum. Christian-Smith (1993) boldly suggests that Newbery winners support the status quo and do not challenge the normal hierarchies of the dominant culture. In *The Girl with the Brown Crayon*, Vivian Paley (1998) describes a yearlong study in kindergarten that focused and studied the work of Lio Lionni in addition to all the other reading that occurred during her last year of teaching. Tico, Alexander, Frederick, Cornelius, Matthew, Pezzettino, Inch by Inch, and Swimmy all have something in common, which sent an embedded and explicit message to her five-year-old listeners. Males star in these books and are adventurers, poets, creepers and crawlers, who can be naughty like Max in *Where the Wild Things Are* (1963). Even five-year-old Reeny, the star of *The Girl with the Brown Crayon*, finally noticed that all of Lionni's characters were male. Paley had never noticed. It took a five-year-old girl to point out the obvious to her, so they went to the library and looked at all of Lionni's books and found one about Geraldine.

Imagine a teacher who fails to notice that there are no female protagonists. Picture the kindergarten curriculum devised and described by Paley that celebrates the active, independent, brave, and intellectual pursuits of males almost exclusively. Whether mice, literary giants, or American heroes, males do still rule the curriculum, and it is what men have done, their deeds and actions, that are worthy of being celebrated. Women's pursuits and interests have not typically been valued, so they have not historically been worth studying in the curriculum.

Reading Against the Grain

As the sixth graders in Cherland's study read the Prydain Chronicles by Lloyd Alexander, Sperry's *Call It Courage* (1940), and Wojciechowska's *Shadow of a Bull* (1964), they were expected to identify with the male protagonists of the books. These stories center on the characters' struggles against society primarily from a male perspective. This curriculum did not include books about female experiences. After reading *The Book of Three* (1964), a fantasy by Lloyd Alexander, the children were told to give a gift to any character in the book. The girls thought long and hard about this task and finally decided to give Eilonwy a sword because she always wanted to fight and didn't want to be considered a little girl. Alexander didn't give Eilonwy her own sense of agency, i.e., a sense of personal empowerment and independence, although he gave her a lot of lip and bravery for the 1970s. The twelve-year-old girls in this classroom wanted more agency for themselves as readers and for one of the main characters in this questing book, so they gave Eilonwy the same means to defend herself that her male peers already had. In their scenario she no longer had to be dependent on the boys and men for the basic right to defend herself from harm. The girls' gift is most revealing about their own sense of self-empowerment and their need to make themselves safe and relevant. These girls do not want to wait for the prince. Rather they want to be responsible for their own safety.

Pinsent (1997) writes about reading oppositionally, i.e., reading resistantly, and gives the example of a female reader taking from the text exactly what she wants rather than what the author may have intended. In this case Alexander's 1970s view of a liberated woman was strikingly different from the way these 1990s girls defined *liberated*.

A common reason given for making girls read books with male protagonists is that boys won't read (or listen to) girls' books but that girls will read anything, as Charlotte Huck states in the introduction. This suggests that teachers perceive girls as being compliant because they will even read books that they don't like. What message does this send to female students about the value of their experiences, interests, stories, and perspectives? Must one always read oppositionally to find one's voice?

I have observed in my own response research that when children read books with male and female protagonists there is greater opportunity for rich discussion about the choices characters face. If boys read and listen to books about the experiences of females their lives are richer and their gender misconceptions are challenged. It is essential that teachers purposefully and thoughtfully offer a wide range of characters and experiences in the books they bring to the classroom. The survival experiences of Clotee in *A Picture of Freedom: The Diary of Clotee, a Slave Girl* by Patricia McKissack (1997), and Yoko and Ko in *So Far from the Bamboo Grove* by Yoko Kawashima Watkins (1986), are no less valid or compelling than the experiences of Brian in *Hatchet* by Gary Paulsen (1987), or Otter in *Dragon's Gate* by Laurence Yep (1993).

Stereotyping Poverty

Many assumptions are made about girls and boys from lower socioeconomic families. Finders (1997) found that girls living in trailer parks, although assigned a pariah status by female peers, were active readers and writers at home and in school. One of the girls lived in a home where literature was so valued that an extra shed had to be built to accommodate all of the family's books. Another girl was active in helping her mother plan home-decorating parties that involved their own kind of literacy, related to lists, invitations, written plans, and shopping orders. Both girls were strong students, read high-quality children's literature rather than magazines and series books such as Nancy Drew and Sweet Valley High, and success in school was very important to them and to their mothers. Teachers seemed surprised when they did well. Family was very important to these girls and they spent a lot of time at home, which has been documented in other research of working-class families. As stated earlier, low income in this instance acts as a double bind for children because they must get past the assumptions of teachers and peers before they are encouraged to succeed.

Boys' Literacies

What characterizes the literacy habits of boys in the sixth and seventh grades? Cherland found that fathers and sons read nonfiction for utilitarian purposes, including magazines like *Fortune*, *The Financial Post*, computer magazines, newspapers and the sports section, biographies, or books on carpentry, woodworking, and electrical wiring. This nonfiction reading has been overstated and has achieved a mythical status for males (Hall and Coles 1999). Both studies found that science fiction and Stephen King novels are also popular with fathers and sons, but the men in Cherland's study did not consider them the same as female fiction. Cherland's interviews revealed that fathers were proud of not reading fiction and did not consider themselves readers, had never liked reading, and believed that their sons were just like them.

Reading is simply not perceived as an acceptable pastime for some men and declines significantly from ages ten to fourteen (Hall and Coles 1999). What then characterizes boys' literacies? Hall and Coles found that boys watch more TV than girls, use computers more frequently than girls, and read more comic books and newspapers than girls.

Female Potential in Literature

How often do girls see their potentials reflected in books? Roberta Trites defines a feminist book as one that gives characters of both sexes options and choices, a definition that offers possibilities for males and females. Feminist children's novels reject the notion that heterosexual relationships are more important and supercede friendships and bonds between women. These relationships include mother-daughter relationships, intergenerational relationships, friendships between women, lesbian relationships, and surrogate sister relationships (Trites 1997). She cites Mildred Taylor's books as being exemplary examples of feminist children's novels. Taylor shows three strong intergenerational connections between Cassie Logan, her mother, and Big Ma, her grandmother. All three African American women learn from each other, provide solid connections of strength for each other, and maintain the family network in the face of severe and often violent racial hatred.

Traditional literature such as *Little Women* views women's relationships as secondary to the love of a good man (Trites 1997). Many traditional books for girls end up with girls turning into women, defined as leaving family and friends behind, abandoning assertive behaviors, staying indoors, giving up one's vocation, finding a man, and becoming his wife, which is, as Huck points out in the introduction, often historically accurate. This is also common of "traditional" female heroes in children's fantasy who give up their own sense of agency once they find their man (Lehr 1995b).

"Feminist" books such as Voigt's fantasy quartet, *Jackaroo* (1985), *On Fortune's Wheel* (1990), *The Wings of a Falcon* (1993), and *Elske* (1999) offer wistful albeit balanced perspectives as female protagonists become independent women able to function successfully in heterosexual relationships and in society. Voigt's mythic medieval world is blighted, as evidenced when pain, frustration, and anger erupt in *Elske*, the latest book in the Kingdom series. Voigt's latest Kingdom book more closely mirrors historical reality than her previous books, as she documents the violence of men as a societal norm. Escaping rape is a central theme in this fantasy as art imitates life. Escaping and avoiding violence is real for women both in history and in contemporary times. Voigt's characters, however, have choices and options within the confines of their societal realities.

Is it unrealistic to document the lives of women who were willing and able to live against the grain? Authors in this volume will explore this question at length. The powerful *Women on the Margins*, by Natalie Zemon Davis (1995), is a scholarly nonfiction book written for adults, documenting the lives of three women in the seventeenth century who were able to transcend successfully the dominant male culture for their own purposes: a Jewish merchant, a Catholic mystic, and a Protestant painter, living on three different continents, living accomplished and confident lives. The author celebrates the potential of women in all ages.

The "Knotted Dilemma"

Cultural expectations for girls and boys are starkly different. Gilligan et al. (1990) capture the "knotted dilemma" faced by young adolescent girls. Gilligan defines the knotted dilemma as the tensions of listening to one's voice and to tradition while also learning to care for oneself and for others. How would girls' and boys' experiences be different if they had access, not sporadically, but consistently, to a wider variety of books with active female protagonists? Would girls perceive themselves differently if teachers explicitly included female content across the curriculum? Would boys' attitudes toward females change if females were equitably represented in literature, history, science, and the arts?

Mem Fox, when being interviewed for an author profile for this book, told me that in Australian universities teachers are explicitly taught how to address gender equitably in their classrooms, because gender equity is a part of the Australian national curriculum. The university students are taught how to lead discussions actively with children about blatant stereotypes found in children's books. Children's books with stereotypes aren't necessarily hidden or removed from the curriculum. Rather, teachers actively promote social justice and equity by inviting children to analyze books through effective questions and discussions of female and male roles in books. Something as simple as asking, "Could a girl have done that?" can invite speculation and role playing by all students.

The wider culture "positions" children to become literate within a heavily gendered social structure. Girls typically read narratives, whereas boys typically read nonfiction. Because different groups of children won't necessarily read high-quality multigenred and diverse literature on their own, assigning high-quality literature as part of the curriculum is imperative. Books with male and female protagonists who have a strong sense of agency should be widely available in libraries, classroom collections, and as a structured part of the curriculum. Ensuring that those male and female protagonists represent many cultures is no less critical. Nonfiction books should be read to both boys and girls as an established part of the curriculum. Can boys and girls read books with female protagonists? Can girls and boys study history that includes the accomplishments and perspectives of females?

A central feature of a balanced literature program includes time for children to have honest and extensive conversations about the themes, settings, and characters found in literature. The questions, concerns, conflicts, and prejudices of the children are all valid topics for conversations. Making children echo politically correct thinking is not the goal of these conversations. What I'm suggesting is not safe teaching. Children are unpredictable. The opinions and attitudes of the children will be as diverse as the number of children in the classroom. Through these dialogues children will be able to think about some of the most basic tenets of what it means to be human. I happen to believe, with John Dewey, that the classroom should be a powerful place where students learn to become active and reflective citizens. Teachers addressing gender equity will offer girls and boys options and choices within a curriculum that reflects the potentials of both sexes.

References

AMERICAN ASSOCIATION OF UNIVERSITY WOMEN. 1992. *Shortchanging Girls, Shortchanging America: A Call to Action.* Washington DC: AAUW.

———. 1995. *How Schools Shortchange Girls: A Study of Major Findings on Girls and Education.* New York: Marlowe & Company.

ARCHER, J. 1997. "The Influence of Testosterone on Human Aggression." *British Journal of Psychology* 82: 1–28.

ARNOT, M., M. DAVID, & G. WEINER. 1996. *Educational Reform and Gender Equality in Schools.* Manchester, England: Equal Opportunities Commision.

BEM, S. L. 1993. *The Lenses of Gender: Transforming the Debate on Sexual Inequality.* New Haven: Yale University Press.

BRANDON, P., & C. JORDAN. 1994. "Gender Differences Favoring Hawaiin Girls in Mathematics Achievement: Recent Findings and Hypotheses." *Zentralblatt fur Didaktik der Mathematik* 94 (1): 18–21.

CHASE, C. F. 1998. *Suncatcher: A Study of Madeleine L'Engle.* Philadelphia: Innisfree Press.

CHERLAND, M. R. 1994. *Private Practices: Girls Reading Fiction and Constructing Identity.* London: Taylor & Francis.

CHEUNG, K. 1989. "Gender Differences in the Junior Secondary Mathematics Curriculum in Hong Kong." *Educational Studies in Mathematics* 20 (1): 97–103.

CHRISTIAN-SMITH, L. K. 1993. *Texts of Desire: Essays on Fiction, Femininity and Schooling.* London: The Falmer Press.

CONSTANTINO, J., D. GROSZ, P. SAENGER, D. CHANDLER, R. NANDI, & F. EARLS. 1993. "Testosterone and Aggression in Children." *Journal of the American Academy of Child and Adolescent Psychiatry* 32: 1217–22.

CULLINGFORD, C. 1998. *Children's Literature and Its Effects: The Formative Years.* London: Cassell.

DAVIES, B. 1993. *Beyond Dualism and Towards Multiple Subjectivities.* In *Texts of Desire*, ed. Linda Christian-Smith. London: Falmer Press.

DAVIS, N. Z. 1995. *Women on the Margins: Three Seventeenth-Century Lives.* Boston: Harvard University Press.

ENCISO, P. 1994. "Cultural Identity and Response to Literature: Running Lessons from Maniac Magee." *Language Arts* 71: 524–33.

EPSTEIN, D., J. ELWOOD, V. HEY, & J. MAW. 1998. *Failing Boys?: Issues in Gender and Achievement.* Buckingham, England: Open University Press.

ERNEST, P. 1998. "Changing Views of 'The Gender Problem' in Mathematics." Introduction in *Counting Girls Out: Girls and Mathematics* by V. Walkerdine. London: Falmer Press.

ETHINGTON, C. 1990. "Gender Differences in Mathematics: An International Perspective." *Journal for Research in Mathematics Education* 21 (1): 74–80.

FAUSTO-STERLING, A. 1992. *Myths of Gender: Biological Theories About Women and Men*. New York: Basic Books.

FINDERS, M. J. 1997. *Just Girls: Hidden Literacies and Life in Junior High*. New York: Teachers College Press.

GILBERT, P. 1989. "Personally (and Passively) Yours: Girls, Literacy, and Education." *Oxford Review of Education* 15 (3): 257–65.

GILBERT, S., & GUBAR, S. 1988. *The Mad Woman in the Attic*. Princeton: Yale University Press.

GILLIGAN, C. 1982. *In A Different Voice: Psychological Theory and Women's Development*. Cambridge, MA: Harvard University Press.

GILLIGAN, C., N. P. LYONS, & T. J. HANMER. 1990. *Making Connections: The Relational Worlds of Adolescent Girls at Emma Willard School*. Cambridge, MA: Harvard University Press.

HALL, C., & M. COLES. 1999. *Children's Reading Choices*. London: Routledge.

HANCOCK, M. R. 1995. "Discovering Common Bonds." *Children's Books in Ireland* 12: 17–18.

HANNA, G. 1989. "Mathematics Achievement of Girls and Boys in Grade Eight: Results from Twenty Countries." *Educational Studies in Mathematics* 20 (2): 225–32.

HEPLER, S. 1982. "Patterns of Response to Literature: A One-Year Study of a Fifth and Sixth Grade Classroom." Doctoral dissertation, The Ohio State University, Columbus.

HICKMAN, J. 1983. "Everything Considered: Responses to Literature in an Elementary School Setting." *Journal of Research and Development in Education* 16: 8–13.

HILTON, M., M. STYLES, & V. WATSON. 1997. *Opening the Nursery Door: Reading, Writing and Childhood 1600–1900*. London: Routledge.

HUNT, P. 1999. *Understanding Children's Literature*. London: Routledge.

JACKLIN, C. N. 1981. "Methodological Issues in the Study of Sex-Related Differences." *Developmental Review* 1: 226–73.

JACKSON, D. 1998. "Breaking Out of the Binary Trap: Boys' Underachievement, Schooling and Gender Relations." In *Failing Boys: Issues in Gender and Achievement*, ed. D. Epstein, J. Elwood, V. Hey, & J. Maw, 77–95. Buckingham, England: Open University Press.

KENWAY, J., & S. WILLIS. 1998. *Answering Back: Girls, Boys and Feminism in Schools*. London: Routledge.

KINDLON, D., and M. THOMPSON. 1999. *Raising Cain: Protecting the Emotional Life of Boys*. New York: Ballantine.

LEHR, S. S. 1991. *The Child's Developing Sense of Theme*. New York: Teachers College Press.

———. 1995a. "Fourth Graders Read, Write, and Talk About Freedom." In *Battling Dragons*, ed. S. Lehr, 114–40. Portsmouth, NH: Heinemann.

———. 1995b. "Wise Women and Warriors." In *Battling Dragons: Issues and Controversies in Children's Literature*, ed. S. Lehr, 194–211. Portsmouth, NH: Heinemann.

LEHR, S. S., & D. THOMPSON. 2000. "The Dynamic Nature of Response: Children Reading and Responding to *Maniac Magee* and *The Friendship*." *The Reading Teacher* 53 (6): 480–93.

LENSMIRE, T., & J. PRICE. 1998. "(Com)Promising Pleasures, (Im)Mutable Masculinities." *Language Arts* 76 (2): 130–34.

LLOYD, B., & G. DUVEEN. 1992. *Gender Identities and Education: The Impact of Starting School.* Hemel Hempstead, Hertsfordshire, England: Harvester Press.

MAC AN GHAILL, M. 1994. *The Making of Men: Masculinities, Sexualities and Schooling.* Buckingham, England: Open University Press.

McCLURE, A. 1990. *Sunrises and Songs: Reading and Writing Poetry in an Elementary Classroom.* Portsmouth, NH: Heinemann.

ORENSTEIN, P. 1994. *School Girls: Young Women, Self-Esteem, and the Confidence Gap.* New York: Doubleday.

PAECHTER, C. 1998. *Educating the Other: Gender, Power and Schooling.* London: The Falmer Press.

PALEY, V. G. 1998. *The Girl with the Brown Crayon: How Children Use Stories to Shape Their Lives.* Cambridge, MA: Harvard University Press.

PINSENT, P. 1997. *Children's Literature and the Politics of Equality.* London: David Fulton Publishers.

ROCKHILL, K. 1993. "Gender, Language and the Politics of Literacy." In *Cross-Cultural Approaches to Literacy*, ed. B. Street, 157–75. Cambridge: Cambridge University Press.

RUDMAN, M. K. 1995. *Children's Literature: An Issues Approach.* White Plains, NY: Longman.

SACKS, O. 1993. "Making Up the Mind." *New York Review of Books* 8: 42–7.

SADKER, M., & D. SADKER. 1994. *Failing at Fairness: How Our Schools Cheat Girls.* New York: Simon & Schuster.

SEWELL, T. 1998. "Loose Canons: Exploding the Myth of the 'Black Macho' Lad." In *Failing Boys: Issues in Gender and Achievment*, ed. D. Epstein, J. Elwood, V. Hey, & J. Maw, 111–27. Buckingham, England: Open University Press.

SMITH, C., & B. LLOYD. 1978. "Maternal Behavior and Perceived Sex of Infant: Revisited." *Child Development* 49: 1263–65.

SMITH, S., & W. WALKER. 1988. "Sex Differences on New York State Regents Examinations: Support for the Differential Course Taking Hypothesis." *Journal for Research in Mathematics Education* 19 (1): 81–85.

STOCKARD, J., & J. WOOD. 1984. "The Myth of Female Underachievement: A Re-Examination of Sex Differences in Academic Underachievement." *American Educational Research Journal* 21 (4): 825–38.

STREET, B. V. 1993. *Cross-Cultural Approaches to Literacy.* Cambridge: Cambridge University Press.

THORNE, B. 1993. *Gender Play: Girls and Boys in School.* New Brunswick, NJ: Rutgers University Press.

TREMBLAY, R., B. SCHAAL, B. BOULERICE, L. ARSENEAULT, R SOUSSIGNAN, & D. PERUSSE. 1997. "Male Physical Aggression, Social Dominance and Testosterone Levels at Puberty: A Developmental Perspective." In *Biosocial Bases of Violence*, ed. A. Raine, P. Brennan, D. Farrington, & A. Mednick 271–91. New York: Plenum Press.

TRITES, R. S. 1997. *Waking Sleeping Beauty: Feminist Voices in Children's Novels.* Iowa City: University of Iowa Press.

WALKERDINE, V. 1998. *Counting Girls Out: Girls and Mathematics*. London: The Falmer Press.

WASON-ELLAM, L. 1997. "If Only I Was like Barbie." *Language Arts* 74 (6): 430–37.

Children's Literature

ALCOTT, L. 1868. *Little Women*. Boston: Roberts Brothers.

ALEXANDER, L. 1964. *The Book of Three*. New York: Holt.

LIONNI, L. 1960. *Inch by Inch*. New York: Astor-Honor.

———. 1964. *Tico and the Golden Wings*. New York: Knopf.

———. 1967. *Frederick*. New York: Pantheon.

———. 1968. *Swimmy*. New York: Pantheon.

———. 1969. *Alexander and the Wind-up Mouse*. New York: Pantheon.

———. 1970. *Fish Is Fish*. New York: Pantheon.

———. 1975. *Pezzettino*. New York: Pantheon.

———. 1991. *Matthew's Dream*. New York: Knopf.

McKISSACK, P. 1997. *A Picture of Freedom: The Diary of Clotee, a Slave Girl*. New York: Scholastic.

MULLER, R. 1984. *Tatterhood*. Richmond Hill, ON: Northwinds Press.

PAULSEN, G. 1987. *Hatchet*. New York: Bradbury.

SENDAK, M. 1963. *Where the Wild Things Are*. New York: HarperCollins.

SPERRY, A. 1940. *Call It Courage*. New York: Macmillan.

TAYLOR, M. 1976. *Roll of Thunder, Hear My Cry*. New York: Dial.

VOIGT, C. 1985. *Jackaroo*. New York: Atheneum.

———. 1990. *On Fortune's Wheel*. New York: Atheneum.

———. 1993. *The Wings of a Falcon*. New York: Atheneum.

———. 1999. *Elske*. New York: Scholastic.

WATKINS, Y. 1986. *So Far from the Bamboo Grove*. New York: Lothrop, Lee & Shepard.

WOJCIECHOWSKA, M. 1964. *Shadow of a Bull*. New York: Atheneum.

YEP, L. 1993. *Dragon's Gate*. New York: HarperCollins.

Author Profile

Virginia Hamilton

The creative process is nearly impossible to explain. This is a combination of the known, the remembered, and the imagined, my literary triad: fact, memory, and imagination, which combine to make plot and characters. Of course I picture characters in my mind, else how could I describe them and know them? Books begin with character. Characters define plot and action and decide the environment lived in and the social action to pursue. "Where do they come from," and "Do they grow and change" aren't pertinent questions. They are created with the creative process, what you know, what you remember and imagine from the other two.

Kids have all kinds of feelings, hidden ones, open ones, bad ones, and good ones. In *Cousins* (1990), Elodie may need affection and be pathetic, but given the opportunity, she turns away from Cammy, who has stood by her. So you see, character will out. I never knew a Little or Fractal. I created them through the process while writing *Second Cousins* (1998). *Cousins* has sold close to a million copies in paperback.

Blended Families

I have always been interested in families, which is why my books are always generational. Blended families are just as good as any other kind. Even if a father or mother is away, missing, gone, comes and goes, the idea of family stays in the atmosphere of the book. I'm interested in how children cope, and they usually do—quite well, in fact. Fractal in *Second Cousins* (1998) is the child who lost out. She will never get back the love she needed from not having a complete family. So she copes. It's up to me to find the ways she copes, which is what writing is all about. My views on forgiveness have nothing much to do with how my characters feel about it. These books are not about me. The defining elements of characters tell us how they feel and why. In other words, whatever is logical for a character is what I write. Has he changed? The point is, he's not perfect and that's what children need to learn. You can love imperfect parents and they can love you. Children learn that parents are human beings.

Contrasting the women adult characters in my books is an unfair method of associating ideas. When I wrote Mrs. Small, I knew nothing about Bluezy. I write one book at a time. Mrs. Small, in *The House of Dies Drear* (1968), was perfect for her environment and her normal, traditional, educated black family. Because she was a homemaker doesn't make her less a person. In *Plain City* (1993), Bluezy's comings and goings make her no less a loving mother. It makes her a mother hard to deal with, a hurtful mother, but one who loves, who made sure her child was taken care of. As I say, in blended families there will be parental figures to take the place of missing parents. I think authors write and what develops from characters and plots is the true story. You don't just include stuff to be putting it there. Maybe some folks do. I don't.

Gram Tut, in *Cousins* (1990), reflects my own mother, who spent her last years in the local care center. I got to know that universe quite well. I projected a child visiting her grandmother in that situation. My mother lived to be 97. She was my children's wonderful grandmother. She was a wonderful source for story. I know many children with grandparents. There are always elders among black families who become the grandparents if not actually so. I wish the propaganda would end about black families not having structure. People should visit churches on Sunday, to view the traditions, the structure.

Origins: M.C. Higgins and Junior Brown

I can tell you exactly where M.C. came from. I was sitting down to write and I saw this youth in my mind. He had lettuce leaves attached to his wrist with rubber bands. And he was running through woods. I started writing that down. Curious it was, but I've learned to trust what I see in my mind. Then, I realized someone was stalking him, invisible off the path. Another boy, smaller. Where was the first youth going? Oh, I thought. The lettuce leaves. He has animals in traps. He's going to bait the traps or free an animal, a rabbit, he's caught. And so it went. *M.C. Higgins, the Great* (1974) was not an easy book to write. But it actually came from that first thought the way I've described it. Books develop from somewhere deep inside. From all one knows and remembers about a place, perhaps, or an imagined situation.

I can tell you something else, which I'm sure has to do with M.C. Driving through hills of West Virginia. I'm in a car, loving the views out the window. Way up high, suddenly, I saw a plane wreck. I mean a plane, that had crashed there, broken apart long ago, perhaps on the side of the high hill. It was so startling. I think it was then I realized what juxtaposition could do in a story. Take something ordinary as a plane and put it on something ordinary, crashed on the side of a hill, and you have an extraordinary sight. So then, you tell me what I did in *M.C.* (1974) with juxtaposition.

Of course there are children like Buddy Clark in *The Planet of Junior Brown* (1971). There are all kinds of children. People are always surprised that poor young people are not dumb. But we tend to equate intelligence with riches, with whiteness. Buddy Clark is one of my best depictions, next to Junior Brown and M.C. Higgins. A very organic book. It does read as if it were written very recently. I'm happy to say that my publisher, Simon & Schuster, put out a special, commemorative, twenty-five-year new edition in 1999. Hard to believe it was written over twenty-five years ago. It seemed to write itself and I think therefore that it is true.

Things have changed. They've gotten worse and we know it. When I wrote *Junior Brown* (1971), people didn't know about the thousands of kids in war-torn cities. American cities are still at war. We don't need to go overseas to see it. We bomb our kids every day. We starve them, abuse them, criminalize and marginalize them. We have some wonderful children in America. Most of them, whether poor or not, are quite wonderful.

Earth's Future Is in the Stars

Children seem to take the Justice books in stride (*Justice and Her Brothers*, 1978). They understand they are science fantasy, I think, with a strong reality base. Someone once said the trilogy starts out as science fiction and ends as fantasy. I like to think the books are a combination. An artful dance is close. It is hard for me to separate out characters, for I write them intertwined, symbiotically. All breathing in and out in rhythm. I have no sense of good and evil, although I do, I think, have a moral sense here. I'm all for Justice! And bemused by "doubting" Thomas. I had two brothers. The younger one, the one I was closest to, was a drummer. There were two sides to him.

Books are put together from strong life forces. To analyze them is to introduce limitations. I accept the book as it is written. As written, it sees earth as wasteland. I do so admire Celester and the Starters. I do see earth's future in the stars.

Painting What I See with Words

I do write fictions and not sociology. Black communities are much like any other kind. If you see the black churches, you may understand the communities that support them. Trouble is, America is so segregated, one part refuses to see the other. I write about the generations. You find them in cities, in the countryside.

"Look and see" is what I tell people. They, we, are all out there, bringing the light. Oh, and I can't speak about most children, or most anything. "I paint what I see," said Rivera. And so I write.

Children's Literature

HAMILTON, V. 1968. *The House of Dies Drear*. New York: Macmillan.

————. 1971. *The Planet of Junior Brown*. New York: Collier.

————. 1974. *M.C. Higgins, the Great*. New York: Aladdin.

————. 1978. *Justice and Her Brothers*. New York: Greenwillow.

————. 1990. *Cousins*. New York: Philomel division of Penguin Putnam Books.

————. 1993. *Plain City*. New York: Scholastic.

————. 1998. *Second Cousins*. New York: Scholastic.

Author Profile

KATHERINE PATERSON

Typical people aren't interesting. That's why I write about atypical people, because I want my books to be interesting. The writer, too, has to be different from her peers. Something has to set you apart from the general run or why write, why be written about? There are certain books, series books, that appeal to the whole middle class of girls whose lives are lived out in what we think of as safe, semiprosperous neighborhoods. These books tend to be plot driven rather than character driven. If the writer cares more about the character, if she thinks character drives the plot, then she's going to have to pick somebody that drives. I've never said that before, but it makes sense.

For example, with *Lyddie* (1991), I had to decide why a person would do the kinds of things she did—why she would leave home and go down to Lowell. A lot of the girls went because they were spinsters and now spinning was no longer necessary to the family's economy. There had been a time in New England when the unmarried daughter who spun the wool from the family's sheep was a very valuable worker in the family unit, but in the middle of the 1800s it was no longer economical to raise sheep in northern New England. The great ranches in the West and the development of the railroads meant that wool could be produced and marketed at prices with which a small New England farm couldn't compete. So these young women had become financial liabilities, and if they had any gumption, they wanted to do something about that. So they went to factories where they could earn money.

A lot of the young women earned enough to pay off the mortgage on the family farm or send their brothers to Harvard, and then they went back home, married a local farmer, and raised families of their own. But some of these women didn't go home, they got sick from breathing the lint-filled air of the factories and died.

But for those who lived, life in the factory had changed their lives. They made money, they got an education, they became strong and independent. A number of them became leaders in the struggle for women's right to vote. Some became writers. Lucy Larcom, one of the more famous of the mill girls, started as a duffer at age ten or eleven, educated herself, and wrote at least two books. She became the editor of the famous nineteenth-century *St. Nicholas Magazine*, the first American magazine for children. Harriet Robinson, who also got her start as a child duffer, grew up to marry a newspaper editor and write books about her factory experience.

There were finishing schools and ladies' seminaries at the time, but a college that would really give women the same quality of education that men received was scarce. At Lowell, Harvard professors taught the classes that the factory girls attended. The girls couldn't get any college credit for their work, but the Harvard professors maintained that the mill girls were better students than the Harvard undergraduates. Of course, the girls were highly motivated.

No matter how much a writer believes in equality of the sexes, she can't rewrite history. Sara Louise, in *Jacob Have I Loved* (1980), was, in effect, a doctor. She wasn't allowed to have the title because of the time in which she lived, but she wasn't stopped from being a doctor, because there was no one else to do the work. So she was more of a doctor than most doctors we know. They are specialists. Louise was doing everything.

When an adult writes for children, she's spanning a gap of experience and perception. A children's book is really a bridge between a child and a wider world, not only between child and author, but between other places, other times. Also a bridge from childhood to adolescence. I'm aware of how reluctant I've been to have adolescents as central characters. To write convincingly about adolescence, sexuality has to be a huge part of what you're describing, and I just don't know if I want to spend that much time on it. It's not that I don't think sexuality is important, but there's a certain reticence on my part to go on and on in print about it.

I'm much more comfortable having a ten- or eleven-year-old as my central character. This is a time when children are still thinking about things other than their own sexual development and when there are other things of importance to them. I remember those years very well because it was a fascinating time in my life. I find when I talk to children of this age they are thinking deeply about many things, but as they get a little older they are much more self-involved. I really like writing for the younger age. I feel they are more ready to trust me.

The book where I tackled adolescence head on is, of course, *Jacob Have I Loved*. I hope kids won't read the book too soon—before, say, seventh or eighth grade. And I think it's a book you want to read and think about on your own and not be required to say what you think about it. So you don't get a standard critical view of it that the teacher approves of. I think it's a very personal story.

One of the most vicious articles that I've ever read about my work was an attack on *Jacob Have I Loved*. It was really an attack on Louise's mother. I tried to shrug it off, but it's always hard to shrug off something like that. The guy simply despised Louise's mother. I don't understand why people don't appreciate Louise's parents. I get a lot of fussing about them, especially her mother.

The trouble is, you see, that people want me to do something that I won't do. They want me to set out examples of what life should be like for children. In other words, they want me to present in *Jacob* the wonderful mother who made a smashing career and is a wonderful role model for her intelligent daughter. I've even known a few such women, and I'm sure I could write a book about them, but in my books I've got all these traditional mothers. Why? Because that's what I know best. I'm very proud of my writing and I'm quite conscious that I have done that, but I wouldn't have considered myself the greatest role model for my children. I certainly wouldn't make a good character in a book. When I was in college I was not allowed to go to seminary. I could take classes, but I couldn't enroll. But you look back at your life and you're not sorry it is the way it is. It would have been quite different if I had been permitted to become an ordained clergyperson.

Well, people are flawed, aren't they? That has been my experience. I have a good friend who is also a good writer. She said to me once, "One thing that interests me about your work is that you don't mind your characters' being flawed. I can't bear to give my characters flaws," she said. And I thought, yeah, that's right, I'm conscious of my own flaws, even though I love myself, and I love those characters. I don't think it makes them less lovable that they have flaws. It simply says that they're human.

I guess if you have difficulty loving people as they are, then you have difficulty creating characters that you can love. Because I have no difficulty loving flawed people, I have no difficulty creating flawed characters.

Even Jimmy Jo (*Come Sing, Jimmy Jo*, 1985) is selfish in a sense. It doesn't come out so blatantly as it does in some of my other characters. His unhappiness with his mother and his wanting to sing the song that his dad wrote for him—which she takes. There's a rivalry there with his mother that even he, a kid, doesn't want to admit, but that's what's going on there. He's really angry with her, and he has very mixed feelings, which I understand. I'm kind of a shy show-off like him. I think probably Jimmy Jo is most like me. It finally dawned on me one day. People said, "You're not shy," and I said, "What do you mean, I'm not shy?" They don't recognize me as shy, which I always have been. I think a lot of performers are shy show-offs. My sister said once, "How can you speak to two thousand people?" Better two thousand than two, because if you're shy, talking to two people is hard, whereas talking to two thousand is fun.

In my books the central character is always me. That's the person whose feelings I know. You don't really know anyone else. You can suspect and imagine, but your own feelings are the ones you really know. And it doesn't mean that I admire all those feelings either, but I understand James and have compassion for him.

Jip (*Jip: His Story*, 1996), however, remains a real mystery to me. The chief criticism of that book was that Jip was too good to be true. Well, too bad, that's the way he came—and he came full blown. He loved not wisely but too well. There are certain characters that appear and you describe them, you don't make them, and Jip was absolutely from the very beginning a wonderful character. Pure of heart. To make him do something wrong, to make him other than good, would have been not my business. That's the way he was, like Trotter (*The Great Gilly Hopkins*, 1978), she also came full blown. She came terribly full of love. I just fell in love with her and that was what she was.

You know, I get accused of writing depressing stories for children all the time. It makes me think of a story. When I moved to West Virginia, which was after I had done my junior year of high school, I went from Richmond, where I was going to a really fine high school that was challenging me in every way, where I had good friends, to

26

this awful high school. I'm not sure I would have survived if the most popular girl in school hadn't taken me under her wings. Because she took me in everyone else had to, because they all followed her. She's still a dear friend of mine. She was a person at a very difficult time in my life who cared for me and made it possible for me to get through what would have been hellacious years. What I didn't know then was that her father was an alcoholic and abused her mom and that she lived in that terror.

She never talked about it. I never much went to her house, but she loved to come to my house. She was crazy about my mom. On the way home from school, we always walked home from school together, we'd get to my house before we got to her house. So it all seemed quite natural to me at that time, that we weren't spending time at her house. After we were both in college she told me. She assumed, however, that I knew or suspected and that was why I had taken her to my house so much. I didn't. I really didn't know. I didn't like her parents much and it was always such a marvel to me that she came from such parents because they were not educated, not personable at all, but I didn't know that they were in bad shape.

A few years ago, I was invited to speak at a correctional center. The inmates had a book discussion group and they were discussing what had happened in *The Great Gilly Hopkins*. The first thing the teacher asked was how many of them had been foster children. It was a mixed male-female group of twenty and every single person raised his or her hand. One young man, who was really involved with the discussion, said that when he was a foster child, he had had a really good foster mother and she had given him *The Great Gilly Hopkins*. He said he was so mad at the world he wouldn't even read it. Now he knew what she was trying to do, but at that time he couldn't hear it. He asked, "Do you think Gilly could have made it if she hadn't had Trotter?" And I said I really didn't know. I think I break one of the cardinal rules on writing for children. One of the cardinal rules they teach you whenever you go to a class on writing for children is that a child has to solve his or her own problems. This never happens in a book of mine. I think it's totally unrealistic. One of the scary things of childhood is that children have so little power.

For each of my young major characters some wise or older person comes and serves the role of the fairy godmother. The minor characters don't get the same treatment. You've got to be one of my central characters. My characters must experience the consequences of their actions, but in every one of my books there's someone who helps the child get through safely. In *Come Sing, Jimmy Jo*, Jimmy had his father and grandmother. So there's nearly always an adult to help, though not always a parent.

Many parents in my books are not biological parents. I didn't set out to do that and maybe it's because we have two adopted daughters. I'd look at a book and say, "Oh look! I've got some self-justification going on here." The mortality rate for parents in my books is notoriously high. The child is an orphan or half orphan, because if you have two loving parents right there all the time, then where is your plot?

I've been asked more than once, where are all the happy families of children's books? Then I think, well, *Little Women* (1868), let's see, if the dad had stayed home like he should have instead of rushing off to war, we wouldn't have had a story, now would we? There aren't a lot of happy families in children's books. But there are a lot of kids that turn out like Jip or Lupe (*Flip-Flop Girl*, 1994) despite their circumstances. My friend Barbara is one of the success stories.

I'm not one of these people who has drawers full of ideas who'll never live long enough to write all these ideas into books. I'm one of those people who finishes a book and says, that was a good career while it lasted. Absolutely, it's the truth. I just sort of do other things, waiting for the book to come to me. It's not that I have no ideas. It's that I want a book I write to be worth my time. I want it to be worth the trees. I don't write just to publish something for the publishing company. I don't think you should treat your readers that way. I don't think you should be that wasteful of time or trees. What I have to do is wait, then. And it is not a single idea. It has to be a complex of ideas that finally come together. The first thing I got for Jip was the image of a child rolling off the back of a wagon and nobody coming back for him. I thought it was going to be an adventure story. I thought, hot diggity dog, I've always wanted to write a real adventure yarn. I just ran to work on it. I went back and reread all the great adventure stories from the nineteenth century that I could put my hands on. I read *Huckleberry Finn* (1885). I read *Treasure Island* (1883). I read *Great Expectations* (1861). *Kidnapped* (1886) was one of the best I read. I said: "This is what I want to do—write a story like *Kidnapped*." The thing was I already had a given—the child rolling off the wagon. When I figured out why that had happened it wrecked my plan to write a rollicking adventure story.

I thought people were going to get on me for writing Jip's story. I mean, there are slave owners in my family tree, not slaves. The protest didn't happen, but it might have. Whether you should write about ethnic and racial groups to which you do not belong is a real issue. It took me a long time to come to grips with Jip's story, but isn't that, after all, what imagination is about—putting yourself into the life of another person?

My first three novels were set in Japan. I was naïve back then. It didn't occur to me that I shouldn't write from the point of view of a Japanese character. After all, I'd lived there for four years and spoke Japanese. I would be shy now going back and writing another novel set in Japan. I also wrote a book set in China, where I was born and lived my early life, though, here again, I'm not sure today I'd set out to write another Asian novel. Still, if a wonderful idea occurs to me, I might just try to get up the nerve to write the story.

Children's Literature

ALCOTT, L. M. 1868. *Little Women*. Boston: Roberts Brothers.

DICKENS, C. 1861. *Great Expectations*. London: Chapman & Hall.

PATERSON, K. 1978. *The Great Gilly Hopkins*. New York: Dutton.

———. 1980. *Jacob Have I Loved*. New York: HarperCollins.

———. 1985. *Come Sing, Jimmy Jo*. New York: Dutton.

———. 1991. *Lyddie*. New York: Dutton.

————. 1994. *Flip-Flop Girl*. New York: Dutton.

————. 1996. *Jip: His Story*. New York: Lodestar.

STEVENSON, R. L. 1883. *Treasure Island*. Boston: Roberts Brothers.

————. 1886. *Kidnapped*. New York: Scribner.

TWAIN, M. 1885. *The Adventures of Huckleberry Finn*. New York: Charles L. Webster.

2

The Unquenchable Source: Finding a Heroic Girl Inside a Man

T. A. Barron

The concept of hero has changed forever. As every reader of mythic tales knows, writers in recent years have developed several convincing, capable, and strong heroes—who also happen to be female.

Joseph Campbell, in *The Hero with a Thousand Faces* (1949), defined a hero as someone whose "visions, ideas, and inspirations come pristine from the primary springs of human life and thought. Hence they are eloquent, not of the present, disintegrating society and psyche, but of the unquenched source through which society is born" (20). Campbell states that this definition applies to girls as well as boys, women as well as men.

But therein lies a problem. Though Campbell was certainly right about the power and importance of heroes—embodiments of that "unquenched source" that creates new worlds—he was writing at a time when few tales featured girls and women in heroic roles. Men almost always did the questing; men normally slayed the dragon, won the prize, or saved the kingdom. Men normally established the rules, as well as the symbols, of victory.

Not every male hero, of course, is the stereotypical warrior—the one-dimensional character who possesses plenty of physical strength, and perhaps some courage, but no depth spiritually, emotionally, or morally. The Arthur portrayed by T. H. White in *The Once and Future King* (1939) is one example: He is compelling precisely because of his vulnerability. Much of Arthur's wisdom flows from his understanding of his own weaknesses; his idealistic vision of a society based on justice, rather than on brute force, stems from his appreciation of humanity's frailties as well as its wondrous potential. Another, more recent example is the protagonist of Katherine Paterson's unforgettable novel *Jip: His Story* (1996). Jip is male—and also gentle, thoughtful, caring, and as openhearted as he is open-minded.

In recent years, characters as rich and deep as Arthur and Jip have been joined by equally compelling female heroes. This has been true in the realm of mythic quests, as well as in historical fiction, but the change has been especially noticeable in the former category. It has been a most welcome shift, with profound consequences for the world of literature—and also, I believe, for the world in which we live.

Madeleine L'Engle, Ursula Le Guin, and Gail Carson Levine—to name just three of the writers who have made important contributions on this front—have deepened and strengthened the concept of the female hero in a mythic context. They have shown convincingly the traumas and triumphs by which women and girls can be great leaders, gifted healers, and also fierce warriors. And such characters need not simply mimic the male hero's journey. They may reject the established patterns, cast aside the old rules, and prevail on their own terms.

In L'Engle's tale *A Wrinkle in Time* (1962), for example, her young hero Meg saves the day (and, not incidentally, her father and her brother) through the power of her love rather than the power of her weaponry. Sometimes, as in the case of Meg, female heroes reveal their greatness through their actions, their direct impact on the world around them. In other cases, their greatness shines through their wisdom, their observations and teachings. Le Guin's wise woman Moss in *Tehanu* (1990), who champions the awesome—and mysterious—wellsprings of female power, comes readily to mind. Ella, the hero of Levine's *Ella Enchanted* (1996), shows her greatness mostly through qualities of character: fierce determination to free herself from the curse she has borne since infancy, unselfishness that causes her to make significant sacrifices for the person she loves, and courage to pursue her dream even when it seems impossible.

These new heroes are very important, not just for literature but for life. All of us need heroes. And all of us, regardless of gender, age, or background, can benefit from such thoughtful portrayals of girls and women who break through the barriers that hold them back—whether those barriers exist primarily within themselves or without. In Meg's case, the barriers are brutally clear: the machinations of a power-hungry opponent determined to destroy her if it cannot control her, just as it has already done to much of the universe. For Moss, the barriers she faces lie more in the social conventions and restrictions that have severely limited her status as well as her access to knowledge. And for Ella, the most serious barriers she must confront are the fears and doubts deep inside herself, which she faces with spirit, intelligence, and humor.

Yet despite the emergence of such remarkable characters in mythic literature, I often despair at the debilitating and demeaning images of girls and women that assault us daily from other sources. Obvious examples flow from the entertainment and product-selling media. How can our young women possibly discover the heroes in themselves if they are continuously told that they are what they buy or wear or look like, rather than what they do and say and strive to become? How can they come to know how much their choices matter—indeed, how much they themselves matter—if they are constantly told that superficial qualities are more important than lasting ones? A hero, after all, is something far more precious than a mere celebrity. A hero cares about ideas and goals and sacred qualities—not the color of her shoes or hair or car.

Creating strong, believable heroes of every gender and description is an immensely valuable enterprise. This I believe, both as a father of five young children and as a writer. The act of weaving bold new threads into our shared tapestry of story, wholly worthwhile for its own sake, may also help us to reweave the tapestry of our lives. Stories can, in surprising ways, enter into our collective consciousness, changing the very quality of our days. Through our stories, we may tap into that "unquenched source," drink from it, and grow through it.

That source is our own mythic imagination. That is what Campbell was celebrating: humanity's universal wellspring of story that flows unfathomably deep, wondrously broad, and endlessly mysterious. Truly, that source is unquenched—as well as unquenchable. How so? Because our power of imagination is nothing less than a variety of the power of creation. Through our stories, we create our own choices, our own lives, our own worlds—with no limits whatsoever.

These unlimited possibilities are especially evident in stories of fantasy (or, as I prefer to call them, "mythic" or "visionary" tales). For while such tales spring from the imagination, they are far more than imaginary. They are, in a fundamental sense, true. If well crafted, they are capable of winning our honest belief at the levels of our emotions, our minds, and our spirits. They can lead us into dark, unknown places—between what is known and comfortable. They can take us beyond the meeting places of femininity and masculinity, youth and age, mortality and immortality, nature and culture. And what occurs in those meeting places is more than a mingling. Rather, it is a becoming. A flowering. A fusion—from which something altogether new can emerge.

All this presupposes that a mythic hero can feel wholly true to an intelligent reader. But how is such a thing possible? This task is never easy (at least, alas, for me). For truth in this context implies a far higher standard than Coleridge's oft-repeated goal of creating a willing suspension of disbelief. To my mind, the hero of a mythic tale, no less than the place itself, must feel so real that the reader willingly and actively *believes*. To accomplish this, a writer must know that character thoroughly—so thoroughly that the character's thoughts, voice, and motivations are as clearly understood as the writer's own.

Is that really an attainable goal? Can a writer come to know a character that well, even if they are different both in gender and background? The answer, I believe, is yes—but not without a great deal of struggle and honest soul-searching.

The greatest challenge I have ever faced in this regard has been in developing the female heroes in my books. As a forty-something man, none of the writing I had done previously came close to preparing me for the difficulties of this challenge. Yet as great as the labor has been, the rewards have been greater still. I have met several characters who have virtually stood up and walked off the pages of my manuscripts and into my life. Best of all, I have experienced the joy of discovering the voice of a young girl within myself.

As a result, I have written three novels—*Heartlight* (1990), *The Ancient One* (1992), and *The Merlin Effect* (1994)—featuring a girl named Kate Gordon as the hero. She is approximately thirteen years old in the novels, which take place respectively on a faraway galaxy, in a mysterious grove of redwood trees, and deep under the sea. From the outset, I knew that for Kate to feel true for my readers, she would need first to feel true for me. That meant, among other things, that she must be strong as well as vulnerable, wise as well as innocent, thoughtful as well as passionate, capable of raging as well as of forgiving. She could not be a two-dimensional character; she must be wholly herself, fully integrating qualities that might seem on the surface contradictory. She must glory in her independence, as well as in her gender, affirming herself naturally and gracefully.

But how to make her come alive? The first thing I did was to interview my wife, Currie, to the limits of her patience, about her life as a teenage girl. Then I spoke with our oldest daughter, and with some nieces, about their own experiences. At last, I began writing the manuscript. I soon concluded, however, that I was still writing out of my own male worldview. My main character seemed more like a boy—albeit a boy with a braid. And if I was not convinced of Kate's trueness, why should anyone else be?

At that point, I set aside the manuscript and began writing a brief biography of Kate. For weeks I labored, trying to understand all the inner motives, fears, dreams, and conflicts that made her fully human. In short, I needed to hear her true voice inside of me, the expression of what Carl Jung called "anima" in works such as *Man and His Symbols* (1964, 220).

To find that voice, I explored the elements of her life. Not the major roles and issues that would be evident to an observer such as Jung, but the microscopic details of her days. What class at school did she most enjoy? Which one did she most detest? And why? What recurring nightmare woke her up, drenched in perspiration? What simple act of kindness had touched her most deeply? When she walked into the kitchen and opened the refrigerator door, what food or drink did she reach for first? Why did her grandfather's Scottish brogue soothe her? Why did his manner of pouring tea intrigue her? And so on.

For me, one of the most striking elements of Kate's voice was its deep intuitive qualities—and, even more important, her willingness to *trust* her own intuitions. For example, at the end of Kate's quest in *The Ancient One*, my original plan showed her taking her final step to triumph in a straightforward, direct manner. But the character I'd grown to know so well clearly wanted to do something else first—to make a sacrifice that just might help a friend. Even though she seemed to be giving up her best chance of prevailing, to do otherwise would not have been true to herself. So she followed her deeper loyalties, and I followed her. In the end, she found another, more surprising way to prevail. And the climactic scene of the book, when she returns to her own time only through the help of a great redwood tree known as the Ancient One, holds richer meaning because of her own earlier sacrifice.

In this way, Kate's voice truly took over. She started telling me her stories, and I started listening. Then I simply got out of the way and let her do the rest.

My most recent novels, the five books of the *Lost Years of Merlin* epic (the first of which was published in 1996), offered me new opportunities to hear strong female voices. Young Merlin washes ashore on the first page of Book One as a completely blank slate, with no memory of his childhood and no idea of his glorious destiny as a wizard, the great enchanter who will one day become the mage of Camelot. How this boy grows in wisdom—discovering his own inner gifts as he learns about compassion, transformation, courage, humility, love, and grief—is the central thrust of these novels. How did Merlin ultimately grow to legendary stature, developing his deep understanding of both human frailty and human potential? That is the underlying mystery, and the framework of his quest.

Much of Merlin's growth comes through the influence of three female characters: his mother, Elen, who dares to combine the healing arts and faiths of people as divergent as Druids, Jews, and Celtic Christians; his sister, Rhia, who lives in the forest and knows the intimate languages of the trees, the animals and birds, and the seasons; and his lover, Hallia, who values deeply her heritage as a deer-woman, and who teaches Merlin how to run and hear and think with the supreme sensitivity of a deer. It is no accident that these three characters represent the archetypal roles of mother, sister, and lover that the wise man must ultimately integrate within himself.

The key metaphor of Merlin's growth in this regard comes during Book Two of the epic, *The Seven Songs of Merlin* (1997). After seeking to master a variety of challenges, codified in the "seven songs of wisdom," Merlin faces the greatest challenge of all. To save the life of his sister, who is dying in his arms, he must somehow take her spirit into himself. He must inhale her very essence. It is by far the most difficult thing he has ever done. He tries, hoping to save her life—but the experience is also about saving himself. For to prevail in this moment, as well as in his quest, he must merge the male and female elements of his innermost being.

As Merlin takes the spirit of his sister into himself, then later releases it, some of her essence remains with him. An abridged version of that scene follows:

> I hesitated, fearing that releasing her spirit would surely mean losing her forever.
>
> Yet . . . the time had come.
>
> I exhaled. Deep within, I could feel her spirit stirring subtly. Then it began to flow out of me, at first like a trickle of water, gathering strength, until finally it felt like a river bursting through a dam. My eyes brimmed with tears, for I knew that whether or not Rhia survived in mortal form, she and I would never be so utterly close again.
>
> Slowly, very slowly, my breath wove into the shreds of mist around us, creating a shimmering bridge linking my chest and hers. The bridge hovered, glowing, for barely an instant, before fading away completely.
>
> Rhia's forefinger trembled. Her neck straightened. Then, at last, her eyes opened, and her bell-like laughter rang out. I realized, in that moment, that I could still feel deep within me, a touch of her spirit. A bit of my sister had remained with me. And, I knew, always would.

Through scenes of this kind, Merlin comes to know his female elements. As that happens, he grows in stature, depth, and ultimately wisdom—all of which must occur if he is, one day, to become the great wizard of lore. His experience, however, is not just limited to legendary wizards. It is open to every human being.

Just like Merlin, all of us harbor within ourselves a variety of voices—and yes, a variety of heroes. Let us honor that fact, and celebrate it, both in our lives and in our stories. In particular, I am hopeful that we will hear many more female voices, voices as compelling as they are heroic.

For while the female hero is not yet a commonplace in mythic tales, she is steadily gaining ground. That is essential, for she has much to teach us—both about herself and about the unquenchable source of her power.

References

CAMPBELL, J. 1949. *The Hero with a Thousand Faces*. New Jersey: Princeton University Press.

JUNG, C. G. 1964. *Man and His Symbols*. New York: Bantam Doubleday Dell.

Children's Literature

BARRON, T. A. *Heartlight* (1990); *The Ancient One* (1992); *The Merlin Effect* (1994); and the *Lost Years of Merlin* epic: *The Lost Years of Merlin* (1996); *The Seven Songs of Merlin* (1997); *The Fires of Merlin* (1998); *The Mirror of Merlin* (1999); and *The Wings of Merlin* (2000). New York: Penguin Putnam.

L'ENGLE, M. 1962. *A Wrinkle in Time*. New York: Farrar, Straus & Giroux.

LE GUIN, U. K. 1990. *Tehanu*. New York: Atheneum.

LEVINE, G. C. 1997. *Ella Enchanted*. New York: HarperTrophy division of HarperCollins.

PATERSON, K. 1996. *Jip: His Story*. New York: Puffin Books division of Penguin Putnam.

WHITE, T. H. 1939. *The Once and Future King*. New York: Berkley Books division of Penguin Putnam.

Author Profile

Gary Paulsen

Survival

When I was a kid, I worried about surviving in the woods, I worried about surviving in school—both academically and socially—I worried about surviving with drunk parents—my parents were alcoholics—but now, I think, young people have a lot more to worry about. The concept of survival—in a world filled with AIDS, guns in the hands of the wrong kind of people, the dangers of predators on the Internet, I could go on and on—is even more important than it was when I was a child.

Hatchet

Hatchet (1987) was based on a real boy, the son of a friend of mine. He came to me when he was about fourteen and said that he had seen his mother kissing another man in a car in a parking lot. He asked me what he should do about his big secret. I said, you know, it's not my call. I can't tell you what to do. This was the seed for *Hatchet*.

I spent a great deal of time in the bush, hunting and fishing and trapping when I was a child and later as an adult, too, so much of what I write about comes from my own life. Almost everything in *Hatchet* has happened to me. I've hunted and trapped and been attacked by moose when I ran dogs in Alaska. I've been attacked by bears and I've been caught in storms. The only things I did in *Hatchet* that were pure research were to start a fire with a hatchet and a rock—it took me four hours—and to eat a raw turtle egg, which was truly awful and tasted like rotten Vaseline, but I had seen the mother lay the clutch so I knew they were fresh.

The Island

The Island (1988) is about my son and these mental islands that he would go to. At first I challenged them because I thought he should be more like me. He was shy and very private and not, I thought, as communicative as he should be. Then I realized that he was right and I was wrong and I went to his island. By that I mean that I quit trying to get him to be like me and I tried to be more like him.

Dogsong

I spent some time in the villages of Alaska running dogs with Eskimos, or Inuits, as is more correct. So many of these villages have gotten rid of their dogs in favor of snow machines. They got rid of the dogs for practical reasons—you don't have to feed a snow machine. But I talked to a young boy who asked me about dogs, wanted me to teach him about dogs. And I thought it was just insane that an Eskimo kid on the Bering Sea would have to ask some white jerk from Minnesota about dogs. He didn't understand about his own traditions and he was curious. He wanted to find out about dogs as a way to learn about himself. From meeting him to writing *Dogsong* (1985) was not a big leap.

The Sea

I've been living on a sailboat for the past six or seven years. I went to Fiji last year, sailed there and back, on this old clunker boat that I've been restoring and repairing. I've noticed some people who buy all these gadgets and electric charts and, instead of actually going anywhere, they sit in the harbor and plan passages that they'll never take. These things are like video games that people buy, and then they sit on their boats and plot pretend trips. It's such vicarious living, something that makes people think they're living when they're really not. I've always believed in personal inspection at zero altitude. If you want to know what it's like to sail, then get on your boat, leave the harbor, and sail.

The Voyage of the Frog (1989) comes from what happened to me on my first boat. When I got out of the Army, after three years, eight months, twenty-one days, and nine hours, I bought a crummy little boat in Ventura. I didn't know how to sail, but I bought this little twenty-two-footer in Ventura, California, took it out, and got stuck in a storm. I was driven south about halfway down Baja when I was becalmed for days and days before the wind picked up and I could start working my way back north again.

Soldier's Heart

The military has come up with many names for what to call a man who has been ruined in combat. In Vietnam, they called it post-traumatic stress disorder. In the Second World War, it was called battle fatigue, and in the First World War, it was called shell shock. But in the Civil War, when a man was shattered by battle, he was said to have soldier's heart. He could never be normal again, and he became isolated. Now the experts have figured out how to treat such a mental blow, or they think they have, but back then the ex-soldiers just walked off, alone.

There really was a Charley Goddard who went through that experience. He was a fifteen-year-old kid who lied about his age, joined the Minnesota First Volunteers, and fought in the Civil War. He got through the war, but he was torn to hell and shot to pieces, both literally and figuratively, because of all the horrible things he'd seen. I just barely fictionalized his story. I moved some times around. Charley was in the Army during all the battles I wrote about but, for instance, he missed the Battle of Bull Run because he had dysentery. I took a little artistic license with that scene. Charley fought through the entire war and died a year after the war was over of soldier's heart.

I get asked what age a book like that is for. I don't do that. A book is a book. When I was young and I finally got turned on to reading, I was about fourteen or fifteen, I read *Moby Dick* and I read Edgar Rice Burroughs and I read *Kidnapped* and I read Zane Grey westerns. I know kids who are eleven and love Stephen King. I had a friend, an adult, and the first book he ever read was *Hatchet*. I feel it's wrong to limit the readers for any book.

The Rifle

My life has been saved many, many times because I had a weapon. I have not shot people, although I know men who have, who are alive only because they have killed other men in combat. But I have been attacked by both moose and bear and had I not had a weapon, I would have died. I would not have merely been hurt, I'm certain that I would have been killed. I've had friends who have been killed like that and I realized how useful a weapon can be in dire straits.

America is, I think, the greatest country that's ever been. There's absolutely no way to dispute that it is the most benevolent, most abundant, the best that's ever been in the human race, even with all of the mistakes and flaws. Part of the reason it's so great, oddly enough, is because of guns. We would not be great were it not for the fact that there were Pennsylvania rifles in the Revolutionary War because they really did help win the war and our independence.

Weapons have worked to save us as a country. But now we have an epidemic of them. Ottawa, Canada, I've heard, has three gun homicides a year, and we have five a night in Washington, D.C. That's insane, it's completely out of control. In *The Rifle* (1995a) I wanted to show how one weapon was necessary and helped us win the Revolutionary War, and yet it killed a child at the end, which, you could say, is what has happened on a larger scale with America.

Guns that were once important to us when we were first a new country have now become a disease. The incorrect use of guns slaughters thousands of people every year in this country. The longer it goes on, the harder it will be to fix it. The gangs are, in many cases, better armed than the cops. Police are supposed to enforce a peaceful life, they're not meant to fight combat. Somehow, ultimately, it has to be controlled and I'm not sure how to do it.

The Tent

When I was in aerospace, I had a friend who wanted to get rich. He saved up a little money and bought an old Army tent; he figured he'd go around running a fake evangelical thing. He thought it was a quick way to make a great deal of money. He got a trailer and a powder blue Cadillac. Then he went around phony-preaching and making quite a bit of money. I got a letter from him years after that and he said that he'd actually started listening to the words of Christ. He went and got ordained as a real minister and studied.

I studied Christ for the research of *The Tent* (1995b). If you read about Christ, the man, his story and his thoughts are really interesting. I studied Christ and I really liked him. I mean, I would like to sit and talk with him. He was an incredible person and a wonderful philosopher. I've never belonged to an organized religion, but much of what he said made sense to me in a way that surprised and impressed and inspired me.

Letters from Young People

I get between two hundred and four hundred fan letters a day. They're all wonderful and I learn from them all. Many of them ask the ordinary questions, such as where do I get my book ideas. Some of them are technical. I made a mistake in the original *Hatchet*: I called a Cessna, the bush plane, a 206; it was a typo, it was actually a 406. I get quite a few letters on that, correcting me, but that's cool.

Some of the letters are from kids in trouble or who are being abused. I answer them all eventually. Most I answer with a letter and a picture and a note about what I'm doing, which I try to update all the time. But the ones who are in trouble I answer personally. I'll call the high school counselor if I think there's an immediate danger. I try to get help for them. It's very ticklish because I don't want to blow a confidence with them. A lot of kids tell me stuff that they wouldn't tell anyone else. They feel very safe writing to me because they know my life, my childhood, and how bad it was, and kids who are in trouble feel that I can relate to that. I'm not qualified to be a counselor or anything like that, but I do try to get them to go to the right place, like a teacher or a principal.

So many young people would do better for themselves if they could realize that this is temporary. Whatever bad is happening to them is really temporary, it's not the end of the world and it will pass.

Living in the Wilderness

I am a function of the wilderness. I can't live in the city. I can't be in crowds. I like people, but I can't live in areas where there are a lot of people. It's very hard on me and I've tried, and failed, several times. I just start pacing like a wild cat in a cage. I just can't handle it. I've been in the bush so long. I've got 22,000 miles on dogsleds and have gone twice across the Pacific on a sailboat, largely alone. I've spent a lot of time in wilderness situations. You go back so far that you become a cave painting, you become very primitive.

I used to maintain that it was a primitive exaltation that happened in the bush or at sea, that you become elevated, not above other people, but above yourself. Wilderness situations are so pure and true, so honest that it becomes very difficult to go back to a crowded place. I just can't do it. So I put those experiences into my writing. It's part of my life to write about what I see and become in the wilderness.

Finding My Obsession

I was sitting with a friend of mine who had done two tours in 'Nam and got shot to hell. We were sitting there talking about how many things we'd done wrong, not morally wrong, but mistakes we'd made in our lives. I figured that the best I can do is about 10 percent right. About 90 percent of my life has been, in one way or another, a mistake.

I became an electronics engineer, which was a waste of time. I joined the Army, waste of time. I've been married twice before I met my wife. These are major blocks of time in my life—we're talking 20 to 30 percent of my life. I worked in Hollywood for a year. I sculpted for a while. I tried acting. I tried carpentry. These were steps along the way, but I should have been writing all that time. I should have been working fifteen to eighteen hours a day trying to find out more about writing. But I didn't have a clue.

Of course, my characters have flaws. They wouldn't be real if they didn't. They're just real to me, these characters in my books, and real people are flawed. Like me.

Sometimes I think I'm getting a handle on writing, and this is after two-hundred–plus books. Sometimes I think I haven't even started to learn. Hemingway used to say that if he could get three or four honest paragraphs in a whole book, then that was just a wonderful thing. He wrote about F. Scott Fitzgerald and how his talent was like the dust on a butterfly's wing. When the dust was gone, he kept flapping his wings and he couldn't understand why he could no longer fly. I have learned that maybe that is true. I'll get a couple of places in a book, maybe a chapter or a page or just a line where it really hits, where the writing really locks in and I know what it means to dance with words.

I can't not write. I work every day. I work on the boat. I have a laptop and I sit on the boat and write while I'm sailing. When I ran dogs and did the Iditarod, I devoted eighteen hours of every day, seven days a week, to the dogs. I did that for eight years and then I developed heart disease and I had to quit running dogs. I suddenly had this eighteen-hour-a-day hole in my life. And I put writing in that hole and started writing like I was running dogs. I work all the time. I'll write obsessively until I die.

Children's Literature

PAULSEN, G. 1985. *Dogsong*. New York: Bradbury.

———. 1987. *Hatchet*. New York: Bradbury.

———. 1988. *The Island*. New York: Orchard.

———. 1989. *The Voyage of the* Frog. New York: Bradbury.

———. 1995a. *The Rifle*. San Diego: Harcourt Brace.

———. 1995b. *The Tent*. San Diego: Harcourt Brace.

———. 1998. *Soldier's Heart*. New York: Delacorte.

3

Deconstructing Harry: Casting a Critical Eye on the Witches and Wizards of Hogwarts

Deborah L. Thompson

I begin this chapter with a disclaimer: I love the Harry Potter novels. I am among the millions of adults (and children) who have been enchanted by the young orphaned wizard with the unruly hair. While I don't consider Harry's stories great literature, they are great reads. What makes them work is a combination of psychology and old-fashioned story telling. They function much like the Hogwarts Mirror of ERISED—in which we see vivid reflections of our richest imaginings. We envision ourselves discovering the joys of flying on a technologically engineered broomstick or studying to become a witch or wizard. We want to join Harry's happy band of friends attending Hogwarts, learning about spells and the dark arts. We would have thousands of uses for the invisibility cloak. Attending Quidditch matches, with its coeducational teams, would be so much more exciting than watching Muggle football or basketball. In other words, being in Harry's world would make our everyday worries secondary. Simply put, Harry is our antidote to real life and its problems.

Harry endears himself to us because he never reaches the end of his novels without his facing numerous obstacles created by Lord Voldemort and/or his minions. We connect with Harry, the underdog. He represents to us what Bettelheim (1977) calls a "fairy tale hero with whom we can identify." Ultimately, he "is the most comforting of fictional heroes: someone whose life, however exciting, is still pretty tough" (Tucker 1999, 25).

However, as I anxiously awaited the fourth installment in the series, I began to replace my unbridled adulation of young Harry and his creator with a closer, more critical look at the three novels. What I have found among the ghosts, spells, and Quidditch matches is a preponderance of gendered images more common to the mid-twentieth century than to the twenty-first.

We Americans so adore Harry and his author that very few criticisms of the works have been generated. There have been the usual evangelical critics who find the world in which Harry lives populated with far too many tools of the devil—witches, wizards, and magic. Some parents have fought against the books without having read a single page. Others have read superficially, overlooking the actual weaknesses in the stories, focusing instead on fantastic plot lines such as Quirrell's drinking unicorn's blood or any of the characters casting spells. Some concerned parents see no redeeming value in the novels and demand their removal from schools and libraries, fearing there are hidden messages that encourage their children to take up childhood witchcraft and wizardry ("Only a Story" 1999). Of course, there are no messages in Harry Potter, hidden or otherwise, that seduce children into drinking unicorn's blood, hatching dragons in the family fireplace, or attempting to turn family pets into plants or toads. However, a small but growing group of critics has focused on one major flaw in the Harry Potter novels—the author's traditional portrayal of males and females (Esmonde 1999; Ramos 2000; Schoefer 2000).

Witches Are Studious, Wizards Have Fun

From ghosts to wizards, the subtext of Harry's novels is that boys have great adventures and girls are studious, weepy, or simpering. It is ironic that these novels have encouraged so many boys to read more, yet the boy wizards Ron and Harry do not really like to read or study much. These are boys of action. They participate in great adventures, but appear clueless when they have to transfigure, cast spells, or write "lengthy" assignments. Harry and Ron are always surprised when they pass their exams: "Harry had almost forgotten that the exam results were still to come, but come they did. To their great surprise, both he and Ron passed with good marks" (*Harry Potter and the Philosopher's Stone*, 222[1]). What a message this presents. Hermione studies excessively and loves to show off her "book smarts." (She was the only student upset when exams were cancelled at the end of the year in *Harry Potter and the Chamber of Secrets*.) Harry and Ron have fun, go on adventures, get into scrapes, and still make good grades. The message here seems to be that it takes little effort for young wizards to be both adventurous and scholarly, but not so with young witches.

Even among the spectral and creature classes, male ghosts have more fun than female ghosts, and male house elves value freedom more than female house elves. Peeves, a Hogwarts poltergeist, has great fun being incredibly ill mannered. He writes rude words on the classroom chalkboards, he throws things at students as they scurry along the halls to class or to their quarters. He annoys teachers and stuffs chewing gum in keyholes. He tattles on everyone. In essence, he is a general nuisance. By comparison, Moaning Myrtle (*Harry Potter and the Chamber of Secrets*) does mostly what her name implies—she moans. She haunts the first-floor girls' bathroom, but she does so because that is where she met her demise. Myrtle doesn't have fun scaring others the way Peeves does. It is her moaning and weeping that keeps the girls from using the first-floor restroom, not nifty pranks. This haunting does serve as a plot device, but Myrtle is little more than a ghostly version of the weeping female who has little or no

43

control over her circumstances. Even Hermione doesn't like to come in contact with her.

Myrtle does moan less in the fourth novel. She even gives Harry helpful hints to pass the second task in Triwizard Tournament, but she still does not get to have the fun Peeves does as he douses the students with water balloons on their return to Hogwarts at the start of the new school year.

The bothersome house elves also exhibit gender differences. In *Harry Potter and the Chamber of Secrets*, the readers meet a most annoying creature named Dobby, a house elf. Throughout the book, Dobby is an obstructionist and a pain, but we learn why and can forgive him by novel's end. A gracious Harry frees Dobby from the tyranny of the Malfoy household, and we are spared his presence in *Harry Potter and the Prisoner of Azkaban*. Unfortunately in the fourth novel, *Harry Potter and the Goblet of Fire*, we are reintroduced to Dobby through perhaps the most annoying fantasy character since Jar Jar Binks—the female house elf, Winky. She tells Harry he has done Dobby no favor by freeing him, because Dobby now wants to do unspeakable things like wear clothes and be paid for his services. She prefers enslavement to freedom, and is among those who turn a deaf ear to Hermione's attempt to liberate Hogwarts' house elves. She obstructs the forces of good by providing aid and comfort to a Death Eater. Worst of all, Winky weeps and wails so much about not wanting to be free that Moaning Myrtle almost pales in comparison.

A "Henrietta Instead of a Harry"

Hermione Granger exhibits characteristics that are unflattering at times and annoying at others. She is the character who raises the ire of most of Harry's critics. Esmonde (1999) wishes that Rowling had named her protagonist "Henrietta" instead of Harry and notes that by taking the conservative route in her novels, she missed her chance to not only "enthrall millions of readers but also to enlighten them" by creating a powerful female hero. Esmonde's critique of the novels is mild compared to that of Ramos (2000) who sees the Harry Potter books as fitting perfectly in the chauvinist world of male literature (like Tom Clancy's novels) where women are either "absent, weak, silly, evil or vaporized by car bombs." Schoefer (2000) extends Ramos's argument. She states that the "range of female personalities is so limited that neither women nor girls play on the side of evil." The only females in the novels exhibiting any characteristics that resemble evil are the female members of Slytherin House. They are described in very unflattering terms—one girl from Slytherin House reminds Harry of a character in the book *Holiday with Hags*. In other words, these girls are not only sinister, but also ugly—a losing combination.

Neither Schoefer or Ramos would be happy with many of Rowling's female characters in *Harry Potter and the Goblet of Fire*. With few exceptions, the females are either temptresses (the veelas), simpering and giggly in the presence of Cedric or Krum, crying because they were not selected to compete in the Triwizard Tournament, or with the Yule Ball. Even the wand of the female Triwizard competitor is considered temperamental, because it contains hairs from a veela. With females breaking down barriers in every field imaginable from Ruth Bader Ginsburg and Sandra Day O'Connor on the Supreme Court to the Williams sisters on the tennis courts, it is disappointing to see such old and negative stereotypes appear in these best-selling children's books (Esmonde 1999).

It is obvious that Hermione is a brilliant student, obedient to a fault, and not particularly athletic—the stereotypical "girl's role." When we meet her in *Harry Potter and the Philosopher's Stone*, she is lending a helping hand to the hapless Neville, who has lost his toad. She stops long enough to annoy Ron and to bewilder Harry. She talks extremely fast and knows-it-all. She has done extra reading before setting off for Hogwarts. She knows more of Harry's history than Harry does (although we can blame the Dursleys for Harry's gap in knowledge about his family history). Ron has an immediate and negative reaction to the loquacious Hermione and fervently hopes that in whichever house he is placed, "she's not in it."

In all three novels, Hermione overachieves and overextends herself to be the best witch at Hogwarts. We are never really sure why she does this. We have no sense that it may be due to her being born to a couple of Muggles who are both dentists. She is just that way. Her knowledge and quick wit do get the three friends out of many dangerous spots. But for all her smarts, she is "hoodwinked" by the con artist Professor Gilderoy Lockhart in *Harry Potter and the Chamber of Secrets*. Lockhart is the smarmy new Defense Against the Dark Arts teacher at Hogwarts. At the beginning of the trio's Year Two, Hermione is the only one who had read Lockhart's assigned readings, so she received "full marks" on a lengthy test full of inane questions related to Lockhart's personal life.

The reader knows that Lockhart's every achievement has been purchased. So too do Ron and Harry, who don't need to read Lockhart's books to recognize a scam when they see one. On the other hand, the "book smart" Hermione is clueless—she has no idea Lockhart is being dishonest. Instead she makes excuses for his poor instruction. When Lockhart's Cornish pixie lesson collapses, Hermione thinks that Lockhart is giving the students "hands-on" experiences. To make matters worse, Hermione is infatuated with Lockhart. When she is in his presence, she blushes and giggles and displays all manner of "silly girl" behaviors.

It is fascinating that in creating Lockhart, Rowling uses particularly negative stereotypes often attributed to women and/or effeminate men. When Lockhart wears a "lurid pink robe" to one Hogwarts affair, the reaction of the other faculty members makes it obvious that real wizards don't wear pink—purple maybe, but never pink. In another scene, Harry goes to Lockhart's room and discovers that all of Lockhart's portraits are running away from the light to avoid being seen in hair rollers. A funny scene, yes, but it also plays on negative images females have struggled to reverse for many years. In the end, when Lockhart is asked to help rescue Ginny Weasley from the Chamber of Secrets, he loses his nerve, packs his bags, and attempts to sneak away, not wanting to be exposed for the sham that he is. It is only then that Hermione comes to terms with who and what Lockhart really is.

In this same novel, *Harry Potter and the Chamber of Secrets*, Ginny Weasley is the weak link that almost is Harry and Hogwarts's undoing. She exhibits few if any traits that would make her stand out among the first-year students at Hogwarts. She has no identity other than being a "Weasley redhead." A normally articulate little girl, she blushes and stammers every time she sees Harry. She makes no friends at Hogwarts, so in her loneliness, she finds and begins corresponding with a diary that can write back. Through this diary Tom Riddle (Voldemort) is unleashed. He gets her to do his bidding, including killing the Hogwarts roosters and writing threatening messages on the walls. By disobeying one of her father's cardinal rules, "Never trust anything that can think for itself, especially if you can't see where it keeps its brain," Ginny endangers herself, Harry, and the students and faculty of Hogwarts. A vapid "Clancy chick" would have done just the same and still have had to dodge bullets and terrorists before being rescued by the hero. It is no wonder that Ramos (2000) charges that the females at Hogwarts would fare better in a Tom Clancy novel.

A Hint of Growth

In the third Harry Potter novel, *Harry Potter and the Prisoner of Azkaban*, Hermione takes overachieving to a new level. She cannot make up her mind (another stereotypical female trait) as to which classes she wants to take, so she packs her schedule. She gives the term "overload" a new meaning by taking two or more concurrent classes. To accomplish this feat, she asks for and is granted special permission to use a "Time-turner." With this device, Hermione can take three classes at 9:00 A.M., two classes at 10:00 A.M., and so on. By the end of the novel, she has overextended herself so much that she becomes weepy and waspish. The boys wonder about her behavior, but not enough to really find out why she suddenly disappears and reappears without apparent reason—even for a place like Hogwarts: "Harry looked around too. Hermione hadn't entered the classroom, yet Harry knew she had been right next to him when he had opened the door. 'That's weird,' said Harry, staring at Ron. 'Maybe—maybe she went to the bathroom or something?'" (*Harry Potter and the Prisoner of Azkaban*, 294). Her lessons are not for naught; she reads so thoroughly that she was the only one of the trio to figure out that Professor Lupine was a werewolf. Her knowledge of the "Time-turner" allows Harry and her to save the lives of Sirius Black and Buckbeak, the Hippogriff. And in the end, Hermione exhibits her first signs of growth and decides that even she cannot take the grueling schedule she set for herself in her third year at Hogwarts.

It is in the fourth Harry Potter novel that we begin to see a less intense Hermione. She even taunts Harry and Ron about homework: "Lots of homework?" said Hermione brightly, catching up with them. "Professor Vector didn't give *us* any at all!" (*Harry Potter and the Goblet of Fire*, 202). Hermione is at her most intense when she champions the rights of the Hogwarts' house elves. But we also see a different Hermione, who gobbles her food quickly to go study in the library. Hermione has her eye on more than just books on these visits. We also realize, along with Harry and Ron, that when Hermione attends to her looks (instead of her books), the results are dramatic. This transformation is demonstrated when she makes her entrance at the Yule Ball: "The oak doors opened, and everyone turned to look as the Durmstang students entered with Professor Karakoff. Krum was in front of the party, accompanied by a pretty girl in blue robes Harry didn't know" (413). We can hope for continued growth of Rowling's favorite character[2] in the remaining novels, but we can only imagine how much better the first three Potter novels could have been had Hermione had the independence of thought and the strength of will of a Birdy or Aerin or Lyddie or Cassie.

Like So Many Ghosts

Various other girls and boys may interact with Harry at times—in class, the commons areas, the sitting room of Gryffindor, or on the Quidditch field (for instance, Ravenclaw's Seeker, who happens to be female, is Cho Chang [We see more of Cho Chang in *Harry Potter and the Goblet of Fire*. Harry has a crush on her, but alas, she only has eyes for Cedric.]), but these interactions are ephemeral, much like the many ghosts that inhabit Hogwarts.

A notable exception is Lee Jordan, the dreadlocked friend of Fred and George Weasley and Hogwarts's resident Quidditch commentator. (He is also Rowling's most prominent ethnic character.) We meet Lee on Platform Nine and Three-Quarters at King's Cross Station in *Harry Potter and the Philosopher's Stone*. He is described as "a boy with dreadlocks." Young Lee appears frequently enough in the novels for us to know that Rowling didn't leave him on Platform Nine and Three-Quarters at King's Cross Station. But beyond what we pick up from his commentaries at the Quidditch matches, we know little else about him other than that he has a giant tarantula and he is a friend of the Weasley twins. In each novel, Lee is always introduced or reintroduced to the reader as being a friend of the Weasley twins. It is as if Rowling has given no significant thought to Lee's place at Hogwarts or in the novels, other than as being a friend of George and Fred.

Other boys do not fare well under Rowling's pen. Neville is hopelessly hapless, and the odious Goyle and Crabbe seem to possess every negative stereotype an author could use to describe characters—apelike, slow-witted, and mean-spirited. They are the puppets of Draco Malfoy, who is also a flat, stereotypical character with no redeeming characteristics. Even the author describes Crabbe and Goyle as "existing only to do Malfoy's bidding." They are both "wide and muscley: Crabbe was taller, with a pudding bowl haircut and a very thick neck. Goyle had short bristly hair and long gorilla-ish arms" (*Harry Potter and the Prisoner of Azkaban*, 79–80). It is perplexing as to why Malfoy needs "muscle." He is, after all, a wizard-in-training. In none of the novels has he shown any hints of being a virtuous character, so why he hesitates to use his magic to wreak havoc is puzzling. He is not one to let some little rule like the one forbidding underaged wizards from using magic to prevent him from doing mischief. Given his father's importance in the wizarding world, his support of and allegiance to Lord Voldemort notwithstanding, it is hard to believe that Malfoy would be afraid to use his magic anywhere he deemed fit, as long as he could get away with violating the rules or aggravating Harry, Ron, and Hermione.

All Quidditch Players Are Created Equal

What little gender equity there is in the novels is displayed on the Quidditch field. This popular wizard sport is coeducational. There are even female members on the competing teams in the Quidditch World Cup (*Harry Potter and the Goblet of Fire*). The positions needing someone with speed and agility—Chasers and Seekers—are often played by girls. These girls give it their all and receive bumps and bruises like the boys. The girls even have to remind some team captains that the sport is played by both females and males, as is highlighted in this passage from *Harry Potter and the Philosopher's Stone*:

> Wood cleared his throat for silence.
> "OK, men," he said.
> "And women," said Chaser Angelina Johnson.
> "And women," Wood agreed. "This is it." (136)

To complete equality on the field, the referee for most of the Quidditch matches is Madame Hooch. Madame Hooch is one of the many teachers at Hogwarts. But like many of the other females in the Potter novels, we know little about her, other than that she always calls a fair game.

Harry Potter—"All-American" Boy

Classic literary references have been made between Harry and such major Dickensian characters as David Copperfield and Oliver Twist or Charlotte Brontë's Jane Eyre (Tucker 1999). And while Harry has had no chances to whitewash (or not whitewash) picket fences, it would not be inconceivable that he would do so, that is, if number four Privet Drive or Hogwarts had picket fences.

Despite his nerdish appearance, Harry exhibits those masculine traits American males so love to call their own: he is self-reliant, a risk-taker, athletic, a leader, independent, defends his beliefs, protects the underdog. In each novel, Harry has exhibited these characteristics on a regular basis. Classic references aside, Harry is, despite his British birthright, an "all-American" boy. He would be at home in many of our best-loved children's stories, most particularly one like Spinelli's *Maniac Magee* (1990).

One could easily envision Harry Potter and Maniac Magee taking apart the giant ball of string at Cobbles Corner, munching on crumpets, or negotiating the two worlds of the East End and the West End. Both boys perform fantastic feats with a wink and a little magic. Maniac's finding a home and love with the Beales is not unlike Harry's finding that he belonged in the world of wizards and witches at Hogwarts School. Each moral dilemma they face tests their courage, challenges their abilities to separate right from wrong, and taps their abilities to do what is right when the wrong thing to do would be the easiest avenue of action. Both boys take risks, whether it is facing down bullies, racists, or mountain trolls. Whether hitting McNab's frogball or catching a Snitch, the two boys are extraordinary athletes. One could see Maniac teaching Harry how to hit McNab's "frogball" properly, and Harry would give Maniac Quidditch pointers. Self-reliant, the boys survive harsh home conditions. And their longing for a safe and loving home is poignant. Maniac finds his; we can only hope that in his quest to be the best of wizards, Harry will also acquire the loving home and family he so strongly desires.

Harry would be just as at home in Flint, Michigan, with Buddy Watson (Curtis 1995, *The Watsons Go to Birmingham—1963*). The two boys have much in common, including their intellect, although Harry rarely displays his intellectual talents the way Buddy does, and their status as outsiders. It would take no stretch of the imagination to see Harry and Buddy engaged in the ultimate dinosaur war or avoiding the derision of Byron and Buphead. Perhaps Harry could drop in on Marty Preston (Naylor 1991, *Shiloh*) to work out how one should make difficult moral choices that involve life or death for a particular character. This "all-American" boy would also find kindred spirits in strong, feisty, "all-American" girls like Dicey (Voigt 1982, *Dicey's Song*) or Salamanca Tree Hiddle (Creech 1994, *Walk Two Moons*), who, like Harry, are on quests of self-discovery, self-acceptance, and closer connections to family.

Four Down, Three More to Go

We know that children begin to assign certain traits to boys and girls when they are young. These beliefs are continuously molded and shaped by what they see, hear, and read (Fox 1993, Turner-Bowker 1996). We have to be careful when a literary phenomenon like Harry Potter takes the literary center stage. We can and should hold Rowling to the standards to which we would hold any children's author whose works have been so lavishly praised. She has a responsibility to portray her fledgling witches and wizards as multidimensional, nonstereotypical characters, because sexism in children's literature negatively affects young readers, both female and male. We can only hope that as Harry's story continues, all of our favorite characters, as well as the author, will mature. The bad news is that we have grown comfortable with the characters as they currently are written—stereotypes and all. The good news is, Rowling has three more chances to break with the old stereotypes and make the world of Hogwarts truly legendary, where wizards and witches can willingly have great adventures and be scholarly at the same time. Rowling has shown us that she can entertain. Now she has to show us that she can entertain with substantive characters who do not adhere to any particular stereotype or gender role. Harry and his millions of fans deserve no less.

Endnotes

1. In this chapter, I used the British title *Harry Potter and the Philosopher's Stone* instead of the American title *Harry Potter and the Sorcerer's Stone*.

2. In an interview with *Entertainment Weekly* (August 11, 2000) Rowling intimates that Hermione is her favorite character.

References

BETTELHEIM, B. 1997. *The Uses of Enchantment*. New York: Random House.

ESMONDE, D. 1999. "The Trouble with Harry (Potter)." *Buffalo News*, 7 November, sec. E, p. 1.

FOX, M. 1993. "Men Who Weep, Boys Who Dance: The Gender Agenda Between the Lines of Children's Literature." *Language Arts* 70 (2): 84–88.

JENSEN, J. 2000. "Hocus Focus." *Entertainment Weekly*, 11 August, 554: 28–29

"Only a Story; Adults Should Worry About Own Fantasies, Delusions." 1999. *Houston Chronicle*, 16 November, sec. A, p. 22.

RAMOS, A. 2000. "The Trouble with Harry Potter—Teaching Our Children Sexism." In *Advancing Women* [e-zine]. Retrieved February 2000. Available wysiwg: //4/http://www.advancingwomen.com/womsoc/review_potter.html.

SCHOEFER, C. 2000. "Harry Potter's Girl Trouble." In *Salon.com* [on-line journal]. Retrieved February 2000. Available http://www.salon.com/books/feature/2000/01/13/potter.

TUCKER, N. 1981. *The Child and the Book: A Psychological and Literary Exploration*. Cambridge: Cambridge University Press.

———. 1999. "Harry Potter: The Boy Who Brought Back the Magic; The Unlikeliest of Literary Heroes Is Bespectacled and Gawky, Yet He Has Hooked Children Again on the Wonder of Reading." *The Independent* (London), 5 December, p. 25.

TURNER-BOWKER, D. M. 1996. "Gender Stereotype Descriptors in Children's Picture Books: Does 'Curious Jane' Exist in Literature?" *Sex Roles: A Journal of Research* 35 (7/8): 461–88.

Children's Literature

CREECH, S. 1994. *Walk Two Moons*. New York: HarperCollins.

CURTIS, C. P. 1995. *The Watsons Go to Birmingham—1963*. New York: Delacorte.

NAYLOR, P. R. 1991. *Shiloh*. New York: Atheneum.

ROWLING, J. K. 1997. *Harry Potter and the Philosopher's Stone*. London: Bloomsbury.

———. 1999. *Harry Potter and the Prisoner of Azkaban*. New York: Scholastic.

———. 1999. *Harry Potter and the Chamber of Secrets*. New York: Scholastic.

———. 2000. *Harry Potter and the Goblet of Fire*. New York: Scholastic.

SPINELLI, J. 1990. *Maniac Magee*. Boston: Little, Brown.

VOIGT, C. 1982. *Dicey's Song*. New York: Atheneum.

4

Popular Series Books and the Middle-Class Children Inhabiting Them: Are Girls and Boys Really That Frivolous?

Jennifer Armstrong

At the beginning of my writing career, I paid my dues—and my bills—by being a ghost-writer for the wildly popular Sweet Valley High and Sweet Valley Kids series. I saw books I had ghosted crop up regularly on bestseller lists. Over the course of seven or eight years, I managed to write approximately fifty of these books, so I have an intimate familiarity with the subject at hand.

Let me assure you from the start that I don't intend to bite the hand that fed me. Writing mass-market series books was never the pinnacle of my literary ambition, to be sure, but I personally benefited in many ways from having written them, and I think they serve a useful purpose for many readers—beyond providing entertainment.

But they are easy prey for literary critics and educators who have a hard time seeing anything worthwhile in them. The boys and girls in these books are so frivolous. But are they?

My first reaction is to refute the statement: in fact, very often the girls and boys in Sweet Valley High or Sweet Valley Kids grapple with very *unfrivolous* issues. The usual laundry list of problem-novel problems moved many of the stories forward, and the characters tried to meet them head-on. Eating disorders, parental abuse, drinking and driving, homelessness, racism—these were not subjects that characters laughed off. On the contrary, they struggled sincerely to resolve these conflicts.

Flip side: A cynical reaction to the above statement might be that yes, girls and boys *really are* that frivolous. Go to any mall or middle school, and you'll see plenty of evidence that nothing occupies teen consciousness except fashion, pop culture, and hormones. Take a sip from the fountain of youth culture and you will instantly feel a million years old. The kids in Sweet Valley High and other mass-market books look like striving, shiny, Horatio Alger characters by comparison.

Of course, the real answer lies somewhere between these extremes. I won't try to persuade anyone that Sweet Valley High books address serious problems in a truly complex and layered way. I also won't paint myself as a creaking old bore by shaking my cane and whining, "In my day, kids had more respect, blah blah blah!" What I can do is tell you what, in my opinion, these books really do, how they work, and what they tell us about gender roles.

To begin with, a definition. These are mass-market books, answering the needs of the marketplace. If a publisher finds sales of a newly launched mass-market series too weak, believe me, that series is dropped like a hot potato. So we are talking about a kind of book that obeys the rules of the marketplace, not the rules of literary taste or artistic integrity. Kids want these books. Why? And why should we pander to that appetite?

These books—SVH and mass-market series fiction in general—have been faulted for presenting stereotypes instead of psyches, clichés instead of characters. But this misses the point, in my opinion, *because stereotypes are just what young readers are looking for* in these books. Just as Dickens gave us many characters who were *characteristics*, such as Uriah Heep or Mr. Micawber, Sweet Valley High has the good/earnest twin and the bad/sexy twin, the sweet jock and the arrogant rich boy, the spoiled brat and the plain but steadfast best pal, the fat girl, the brainiac, and so on.

What are these types for? I think they serve as convenient and simplistic psychological *costuming* for readers. Wouldn't it be fun to be the naughty, ne'er-do-well, bold, and tempestuous Jessica Wakefield for a few hours? Wouldn't it be fun to play the role of smart and compassionate (but still beautiful and popular!) Liz Wakefield for a while? As readers mature, they begin to look around and see where they fit in. Using stereotypes as a sort of psychological menu (I'm smart like Liz, although a little nerdy, like Enid, but also kind of snotty, like Lila, etc.) is easy and fun. It's helpful.

In any series with star characters, each book provides a description in the early pages. (How many times did we read that Nancy Drew had Titian hair and that her housekeeper was named Hannah Gruen?) Sweet Valley High is the same. The stars, Elizabeth and Jessica Wakefield, are introduced in the first pages of each book. In *White Lies*, Sweet Valley High #52, I wrote these very typical descriptions which establish not only the twins' California-girl good looks but their attributes as well:

Even though it was officially a gossip column, "Eyes and Ears" was never spiteful or malicious. Elizabeth always kept it lighthearted, and as a rule, most people were thrilled to be featured in it. Elizabeth's blue-green eyes sparkled with amusement as she typed. (1)

With Jessica, everything was absolutely urgent, whether it was wearing the perfect outfit or waiting to make a grand entrance at a party. And sometimes little details got overlooked, like whose clothes she was wearing or who she was causing to wait for her. She was tempestuous and exciting, a self-centered five-foot-six whirlwind. (2)

While Jessica was flighty and inconsistent, Elizabeth was steady and thoughtful. She enjoyed reading, thinking, talking with her close friends, and doing things with her boyfriend, Jeffrey French. People instinctively knew that Elizabeth was a sympathetic friend, and everyone turned to her for advice. By contrast, Jessica was known to be interested in only one person—herself. (3)

Sweet Valley Kids followed the same technique of painting the twins with broad brushstrokes at the start, although with the Wakefield twins here in second grade, their characteristics are naturally younger. Here they are introduced in *The Sweet Valley Cleanup Team*, Sweet Valley Kids #27:

Elizabeth and Jessica were in second grade at Sweet Valley Elementary School. Both of them had blond hair and blue-green eyes. They looked almost exactly alike. In fact, even their close friends sometimes had to check the twins' name bracelets to tell them apart.

On the inside, though, Elizabeth and Jessica were as different as could be. Elizabeth studied hard in school and was proud of the good grades she got. Jessica liked school, too, but only because it gave her a chance to talk to her friends. (2)

Liz and Jessica, and the other characters in these books, are no more layered or nuanced than the wicked stepmothers or steadfast woodcutters or patient third daughters who are as thick on the ground in folklore as mushrooms on the enchanted forest floor. And just as those types do, these mass-market teen characters stand in for personality traits. Young readers *want* books with types in them so they can try the types on for size.

Furthermore, this is not limited to the putative unsophisticated reader who finds Lois Lowry or Philip Pullman too challenging. *Pas du tout*. I was an exceptionally sophisticated child reader, but I still gobbled Nancy Drew and many of the grossly sentimental series books of the early part of this century (I think particularly of the Maida books, which my mother had collected). Every teacher has no doubt found a favorite "great reader" hunkered down with a Babysitters Club or a Silver Skates. These books are entertaining tools. They are as useful for the good readers as for the not-really-readers.

So are these books and their characters frivolous? Compared to *The Giver*, compared to *The Golden Compass*, of course they are. But I think this is the classic apples and oranges bugbear. It just ain't the same animal. Don't blame the turtle if he doesn't have a graceful gait. These books are telling girls and boys about girls and boys in a schematic way—as Horatio Alger did, not as Madeline L'Engle does.

And so what *are* these books telling girls and boys about girls and boys? I can tell you one thing I was always sure to do: for all the times girls played with dolls (Sweet Valley Kids) or fluttered their eyelashes at boys (Sweet Valley High), I made sure to counterprogram. Girls played soccer, became obsessed with video games, ran for school office, planned for professional careers. In *Jessica's Unburied Treasure*

(SVK #30), when the Wakefields took an airplane to Arizona, I made the flight attendant a man and the pilot a woman. The elementary school principal in Sweet Valley Kids was a woman (Mrs. Armstrong!). In *Elizabeth's Super-Selling Lemonade* (SVK #9) I made sure it was clear that Liz was really good at math. In *Olivia's Story* (Sweet Valley High Super Star) Olivia buys lunch for herself *and* her boyfriend. In *Friend Against Friend* (SVH #69) I had the members of the school newspaper staff have a heated debate about the discrepancy in school funding (and attention) for girls' sports versus boys' sports. Whenever possible, I tossed in bits of girl power. Of course they were sops to my feminist conscience—but it was a great opportunity to exploit the power of the mass market and reach a lot of readers with those sops.

Bear in mind who the ghostwriters of these books are. On the whole, they are people like me: well-educated, ambitious authors. They like books. They work hard. Most of them are women who want only the best for girls. These are values that the ghostwriters can't help building into the books they write.

A close girlfriend of mine, who writes for the new Nancy Drew mysteries, agrees with me strenuously on this subject. In the books my friend writes, Nancy Drew never lets a put-down pass unchallenged, especially put-downs making fun of the girl detective. My friend always tries to include girl characters who want to go to medical school, or who have other ambitious career goals, and she salts her books with women CEOs and business owners as well. Nor are the boys always as hunky as Jockey underwear models. Some of them are geeky, but nice. In other words, regular kids. The characters in these books don't need to go by society's dicta about who's hot and who's not.

In Sweet Valley High, the underlying message is as persistent and noticeable as the bass line of a Backstreet Boys song: however attractive and tempting it might be to be Jessica Wakefield, *the naughty girl is the loser time and time again.* Goodness and generosity are rewarded. Cruelty and selfishness are punished. Jessica's comeuppances may often be comic, and she may laugh them off with many a blithe and tinkling laugh; but if you keep a tally of who comes out ahead in book after book, it is almost always the good characters, the characters who typify kindness, decency, diligence, punctuality, honesty, unselfishness, and courage. And what does winning mean, in these books? Material gain is not to be chased after, although it's nice to have a cool car; no, winning means landing a steady heterosexual partner.

A sinister, Marxist, and quite possibly paranoid interpretation of this is that the mass market is colluding to brainwash young readers to grow up into hardworking, married, straight citizens who follow the rules, pay their taxes on time, and don't complain.

Of course, there's nothing wrong with being hardworking, straight, married, following the rules, paying taxes on time, and being a good sport. Far from it. The specter of brainwashing might raise a few hairs on the back of your neck, though—especially if you concur with the argument that this marriage imperative is damaging to female-female relationships. But if these books are tools, then readers have to know how to use them. I think it *is* helpful to have stereotypes to hold up for comparison: the trick is not to get stuck up there on the surface when there are many fathoms to plumb down below. Such a tool used wrongly can lead to mindless conformity. Used rightly, it might provide a little helpful growth inside a package of light entertainment.

So how can we be sure kids will know how to use these tools, and recognize these books for what they are? By doing what adults should always do with young readers: guide them toward progressively more challenging books. By exposing kids to other examples of fictional characters, personalities that are much more complex and much closer to real, we can give them more stimulating models to examine. Start with training wheels. Then take them off.

Kids do generally read these books on their own time, I know that. But if parents and teachers are ignorant of what their children are reading extracurricularly, be they get-married romances or bomb-making manuals, then we have more to be concerned about than literary criticism, in my view.

I would no more argue for doing away with Sweet Valley High and its ilk than I would argue for banning training wheels. Growing up is a hard thing to do. Claiming an identity is a challenge. When people say kids need role models, many of them are looking for Michael Jordans, not Henry Kissingers. *Work hard and be nice.* Complexity is not what a lot of people look for in models. We have been returning to the same stock of folktales for centuries, to the warty witch, the fair princess, the valiant peasant. The mass-market books of today are not so very different. Yes, we all must learn that not all pretty girls are princesses in disguise; there isn't always a handsome prince and a golden reward; yes, those are all truths we must grow into. We're none of us really Liz Wakefield or Jessica Wakefield, either. But we understand that, too.

A steady diet of these books can be stultifying. But few readers subsist purely on series books (and those that do are reading these books not at the expense of Alcott and Voigt, but of hanging out at the mall). Sales of the early books in the Sweet Valley series remain consistently strong, but sales of later titles peak early and then dwindle. This is because by the time a reader has devoured ten or twenty of these titles, she usually moves on. Readers generally want to start from the beginning of a series, so although the first book in hand might have been #56, the reader will probably seek out book #1 and proceed to read in order. After a while, she has made sufficient use of the books and stops reading them.

I was the same with Nancy Drew. I read those mysteries eagerly for a couple of years; then I outgrew them. But I was left with a strong impression of this girl. She was strong, brave, smart, and serious. I adored her. I *still* want to be like Nancy. And if there are girls who still want to be like Liz Wakefield, that's okay by me. I don't think that's frivolous at all.

Children's Literature

N.B. These are series pseudonyms.

STEWART, M. M. 1990. *Elizabeth's Super-Selling Lemonade* (Sweet Valley Kids #9). New York: Bantam Doubleday Dell.

————. 1992a. *Jessica's Unburied Treasure* (Sweet Valley Kids #30). New York: Bantam Doubleday Dell.

————. 1992b. *Sweet Valley Cleanup Team* (Sweet Valley Kids #27). New York: Bantam Doubleday Dell.

WILLIAM, K. 1989. *White Lies* (Sweet Valley High #52). New York: Bantam Doubleday Dell.

————. 1990a. *Friend Against Friend* (Sweet Valley High #69). New York: Bantam Doubleday Dell.

————. 1990b. *Olivia's Story* (Sweet Valley High Super Star). New York: Bantam Doubleday Dell.

5

Picture Books for Preschool Children: Exploring Gender Issues with Three- and Four-Year-Olds

BARBARA CHATTON

Jamie Lee Curtis begins *When I Was Little: A Four-Year-Old's Memoir of Her Youth* with this insight from the character: "When I was little I didn't know I was a girl. My mom told me" (Curtis 1993). By the age of three, with help from adults, children know their own gender, have learned the gender labels for boys and girls, and can use the terms *he* and *she* with increasing accuracy. Young children typically assign gender by appearance and behavioral traits. Preschool children pay close attention to such items as character names, behaviors and attitudes, dress, toys, and other forms of play, ascribing them to girls or boys. Because young children are in the process of consolidating and making sense of their gender identity, they typically assign gender to characters in books using gender stereotypes. When I read Maurice Sendak's *Where the Wild Things Are* (1963) to my three-year-old nephew, for example, he stopped the reading to assign character names to the wild things based on family members. Long hair was a marker of female characters: The wild thing with the reddish long hair was Mommy and the green-faced, long-haired one with the rhinoceros horn was Aunt Barbara. The characters with beards were male.

Children generally pay more attention to the way that characters are portrayed in the illustrations than in text references to gender as they focus on these external characteristics. A three-year-old boy, for example, thought that the baby pig in Pat Hutchins's *Little Pink Pig* (1994) was a girl in spite of the repetition of the words *he* and *him* in the text because "pink is a girl color." A four-year-old girl thought Hutchins's Titch in *Tidy Titch* (1991) was a girl because, although described as *he* in the text, he has longish hair, wears sandals that look like girls' shoes, and "she's tidy."

Exploration of gender roles occurs in all preschool children's activities. Physical and social environments, reinforcement of gender roles provided by the occupations

57

and concerns of parents and other significant adults, the toys with which children are encouraged to play, television and video programming, and relationships with peers all influence their understanding of gender roles. Adult responses to books shared also play a role. Because books for this age group are largely read to children, the ways adults use language during this activity can be crucial. DeLoache and others (1987) found, for example, that mothers reading aloud to their young children labeled as male 90 percent of the characters who appeared in groups or without specific markers such as clothes, even Mama Bear in the Goldilocks story. Amy Sheldon (1990) has noted that her own child responded to the dominant use of the male gender for generic descriptions of animals and working people by automatically assuming that these beings were all males when she encountered them in other situations. Questioning and discussion with children will often turn this around. Sheldon began to more carefully model and question her daughter whenever these assumptions of gender arose until her daughter began to question them on her own. When the mother whose child had mistaken the pig for a girl in Hutchins' book pointed out to her son that the text said "he" and that little baby pigs were indeed pink, the boy accommodated that information and referred to the pig as a boy in subsequent readings.

Previous studies of recent children's books have indicated there are more strong girl main characters than in the past. However, they also have found that minor female characters are still largely passive and traditional, and that active boys still dominate by about two to one (Collins et al. 1984). These studies have not focused on books for young children. This chapter is intended to open the discussion of gender images in books for young children with a brief look at some current books for this age. The books have been published in the past ten years by authors and illustrators who have been praised for capturing the experiences of young children. These include recent works by Molly Bang, Marc Brown, Donald Crews, Jamie Lee Curtis, Lois Ehlert, Denise Fleming, Mem Fox, Eloise Greenfield, Kevin Henkes, Shirley Hughes, Pat Hutchins, and Rosemary Wells. Several classics that have been given new publicity or appeared with new illustrations during this period have been included in the discussion as well.

Gender of Animal Characters

Books for young children have traditionally featured animal characters as often as humans. As in folktales, the characters typically act as humans would. A number of books in this selection include animal characters. In some cases the animals are not clothed, and gender is implied in the text or inferred by the reader. In recent editions of Margaret Wise Brown's *Big Red Barn* (1989) and *Little Donkey Close Your Eyes* (1995) animals are not clothed in any way and appear in their natural habitat. Gender is only implied in family groupings of animals when young readers assume the nurturing adult with the baby animal is a female.

In other books, the clothing is neutral, not revealing gender. Margaret Wise Brown's classic *Goodnight Moon* (1947) shows a bunny child in blue-and-white-striped pajamas in a room with both a toy house (a possible girl's toy) and a picture of someone fishing (a possible male image) as well as a number of gender-neutral toys and objects. Preschool children with whom I have spoken are about equally divided on whether the bunny is male or female based on these markers. Generally they choose to see the bunny as their own gender.

In still other stories with animal characters, the illustrator resorts to gender stereotypes in order to distinguish male from female characters. Rosemary Wells's mouse Nora, Arthur's sister D. W. in Marc Brown's series featuring a very human family of aardvarks, and Kevin Henkes' Lilly and other female mice in his stories wear dresses to set them off from other animal characters. But these conventions of dress hide characters who move beyond stereotypes. In *Noisy Nora* (1973), recently rereleased, Nora struggles to regain the attention she has lost as her parents focus on her baby sister. Nora, clothed in a long dress, resorts to mischief, and comes across as a lively and engaged child. While Marc Brown's D. W. wears dresses, she is adventurous, curious, smart, and often dirty. Lilly, the mouse featured in Henkes's *Chester's Way* (1988), *Julius, the Baby of the World* (1990), and *Lilly's Purple Plastic Purse* (1996), is a strong female character. Lilly wears a dress in most pictures, but her crown, cape, and red cowboy boots suggest that she is not a passive girl. Lilly is by turns jealous, bright, imaginative, uncooperative, loving, and misunderstood; she is also a creative problem solver. She contemplates a variety of careers including teacher, surgeon, pilot, and hairdresser. Her closest friends are two boy mice. These girl animal characters are popular with both boys and girls. While the children clearly identify the characters as girls, they recognize the behaviors as universal.

Animal characters in a number of the selected books are identified with male pronouns in the text although the illustrations may show no particular gender characteristics. Denise Fleming features a male mouse in *Lunch* (1995), and the sleepy kitten Boris in her *Mama Cat Has Three Kittens* (1998) is male. In Lois Ehlert's *Nuts to You* (1993) the squirrel is male. In Pat Hutchins's *Shrinking Mouse* (1997) all of the animal characters are male. The lost puppy McDuff in Rosemary Wells's *McDuff Moves In* (1997a) is male, although the animals he meets before his adoption are not identified by gender in text or illustrations. The use of male pronouns to represent animals in this small sample supports DeLoache's and Sheldon's findings that we generally ascribe male gender labels to animals. Mem Fox's *Time for Bed* (1993) invited discussion with a three-year-old girl about animal gender. This bedtime book pictures animal parents in loving poses urging their babies to sleep, with the last two pictures showing a mother tucking a child into bed. I asked the child which characters were girls. She said all of the mothers were girls and the child who went to bed was a girl, because, although the blue night shirt and shortish blonde hair might have been a boy's characteristics, the character had on "lipstick" (the picture shows the child's lips as a definite rosy pink). She labeled most of the baby animals as boys, the exception being the cow and horse that had "girls' eyelashes."

Images of Girls

In the case of human characters, dress and activities can cause a strong response in child readers. Jamie Lee Curtis, for example, features little girls in all three of her popular picture books. While these books are full of nail polish and hairstyles, high heels, dressing up, and lots of pink, the little girls who star in them are also opinionated and active. Girls with whom I have shared these books find these characters appealing. Young boys tend not to care for the first two books, which they describe as "for girls." Although Curtis's third book, *Today I Feel Silly & Other Moods That Make My Day* (1998) also features a girl and lots of girl activities, boys with whom I've shared the book enjoy it. Perhaps the fast pace, rhymed text, and the interactive mood wheel included in the back increase its appeal.

Sometimes an author for young children will deliberately confront the child's reliance on outward trappings to discuss gender. In Mem Fox's *Shoes from Grandpa* (1990), Jessie (a name that can be given to a boy or a girl) is given a pair of red boots by her grandfather. This leads to an accumulation of gifts of clothing, many of them clearly only worn by girls. But Jessie finally asks for and receives what she truly wants: a pair of jeans she wears with her red boots to go skateboarding. The subtle story allows young readers to absorb a simple lesson about clothing not "making the man."

Heine and Inkster (1999) suggest that strong female characters should show a range of emotions and abilities, be "perseverant, courageous, feisty, intelligent, spirited, resourceful, capable, and independent," wrestle with significant problems, find solutions through their own initiative, and grow in the course of the story. *Madeline* (Bemelmans 1939) is a classic heroine for children who exhibits these characteristics, and her popularity has been renewed by the recent movie. Madeline lives in a world populated almost entirely by women, most of whom defer to her superior imagination and daring behavior. It is as if Madeline were an aberration, an unusual girl in a world of more passive female followers. While minor female characters in the books in this sample do not necessarily follow the lead characters, they are still portrayed more traditionally. Nora's older sister, Lilly's schoolmates, and the featured mothers in these books tend to exhibit more stereotyped female traits than do the main characters.

Two books by Molly Bang feature characters who solve problems on their own initiative. When Sophie in *When Sophie Gets Angry—Really, Really Angry* (1999) is angry about sharing with her sister, she starts to have a tantrum, then runs awhile, cries a little, climbs a tree, finds that the wild world comforts her, then goes home having worked out her feelings herself. The female goose in Bang's *Goose* (1996) is also a problem solver. When she feels different from the animals who have adopted her, she too sets off on a journey to see what she can "figure out for herself." When she learns she can fly she returns home with this new knowledge and is able to live happily with others who are different from herself.

Images of Boys

What do male major characters in these books reveal about gender roles for boys? By and large three- and four-year-old boys are portrayed as multidimensional, exhibiting the proactive and energetic characteristics stereotypically thought of as male but showing emotion and imagination as well. In the sample of books reviewed, boys like Max in Maurice Sendak's classic *Where the Wild Things Are* participate actively in a world in which imagination and the need for love and reassurance are also clearly important. In Eloise Greenfield's *On My Horse* (1995), for example, a little boy rides a horse at a stable, aided by a quietly supportive older man. The boy imagines himself freely running and jumping as he rides as one being with the horse, rather than controlling it. Kevin Henkes's *Owen* (1993) and *The Biggest Boy* (1995) both feature male characters who engage in activities typically labeled as feminine including imaginative play, drawing, and doing the dishes, and who experience sadness, fear, and the need to be comforted even as they venture out on their own. Marc Brown's Arthur is also a well-rounded character who has friends of both genders, tries hard to please his male teacher and his parents, and worries and makes mistakes as he tries out new roles. All of Marc Brown's characters are well rounded. Arthur's mother works outside the home and often wears pants, his father runs a catering business from their house, and his sister D. W. is assertive and sassy.

Alfie in Shirley Hughes's books is another boy with these qualities. Alfie is both an adventurous problem solver who loves to play in puddles and can work out how to unlock the door when he "gets in first," and he is also a softhearted child who takes care of his sister and cries before he begins to solve his problems. While Alfie's mother is a traditional stay-at-home mom and his dad goes off to work, his home life and the other characters in these stories reflect a fairly gender-neutral environment. The illustrations in the Alfie books feature apple-cheeked children playing in rooms cluttered with both boy- and girl-oriented toys as well as lots of natural playthings such as vegetables and pans. Alfie's plucky babysitter, Maureen, an initiating problem solver, is considering becoming a plumber. Alfie's father spends a great deal of time with his children in these stories, and his gentle neighbor, Mr. McNally, openly nurtures not only his own daughter, Maureen, and his beloved old cat, but also Alfie and his sister.

Of the books selected to review here, Margaret Wise Brown's *The Little Scarecrow Boy* (1998) includes the most stereotypically male characters. Although the text is newly illustrated by David Diaz, the illustrations are strongly restricted by a story line written in the forties. In this story a strong, active, male scarecrow fiercely faces off with crows, and his son strives to follow in his "footsteps." The boy's passive mother offers encouragement but never leaves her stake. At the other end of the spectrum, Mem Fox plays against traditional male stereotypes in *Tough Boris* (1994). Boris, a tough, massive, scruffy pirate ("all pirates are tough") also cries when his parrot dies ("all pirates cry").

Images of Adults

Critics of gender images in books for children have pointed out that even when girls themselves are portrayed more positively, parents, teachers, and neighbors who might serve as role models are often more stereotyped with stay-at-home moms in dresses doing housework and errands, while fathers go off to work. The mothers in Eloise Greenfield's *Honey, I Love* (1995), in Jamie Lee Curtis' *When I Was Little*, in Donald Crews's *Bigmama's* (1991), in Kevin Henkes's Lilly books, and in Shirley Hughes's Alfie books are all engaged in domestic chores as they interact with their children. In this sample, only the Arthur stories and Jamie Lee Curtis's *Today I Feel Silly* make clear mentions of mothers' work outside of the home.

I gave a four-year-old boy a handful of these books to look at. I then asked him what the mothers in the stories did all day. He replied, "They go to work and then they come home and play with their children and take care of them." He was more focused on what the parents did with their children than when they did it. As this child suggested, the authors of these books may have focused on the concerns of the child reader, offering three- and four-year-olds images of adults who care for them and nurture them, rather than models for parents' careers.

The most obvious example of female nurture is in the bedtime stories that feature animals. In Margaret Wise Brown's *Big Red Barn* and *Little Donkey Close Your Eyes*, Denise Fleming's *Mama Cat Has Three Kittens*, and Mem Fox's *Time for Bed*, the animals are shown with a single female parent. While the mother mammal typically is the one who stays with the young in order to nurse them, the consequence is that these books can leave children with notions that human mothers do all of the nurturing. Ashley Wolff tries to disavow this notion by dedicating *Little Donkey Close Your Eyes* to two boys, with a picture of them cuddling as they read, and including a male shepherd with the sheep and a family camping beneath the birds' nest. Other authors, including Jamie Lee Curtis, Molly Bang, Marc Brown, Shirley Hughes, and Kevin Henkes, have included fathers in bedtime rituals.

A number of these books include portraits of nurturing fathers and other male role models. From the gentle, playful fathers in Molly Bang's *Ten, Nine, Eight* (1983) and *Yellow Ball* (1991) to the fathers and Lilly's teacher Mr. Slinger in Kevin Henkes's stories, from the work-at-home dad of Marc Brown's Arthur and D. W. stories to the neighbors and helpers in Eloise Greenfield's and Shirley Hughes's stories, kindly men play consistently strong roles.

A long tradition in children's books that plays to children's egocentricity consigns parents to little or no role in some stories. Books with orphans such as Madeline and children with babysitters as in *Goodnight Moon* remove parents from the picture. In a number of contemporary books, the parents appear only as voices or legs, just provided to move the action of the story along. This is the case in Sendak's *Where the Wild Things Are*, in Henkes's *The Biggest Boy* and *Chester's Way*, and in Pat Hutchins's *Tidy Titch*. Jamie Lee Curtis's *Tell Me Again About the Night I Was Born*, on the other hand, about adoption, supports the idea that love and caring are the most important aspects of any family.

Multiple Possibilities

Several of the books use narration or illustration that gives no indication of gender. Lois Ehlert uses first-person narrators in *Red Leaf, Yellow Leaf* (1991) and *Snowballs* (1995), books that explore aspects of nature. In the first, all of the activities are gender neutral, while in the second, snow figures of dad, mom, girl, boy, and baby use artifacts of dress to indicate gender, while the "we" who tell the story could be girls, boys, or both. Denise Fleming, who also has her characters explore the natural world around them, features a character in her illustrations for *In the Small, Small Pond* (1993) and *In the Tall, Tall Grass* (1991) who might be either a boy or a girl.

Donald Crews's *Bicycle Race* (1985) features both men and women bicyclists, and the race is won by a woman who overcomes an early problem with her bicycle. His *Night at the Fair* (1998) includes people of all ages, races, and genders engaged in a variety of activities. Mothers and sons, fathers and daughters come together. Both boys and girls toss for prizes and ride the scariest rides. Crews even puts himself, camera around his neck, in the middle of the action. Mem Fox's *Whoever You Are* (1997) is a richly illustrated picture of ethnic and gender diversity, showing both men and women with children from around the world playing a variety of roles. A female doctor smiles at the reader, a father in a business suit hugs his daughter, and a boy cries over his scraped knee in this world of possibilities.

In Lois Ehlert's *Hands* (1997), the child narrator, who might be a boy or a girl, suggests that children receive gifts from both parents that will become less gender bound in their own hands. This child learns to build from the father and to sew from the mother and accepts these gifts from each parent, saying at the end, "I want to be an artist. Then I'll join hands with my mom and dad."

Conclusion

Children working to make sense of their gender identities rely on picture books as one of the ways to add to their understanding. As shown in this small sample, authors and illustrators for this age group provide children with a range of images of boys and girls, men and women. They may create stories of strong girls such as Kevin Henkes's Lilly or Molly Bang's Sophie. They may show well-rounded boys, who are imaginative and emotional, active and assertive, such as Shirley Hughes' Alfie or Marc Brown's Arthur. Sometimes they may fall into cultural patterns that show boys and girls, men and women, and even animals more stereotypically. Some authors consciously provoke children to question gender stereotypes, as Mem Fox does in *Shoes from Grandpa* and *Tough Boris* or, like Donald Crews, quietly show children that anything is possible. Research and conversations with children suggest that any book can provide for discussion of gender roles and identity. When adults pay careful attention to the sense children make of their books, they can guide them to consider a world of larger possibilities through questions and comments on the text and pictures.

Generally, books for young children tend to give gentle instruction on how to behave while reassuring them that they are uniquely themselves and they are loved. At times, this assurance may take precedence over gender issues. The young girl in Eloise Greenfield's *Honey, I Love*, for example, dresses and plays in a more conventionally girlish way but is learning to understand her individual and cultural identity. The ending of the original version of the poetic text (1978) has been altered from "And honey, I love you, too" to "And honey, I love ME, too" reinforcing that this theme predominates.

Picture books for young children tend to be brief and to focus on a single theme. At the same time children are developing their gender identity, they are striving to understand their cultural identity, role in the family and community, and use of language. A critical element in picture book sharing is the encouragement and reinforcement of the value of reading. Rosemary Wells's *Read to Your Bunny* (1997b) puts this theme first but subtly encourages children to pay attention to gender. The book features both mothers and fathers reading to both boys and girls. The bunny characters wear the clothing of a variety of roles such as pilots and cooks without being clearly male or female. In her note to parents in the back of the book, Wells says, "Trusting, singing, laughing, and language are the most important things in a young child's life." Her final sentences suggest she consciously chooses to cross gender stereotypes in her stories. She ends her comments on reading to young children with, "Your daughter will learn, and imagine, and be strong in herself. Your son will thrive, and give your love back forever."

No one book can be the text that explains all aspects of the complexity of identity. Interactions with adults play a significant role in children's developing understandings, including their understandings of gender. The conversations we have with children, the types of questions we ask, the variety of stories we share, and the language we use are all models from which children can make sense of who they are.

References

COLLINS, L. J., B. B. INGOLDSBY, & J. C. DELLMAN. 1984. "Sex Role Stereotyping in Children's Literature: A Change from the Past." *Childhood Education* 60: 278–85.

DELOACHE, J., D. J. CASSIDY, & J. C. CARPENTER. 1987. "The Three Bears Are All Male: Mothers' Gender Labeling of Neutral Picture Book Characters." *Sex Roles* 17: 163–78.

GOLUMBOK, S., & R. FIVUSH. 1994. *Gender Development*. New York: Cambridge University Press.

HEINE, P., & C. INKSTER, with F. KAZEMEK, S. WILLIAMS, S. RASCHKE, & D. STEVENS. 1999. "Strong Female Characters in Recent Children's Literature." *Language Arts* 76: 427–34.

HIBEN, L. S., & M. L. SIGNORELLA. 1987. *Children's Gender Schemata*. San Francisco: Jossey-Bass.

SHELDON, A. 1990. "'Kings Are Royaler Than Queens:' Language and Socialization." *Young Children* 45: 4–9.

Children's Literature

BANG, M. 1983. *Ten, Nine, Eight*. New York: Greenwillow.

———. 1991. *Yellow Ball*. New York: Morrow.

———. 1996. *Goose*. New York: Blue Sky.

———. 1999. *When Sophie Gets Angry—Really, Really Angry*. New York: Blue Sky.

BEMELMANS, L. 1939. *Madeline*. New York: Viking.

BROWN, M. 1993. *D. W. Thinks Big*. Boston: Joy Street.

———. 1995. *Arthur's TV Trouble*. New York: Little, Brown.

———. 1996. *Arthur Writes a Story*. Boston: Little, Brown.

———. 1998. *D. W.'s Lost Blankie*. Boston: Little, Brown.

BROWN, M. W. 1947. *Goodnight Moon*. Illustrated by C. Hurd. New York: HarperCollins.

———. [1956] 1989. *Big Red Barn*. Illustrated by F. Bond. New York: HarperCollins.

———. [1959] 1995. *Little Donkey Close Your Eyes*. Illustrated by A. Wolff. New York: HarperCollins.

———. 1998. *The Little Scarecrow Boy*. Illustrated by D. Diaz. New York: HarperCollins.

CREWS, D. 1985. *Bicycle Race*. New York: Greenwillow.

———. 1991. *Bigmama's*. New York: Greenwillow.

———. 1998. *Night at the Fair*. New York: Greenwillow.

CURTIS, J. L. 1993. *When I Was Little: A Four-Year-Old's Memoir of Her Youth*. New York: HarperCollins.

———. 1996. *Tell Me Again About the Night I Was Born*. Illustrated by L. Cornell. New York: HarperCollins.

———. 1998. *Today I Feel Silly & Other Moods That Make My Day*. Illustrated by L. Cornell. New York: HarperCollins.

EHLERT, L. 1991. *Red Leaf, Yellow Leaf*. San Diego: Harcourt Brace.

———. 1993. *Nuts to You*. San Diego: Harcourt Brace.

———. 1995. *Snowballs*. San Diego: Harcourt Brace.

———. 1997. *Hands*. San Diego: Harcourt Brace.

FLEMING, D. 1991. *In the Tall, Tall Grass*. New York: Holt.

———. 1993. *In the Small, Small Pond*. New York: Holt.

———. 1995. *Lunch*. New York: Holt.

———. 1998. *Mama Cat Has Three Kittens*. New York: Holt.

FOX, M. 1990. *Shoes from Grandpa*. Illustrated by P. Mullins. New York: Orchard.

———. 1993. *Time for Bed*. Illustrated by J. Dyer. San Diego: Harcourt Brace.

———. 1994. *Tough Boris*. Illustrated by K. Brown. San Diego: Harcourt Brace.

———. 1997. *Whoever You Are*. Illustrated by L. Staub. San Diego: Harcourt Brace.

GREENFIELD, E. [1978] 1995. *Honey, I Love*. Illustrated by J. S. Gilchrist. New York: HarperCollins.

————. 1995. *On My Horse*. Illustrated by J. S. Gilchrist. New York: HarperCollins.

HENKES, K. 1988. *Chester's Way*. New York: Greenwillow.

————. 1990. *Julius, the Baby of the World*. New York: Greenwillow.

————. 1993. *Owen*. New York: Greenwillow.

————. 1995. *The Biggest Boy*. Illustrated by N. Tafuri. New York: Greenwillow.

————. 1996. *Lilly's Purple Plastic Purse*. New York: Greenwillow.

HUGHES, S. 1997a. *Alfie and the Birthday Surprise*. New York: Lothrop.

————. 1997b. *Alfie's ABC*. New York: Lothrop.

————. 1997c. *All About Alfie*. New York: Lothrop.

HUTCHINS, P. 1991. *Tidy Titch*. New York: Greenwillow.

————. 1994. *Little Pink Pig*. New York: Greenwillow.

————. 1997. *Shrinking Mouse*. New York: Greenwillow.

SENDAK, M. 1963. *Where the Wild Things Are*. New York: HarperCollins.

WELLS, R. 1973. *Noisy Nora*. New York: Dial.

————. 1997a. *McDuff Moves In*. New York: Hyperion.

————. 1997b. *Read to Your Bunny*. New York: Scholastic.

Author Profile

Mem Fox

I think my statement to young girls is the old cliché, that girls can do anything. Girls *can* do anything and there are a lot of American teachers whom I meet, who are predominantly female, who haven't heard that message. I think our Australian girls have a lot of fun. They're much less conditioned into their gender roles, particularly the generation in their twenties and thirties. They're almost terrifying. They're encouraged to be widely and deeply aware that gender doesn't have to make a difference. I'm really impressed by it.

My relationship with my daughter is very open and loving. We're very good friends and I think the depth of the relationships that I write about occurs because my own family—my husband, my daughter, and I—have such a strong relationship with each other: very loving. Tempestuous, but very loving! Like Koala Lou and her mother.

The theme in *Koala Lou* (1989) arises from a deep and hidden wound. Koala Lou began as a male character and it did not become a real character to me until I made her female. She did not become a true character until I made her the oldest character in the family, which is me. I basically made her me. My mother was not affectionate—well, not overtly affectionate. She loved me and I knew that and she still does. You know, she's eighty-five and I'm fifty-four and you would think that I would have got over it by now, but no, I haven't. She would not say that she loved me under any circumstances because she would think it unnecessary. She thinks that I ought to know that she loves me. Deep down there is this anguish in my own view of the relationship between my mum and me, so some of the relationship themes in my books are quaintly sad. But you know the world that we live in now is different, more open, thank heaven.

After writing *Koala Lou* I realized from then on, if I could possibly do it, if it fitted, I would make the main character a girl, to show people that girls could be active and interesting. Not could be, but just *are* active and interesting, courageous, feisty people. I think one of the most important things that women need to be is interesting. So many women subsume their own personalities under other people, either their husbands' or their children's. One of the reasons why women aren't liberated is because they're often boring, because they're too frightened to be interesting. They are so beautifully brought up they don't want to stand up to be challenged or anything like that.

My parents had three girls and they were incredibly interested in sexism and feminism before those terms were really obvious. When my mother was a young girl, Christobel Pankhurst, the niece or the daughter of Emily Pankhurst who fought for the woman's vote in England, stayed in my mother's house on a tour of Australia back in the 1920s when Mum was a girl. My mother is the fiercest feminist that you can imagine and so is my sister. When my father left Africa in 1990 he set up a fund for education, specifically for women in Africa who want to be teachers. Some of the people my father educated are in the highest positions in Zimbabwe at the moment, which is a testament to him. He was the principal of the Teacher's Education College, a college for African people only.

I'm married to an absolutely adorable, completely unambitious man who is perfectly happy with his position at the university and never plans for a promotion, and couldn't be bothered. He loves his work, and one day we were checking in at the airport and of course my card says Professor M. Fox and of course they turned to my husband. And we just laughed and laughed. And my husband said, "She's the professor, I'm the lecturer," and the man apologised profusely, but it's just ridiculous, you know, it goes on and on. There are times when I really do bristle and others when I find it funny. I try to just laugh about it. Life's too short.

I guess my respect for the old came about because my grandfather was absolutely alert, sharp, and brilliant at ninety. He wasn't floundering in any way in his brain, nor his ability to speak about matters ranging from an ant to world politics. He lived in a retirement home, which had various stages of care. He was living in a completely self-contained unit and I would visit him once a week. I'd be almost terrified by his intellect, really, he was so wonderful and so funny. Then the nurses would come to his room and say in a singsong patronising voice: "How are we today, Mr. Partridge?" You know, treating him as if he was one of the demented inmates. That just used to drive me insane. I do have an incredible affinity with the elderly. I adore them, but I also have a massive respect for them. That is really a part of who I am.

In the state of South Australia, we do overt teaching about gender. It's part of the active curriculum. When kids are just five years old, the teachers will read a book and say, "Kids, don't you just love the characters in this book? What a great story! Isn't it fabulous? Now I wonder if we could read it again and if we could just notice what the mother does and what the father does. Is that really how mothers and fathers act these days?" Gender is actually part of the curriculum; it is embedded in the curriculum. In teaching language arts to university students it's a topic that has to be covered: we have to teach preservice teachers how to do that.

I think you can ruin a good book by too much analysis of sexism because a book may have a great many other wonderful attributes that are swept under the carpet simply because of one aberrant piece of sexism. You've got to look at the whole book and say, "Well, for this reason and this reason, this is a great book and it's a pity they slipped up here." From the time that they start school, and that's five years old in my state, we want to make children more aware.

We have a lot of research about boys who are now doing so badly, particularly in their last days of high school. We're now saying to ourselves that if girls are doing so well, then what is happening to boys? They are increasingly doing very badly at school in relation to girls. It's absolutely astounding and it's a serious problem. The exam results come out in mid-January, and now there's always the question of why are boys doing so badly. In Australia now girls are so fantastically confident that boys are withdrawing as a form of self-protection. They are just so confused about who they are and what they're supposed to be that they're not making an effort, because no matter what they do, they can't do the right thing. The right role is so indistinct for guys. It must be a very confusing age for them to live in the world as we currently know it.

There's been a lot of research about girls and education, about the amount of attention given to boys in the classroom instead of girls. I still think in every single classroom that you'd come across in Australia that boys would get more attention than girls, because boys are allowed to be interesting and you pay attention to the kids who are more interesting. Girls are still toeing the line even though they've become more confident and more aggressive. I think they turn into more interesting women but I don't know that they're naughtier in school than boys. And of course it's the people who attract the attention that get the attention.

My daughter Chloë was born in 1971 so she was twelve in 1983 and starting high school. I said to her the night before she started high school, "Chloë, you must be as bad as the boys; you must make noise in the classroom; you must draw attention to yourself, because then you will get the kind of attention that the boys get. If you receive any aggression from boys I give you total permission to answer them in kind. You can either use words or you can actually hit them if anyone touches you. Please be as aggressive as you like. I give you permission to be physically violent!" Of course she never was but she still remembers that conversation. She was a live wire in school and has continued to be one. I was aware of the research then, and I knew that if you were not noisy you wouldn't get any attention; the brilliant ones get attention and most of the girls in the middle range of a class don't.

I remember a particular book called something like *Colleen the Question Girl* that Chloë had when she was little—it was an Australian feminist book for little girls. It was so overtly sexist that she threw it against the wall and said: "It's all so stupid, they think that we can't see through them," because its intention was overtly to make girls think that they were okay. I think when literature is as crass as that it's particularly useless. I have noticed "good antisexism attitudes" in many of the books I've read, which have been marvelous about sexism because the antisexist attitudes have been embedded in the text. It's been so much part of the text that it's not something that leapt out of the text because the text itself was so good.

I talk a lot about censorship and sexism in the United States; if you let this get a hold, where you end up eventually is the Afghanistan situation, where women are enshrouded from top to toe, where they cannot be educated, and where they can scarcely leave their homes. We need to be very careful because such a scenario is a creeping thing, you don't realize it's happening and if you let something pass and then you let the next thing pass, the sexist power brokers have control and you're finished.

I was in Yemen shortly after Christmas on vacation and we passed a girls' high school as we were driving home from the center of the city. All these girls were talking and laughing with each other, as any high school kids would around the world, but the difference between these and any high school kids around the world was that they were covered from head to toe in chador. You couldn't even see their eyes. We were flabbergasted. We were absolutely flabbergasted. There are physical, climatic advantages to it, which have been appropriated by men to become a source of subjugation of women. I'm sure that when the chador was invented there was a good reason for it physically in those climates.

My liberated friends are interesting people because they work hard and their minds are active and they don't mind speaking out. Being opinionated is being interesting, really: it shows a mind that isn't flabby or compliant. I like a woman to have an opinion and not to be afraid to speak out rather than being just a biddable little woman.

It's my hope that through the things I write I'll be able to give a glimpse of a liberated and interesting world to all the girls who read my books.

Children's Literature

Fox, M. 1989. *Koala Lou.* Illustrated by P. Lofts. New York: Harcourt Brace.

Illustrator Profile

Jerry Pinkney

In the very beginning most of the stories that were offered to me were about young girls. I think it has a lot to do with the watercolor as my medium, the light touch that I have. There was a conscious effort once I had those stories to bring a certain respect and dignity and expand on the roles of young girls in books about the African American experience. That was a conscious effort on my part. It was much later that I sought stories about young boys and men.

Gloria and I collaborated on two children's books, *Back Home* (1992) and *Sunday Outing* (1994). The stories are inspired by events in her growing-up years. Gloria Jean lost her mother at the young age of eight and was raised by her great-aunt. Shortly after her loss she traveled with her father by car to a relative's farm in Lumberton, North Carolina, for a week. It was that visit that inspired the first book, *Back Home*. Both books are based on real people and true events with some invention, so the story has a beginning, a middle, and an end. In both books she also created a complete family with a mother and father that she would have liked to have had in her growing-up years. Gloria Jean, over the forty-odd years we have known each other, has told me of the adventures of her growing-up years. I also knew her aunt and remembered her with great affection. I later met her aunts, uncles, and cousins of Lumberton, North Carolina. Knowing the stories and the people who were to be the models for the characters helped to energize my role in the collaboration.

Females have always played a large role in my life, my mother being the inspiration in my growing-up years for how I live my life today. She was also the one who instilled in me a sense of responsibility as well as possibility. I also have a very close relationship with my aunts on both sides of the family. I have three sisters who I am very, very close to, and there is truly a bond and a real concern for each other. The positive female experiences throughout my life include a loving marriage for forty years and a strong relationship with our daughter, Troy.

These experiences enabled me to empower the heroines in the stories I've illustrated. These stories are filled with the showing of love and care. It is interesting that, as supportive and caring as my mother and father were, there was little touching at home, no demonstration of affection in that manner; therefore, I make a genuine effort to show affection to my family. You will find in the books that I have illustrated that the characters show affection for one another, usually an embrace or a touching of one another. What I try to do in the stories is to make sure that the characters have full and deep ways of communicating with one another. Gloria and I both, in the books that we've created, have tried to show the events that were very positive in our lives. We are also responding to the things we didn't receive in our young lives and we put those things in the stories that we create.

I live in a place where you can truly enjoy spring and eagerly wait for it. *In for Winter, Out for Spring* (Adoff 1991) is a joyous book, for the whole family. In each of my books, what you find is that the book very much parallels how I'm feeling and what I'm experiencing at a given time. Arnold Adoff is a master at writing poetry. You find the anxiousness of spring coming, the anticipation of weather and its many changes. It's very exciting. A lot of the situations that happen in the book I have witnessed. I've seen our children sledding so I am drawing upon my own experience seeing my children at play, and my own relationship with Gloria Jean. I find those scenes very easy to do. I know what the actions should be. The idea of family and closeness is very natural for me. I don't look for that or try to get it; it comes out naturally.

Arnold insists on how the type is laid out and it's done in a way that's very easy to read in the tempo that he wants it read. So he is probably the first author that I've worked with who actually made the decision of how the type looks on the page. In some respects it's very challenging; in the beginning it seemed like it would get in the way. It turned out that I was able to use it in an interesting manner; it's usually always true when you're posed with the most difficult challenges that you have the most creative results. So I designed the spreads in a way to suggest a page on a page. You'll see a vignette that goes underneath another illustration that is bordered with a line and comes out on the other side. The desired effect was to make sure that there was a real marriage between the way Arnold envisioned the text and how I visualized the poem.

What I try to do with my art is have it parallel the text where the words are expressing one thing and my art is saying another, but they come together to create one idea. When I use models, I try to involve them as much as possible. Part of the magic is working with people, getting them to understand and to be excited about the project. With all of my figurative work I use models, so that the characters are consistent in how they look. There's a thing that happens when I'm in the studio with models, and they are responding to the story. In *Minty* (Schroeder 1996) you see it; even in the harshness that accompanied the cruelty of plantation life, there's a sense of warmth and intimacy between Minty and her parents. That is part of what my work attempts to speak to.

Red and yellow are two colors that will really make you pay attention to a character and her or his situation. Sometimes I use it to direct the eye to a certain action on the page. Most importantly I use it to focus attention on the main character—red and yellow will do that. Also the use of the colors around it will enhance and make the reader focus directly where I want them to focus. Red will do something that's impossible for yellow. And yellow will do something that's impossible for red to do.

The book *Drylongso*, by Virginia Hamilton (1997), is set in a time of drought and hardship; yet Lindy and her father are holding hands and looking at the sky hoping for rain. One thing I find is that people do things in times of adversity that don't occur at other times. People support each other and band together. If you are going to try in some way to inspire or lift people up, the idea of hope becomes important. So that what you find in the book *Drylongso* is a sense of hope. It's about my feelings that when things look dreary you reach for something to feel uplifted, you reach for something that has a possibility. I find children will pick up on those things more quickly than adults will.

The mythic quality in black literature is something I am very much interested in. One of the things that happens, especially in African American literature, is this lack of myth, because our history as an African American culture is relatively young. We think in terms of the late 1700s, the early 1800s, plantation life, and the migration period beginning in the late twentieth century when people were moving to the large cities of the North to seek employment and a better way of life. We don't have a very long history, and myth takes hundreds and hundreds and hundreds of years to evolve. So I look for stories that would suggest myth, and I'm also doing something that satisfies me as an artist, but also extends the kind of literature that we have about black Americans. I love the ending where we find Drylongso has disappeared and we imagine him somewhere tending to the need of others. He's moving on.

What attracted me to The *Hired Hand* (San Souci 1997) was the magic in it. It was one of those attempts to find and enlarge the kind of projects that I would illustrate. I always wanted to find a story that suggests once upon a time, like in fairy tales. It's the once-upon-a-time quality that we need in African American subject matter in children's literature. So in that particular book I actually did some research and found Waterford, Virginia, which was a Quaker town that had free black craftsmen living there, and I was able to stage the story early in American history. My story could take place in Waterford or a town like Waterford since it did exist, and the book is therefore set in the late 1700s.

Julius Lester and I have collaborated on a number of projects, so there's a real connection that I have with Julius. We are of the same age, so we've experienced a lot of similar things. He grew up in the South and I grew up in the North. That does bring different perspectives to things, but I think the fact that we grew up in the time period has helped shape our shared interests.

I have been drawn to the West since the 1970s, when a lot of research all of a sudden surfaced about black cowboys. Julius and I came together because we were both inspired by the West. He had written a story about Bob Lemmons and he was thinking about rewriting it for a picture book. Julius would write a text and then I would do so some sketches, and the process would continue until the art was completed. The next book has to be a story about the Mexican cowboys who played such a large role in the West, as one out of every three cowboys was black or Mexican.

I've always had some trouble trying to explain what happens when I connect with a subject matter. The process is intuitive for me. The text is my inspiration. I try to create a visual story that parallels the text and at the same time enlarges on the idea of the story. The more inspiring a story is, the easier it is to visualize. The research involved in illustrating Bob Lemmons' work included watching films, studying photography books on horses, and talking to people to get an understanding of how horses behave in certain situations and conditions. I knew how the herds would respond in different circumstances.

I saw Bob Lemmons as a loner. You see him in the opening on the dedication page, as he is riding away from the ranch. What I wanted to show is his isolation from the process of the cruelty of breaking in the horses and yet his job is to bring in the herds of mustangs. When the book ends one day he may keep going, he may not return. I wanted to show that as well. He'll ride with the horses. He is alone, but connected to his environment. He has tremendous respect for nature. Finding that project that excites and challenges one is not easy. Now I'm much more patient in finding a project that will in some way connect with an interest of mine at a given time or need I have to express a view or idea. I now wait for these kinds of projects and they always present themselves to me.

In illustrating a picture book, I try to create a picture that allows you to expand your perspective. That's very important. I'm trying to express action or mood using my abilities and talent to convey that. But it only works when the viewer begins to enhance what I've already done. I try to do my illustrations in a manner that keeps them open, to invite you to interpret it. It works when you interpret it and it parallels my intent. What should happen with the text of the story is that there's my interpretation of the text, and there's the reader's interpretation of the text, and pictures, which are a third element.

One of the things you'll find in my work, if you search, is that I'm trying to always tell another story with my pictures. In other words, we know what the main action is, the text describes that, but my illustrations give the reader some sense of where that person lives, what the culture is about, and enlarges on the story itself. When I started illustrating there were very few books that expanded on the African American culture.

Let me tell you a little bit about that process. In each case Gloria plays a very large role. There's a discussion between me and Gloria about what the characters should feel like, how they should act. Gloria has a way of finding children that have not only the stature of what we think would work in the story, but also we try to catch the spirit of what the character is about. I do a dummy book where I will draw in very loosely what I think the action should be. A very particular part of my talent is to be able to figure out how a child might express a certain action. Then we get the child into the studio to communicate that to the child and also allow the child, the model, to respond to the text. Sometimes we read from the story and sometimes we simply tell what the action should be, and I photograph the children. Those photographs are used for my figurative reference for the backgrounds. For the setting I use photographs from that particular part of the country or the world.

I've always been in love with the photographs of black families in the 1920s and '30s, when the black folks would get dressed up, go out and have their portraits done.

I was thinking about that when I decided to do that time period for *Sam and the Tigers* (Lester 1996). I wanted to suggest that stylish period. I have photographs of my mother and father when they were young adults and I wanted to suggest that Sam's choice of clothing was not only his own choice, but was also at a time when style was very important.

In my drawings I'm trying to make the tigers believable even though they are personified. The stripes became a way of getting you to believe in these tigers. If you look at the stripes, the stripes are pretty realistic to real tigers, even though what they're doing is not.

In my research on the project *John Henry* (Lester 1994), I came to the belief that there was a John Henry and that he was a workman on a railroad work crew. There were ballads written as work songs, and John Henry was possibly the subject for such a ballad. Julius came to the conclusion in his research that there was no John Henry, so we created our John Henry as a legend, meaning that the person could be real or not, but there is no definitive research that says one way or another that he was a real person. There was probably never a contest as the tale suggests of man against a machine. The story is a tall tale that can't be proven. He is a part of American folklore. In *John Henry* you notice that animals almost always follow him, and they're on almost every page in that book. Doing something and responding. They have a connection with him.

I guess it's a place where invention comes in. I think it is the place where dreams actually become very powerful, in terms of imagination. It's the possibility in all of those dreams to find something that inspires us to make us think all things are possible. Folktales and the world of fantasy allow us to find our spiritual selves, to find our individuality.

When I was a kid growing up I grew up in a very small house. There were six of us and very little private space. My mother was a reader and I only appreciated the importance of that much later in life. I don't recall being interested in reading, so I did not grow up as a reader. That came much later in my life. I'm a ferocious reader now with a library of over two thousand books. My private space became my imagination. I think that allowed me to think about the possibilities or have dreams come true. Stories do that.

Children's Literature

ADOFF, A. 1991. *In for Winter, Out for Spring.* Illustrated by J. Pinkney. New York: Dial.

HAMILTON, V. 1997. *Drylongso.* Illustrated by J. Pinkney. New York: Harcourt Brace.

LESTER, J. 1994. *John Henry.* Illustrated by J. Pinkney. New York: Dial.

———. 1996. *Sam and the Tigers.* Illustrated by J. Pinkney. New York: Dial.

PINKNEY, G. J. 1992. *Back Home.* Illustrated by J. Pinkney. New York: Dial.

———. 1994. *Sunday Outing.* Illustrated by J. Pinkney. New York: Dial.

SAN SOUCI, R. D. 1997. *The Hired Hand.* Illustrated by J. Pinkney. New York: Dial.

SCHROEDER, A. 1996. *Minty.* Illustrated by J. Pinkney. New York: Dial.

Author Profile

ANDREA PINKNEY

My husband, illustrator Brian Pinkney, and I frequently get asked how we collaborate on our books. Authors and illustrators seldom meet each other and they don't collaborate. Publishing houses keep them apart so that each is free to have their own creative vision. In our case, Brian and I have come up with a very good system of working together.

We have a studio in our home, which we share. To discuss projects we have a meeting once a week at our dining room table. In preparation for the meeting, Brian reads whatever manuscript I've been working on and I look at whatever artwork he's been working on. Then we bring these to the table and we have a meeting as you would in an office. There are certain rules for the meeting. There is no crosstalk—you can't cut the other person off when they are speaking. We always start the meeting on a positive note; I treat Brian as I would a coworker in an office—with respect and courtesy. Another rule for the meeting is that Brian starts his comments by saying, "Honey, I think you're off to a great start." The final rule is that when the hour meeting is over, it's over. Because we work at home, we could potentially talk about work all the time. The weekly meeting and the rules help us keep our personal family life and professional life separate. The meeting gives us a time and a place to discuss our work, and helps us to keep a sense of humor.

When I write any nonfiction book it starts with an idea. In the case of *Dear Benjamin Banneker* (1994), my editor at Harcourt Brace, Liz Van Doren, approached me and said, "Let's do a book on the scientist, Benjamin Banneker, and let's focus on Banneker's correspondence with Thomas Jefferson." What I knew of Benjamin Banneker was what most people knew of him—that he designed the first working clock in the United States, was an astronomer, taught himself mathematics, wrote almanacs, and helped lay the plans for the city of Washington, D.C. This was all too much to fit into a thirty-two-page picture book, so I focused the book on the letters he and Thomas Jefferson wrote to each other.

I am a real stickler for research. I usually research a book for about a year before I start writing it. I leave no stone unturned. I research as fully as I possibly can. I go to the library and I make an effort to speak to as many people as possible who are either experts in the area or who knew the figure in question. In the case of *Alvin Ailey*

(1993), for example, I spent a lot of time speaking to his mother, Lula Cooper, who gave me a lot of anecdotal material about what Alvin was like as a little boy. My husband and I learned all of the choreography from "Revelations," which is Ailey's signature ballet. Every turn of the hand, every position of the foot, every head, every shoulder, is correct in the illustrations. To get an even better grasp on the choreography, we took dance lessons with Ella Thompson Moore, who was one of the original Alvin Ailey dancers.

We do research in every form. In the case of *Benjamin Banneker* we took a field trip to his homestead. We visited Oella, Maryland, where Banneker lived. We always try to go to the source. Our research is a combination of reading books, doing practical hands-on research, and talking to people.

For our book *Bill Pickett, Rodeo Ridin' Cowboy* (1996), we went to the Black Cowboy Museum in Denver. I interviewed Pickett's great-great-grandson, who I mention in the book. I spoke to his biographer. We studied the rodeo, and Brian learned the actual techniques of bulldogging. Through research, Brian discovered that after a certain date, bulldoggers didn't jump off one side of the horse, they jumped off the other. He had depicted this incorrectly in his initial illustration, so he had to go back and do the illustrations over. Bulldogging is still one of seven rodeo events, but bulldoggers today don't bite the steer's lips like Bill Pickett did.

Brian and I chose to create a book about Duke Ellington because he's an icon of American music. He is the father of jazz, and when we worked on that book, we had a lot of fun. The research was extensive. We studied not only Duke Ellington, but also the history of jazz, the history of Harlem, the history of the Cotton Club. We had two goals for that book. The first was to convey Duke Ellington's use of music as painting. Duke thought of notes and instruments, and the sounds that they make, as colors. This was the mindset he used when he composed music. Brian's illustration palette for *Duke Ellington* (1998) is very colorful. The second goal for the book was to help the reader enter a world of music. When we collaborate on a book, the research is so long and so extensive that usually by the end I'm burned out and tired and just want it to be over. But when we finished *Duke Ellington*, I felt a bit sad, because the fun of making the book had ended.

I was thrilled when *Duke Ellington* won the Caldecott Honor Medal and the Coretta Scott King Honor. In addition to my work as an author, I am a children's book editor, so I was at the ALA conference when the awards announcements were made—what a thrill!

I also write novels for children. The idea for *Hold Fast to Dreams* (1995) came from an essay I wrote about growing up in a small town in Connecticut, where my family was one of a handful of black families. On a lark I sent this essay to the *New York Times*. Within a week somebody called me from the *New York Times* and told me they were publishing my essay in the Sunday *Times*. It was the first thing I'd ever published. After the piece ran in the paper, neighbors and friends called me. My parents had the piece framed. I hung it up by my computer. Then ten years later, a book editor asked me if I'd ever thought of writing a novel that has to do with race. I looked up at this little framed essay, and thought, why not?

I didn't understand the impact of the article when I did it. First of all, I didn't think anything would happen to it. But strangers called to tell me how much they liked it.

I wanted to write a story about a positive black family, which is what I'm from. The *Hold Fast to Dreams* story is not unique to me or to many people I know. I hear that story over and over, different scenario, different people, a different scene, but it's the same story.

Writing is a most gratifying thing, especially when a seventh grader, or a parent of a seventh grader, or a teacher, writes me a letter and says, "This same thing happened to me." We have to embrace our differences, and at the same time, we, meaning everybody, we really have to be who we are, in any situation. The true way to be is to be who you are.

Bob Fosse, the choreographer, once said about the creative process, "The pain is excruciating and I hope it never ends." I embrace that quote because it's so true. Every time I'm working on a novel or book I'm sitting at my computer saying, "Why do I do this?" I think that it's because I hope the pain never ends.

Children's Literature

PINKNEY, A. D. 1993. *Alvin Ailey*. Illustrated by B. Pinkney. New York: Hyperion.

———. 1994. *Dear Benjamin Banneker*. Illustrated by B. Pinkney. San Diego, CA: Gulliver Books.

———. 1995. *Hold Fast to Dreams*. New York: William Morrow.

———. 1996. *Bill Pickett, Rodeo Ridin' Cowboy*. Illustrated by B. Pinkney. New York: Dial.

———. 1998. *Duke Ellington*. Illustrated by B. Pinkney. New York: Disney.

6

Are Authors Rewriting Folklore in Today's Image?

MARGARET CHANG

The feminist movement is about change—while the serious writer must deal with what is permanent . . .

SUE MILLER (QUOTED IN BIRKERTS 1993)

My mother-in-law, Li Jú-fen, born in China when there was still an Emperor on the Dragon Throne, spoke no English. Since I, the American wife of her Chinese-born son, spoke just a few words of Chinese, I heard her reminiscences only through oral translation. During her lifetime, China, buffeted by the wild winds of history and social change, was swept into the modern world. The portrait of her in our novel *In the Eye of War* (1990) is drawn from her children's memories, from my knowledge of the events she witnessed, and from my attempts to imagine how she felt during the turbulent years of World War II. This complex, contradictory, and very real woman is my touchstone as I consider images of girls and women in children's books about imperial China.

A children's book writer and teacher of children's literature, I pay critical attention to fiction depicting China for the American audience. Here I will focus on stories about girls and women set before the fall of the Qing, the last imperial dynasty, in 1911. Li Jú-fen, like generations before her, took her place in a hierarchy articulated by the seminal philosopher Confucius (551–479 B.C.E.). Confucius placed women below their fathers, husbands, and sons. Chinese marriages were arranged, and once she left her childhood home, a woman contributed her labor and her children to her husband's family. A well-known female scholar of the Han Dynasty, Pan Chao, who died in C.E. 116, expounded on Confucian virtues for women: humility, service to a worthy and righteous husband, conjugal respect based on mutual affection, devotion to wifely duties, obedience to her husband's parents, and harmonious relations with her husband's brothers and sisters. Pan Chao's writings became classic models for female behavior for two thousand years (Guisso and Johannesen 1981, 67–71).

Meanwhile, eighteenth- and nineteenth-century Europe was flooded with images of a magnificently mysterious land known as China. The dream country portrayed, exotic and far away as the moon, in porcelain painting, wall coverings, landscape design, book illustration, and literature, is not a place Li Jú-fen would recognize, though it is comfortably familiar to Americans. Decorative art historians call this passion for "things Chinese" *chinoiserie*. *Chinoiserie* is alive and well in modern American children's books. Because the ersatz has been with us so long, we frequently mistake it for the real thing, and many modern examples of *chinoiserie* are frequently offered to teachers and children as authentic depictions of China's past.

A good example is Marianna Mayer's picture book retelling of Italian Giacomo Puccini's opera *Turandot*. The story, perhaps of Persian origin but first dramatized in Italy in 1762, tells of a powerful Chinese princess, Turandot, who demands that her royal suitors guess three riddles or die. All through the eighteenth century, European writers had freely used the China they imagined as a setting for philosophical fantasies and fables. English playwright Aaron Hill wrote in the introduction to his 1716 play set in China and produced in London: "our distance from, and dark ideas of, the Chinese Nation . . . tempted me to fix my scene in so remote a location. The fable is fictitious and the characters are all imaginary" (quoted in Honour 1961, 126). The same could be said of Puccini's opera, first staged in 1926. Winslow Pels's illustrations for Mayer's picture book resonate with Twenties fascination for exotic decadence, showing the Chinese princess draped in pearls, accompanied by a white tiger, her lovely white arms tattooed with curving forms. Pels portrays Turandot as Puccini did: compellingly seductive and cruel, a fantasy about Chinese women familiar in Western popular culture, but one that bears little resemblance to the real aristocratic maidens depicted in Chinese art for centuries. Though Mayer's afterword makes clear that the story is of Western origin, and really no one expects an opera to draw an accurate picture of China's imperial succession, Mayer's *Turandot* found its way into a list of folktales that followed a useful *Book Links* article outlining teaching activities for Laurence Yep's outstanding novel about a Chinese-American girl, *Child of the Owl* (Scales 1996). The title was not suggested by the author of the article, but inserted by the editor, Barbara Elleman, because "it is set in Peking . . . [and] we don't include enough music connections . . ." (Elleman 1996). By assuming that an Italian opera in the Western tradition, fancifully plotted and set in a distant, dark, and remote country, could shed light on the Chinese American experience, Elleman is tacitly asserting that Western writers, even opera librettists, are more capable of describing China than are the Chinese themselves.

Early in the twentieth century, other groups, both inside and outside of China, created their own versions of Chinese history. Reformers within China, eager to further their own political and social agendas for modernizing China, wrote historical narratives identifying women who lived in previous centuries "with backwardness and dependency" (Ko 1994, 1). Both Republicans and Communists sought to resist domination by foreign powers in part by reforming Chinese society from top to bottom. Freeing women from the strict confines of the Confucian hierarchy was high on both agendas. To justify their revolutionary causes, these groups painted the lot of previous generations as uniformly miserable, a reading of history that has shaped contemporary ideas about women in China in both East and West. Dorothy Ko's (1994) detailed "study of wives and daughters of scholar-official families in seventeenth-century Jiangnan" (7), a fertile region surrounding the Yangzi River delta, asserts that they faced a "range of constraints and opportunities" (4). Her book presents a richly colored, nuanced mural of women's lives. She writes: "It is my contention that the deep-seated image of the victimized 'feudal' women has arisen in part from an analytical confusion that mistakes normative prescriptions for experienced realities . . ." (3).

Protestant missionaries traveled to China early in the last century, replete with normative prescriptions of their own, determined to convert Chinese to Christianity and imbue them with American values (Hunter 1984). Women missionaries, as invested in negative depictions of the Chinese past as were Chinese reformers, interpreted China for American readers. Pearl Buck's *The Good Earth* (1931) is the most famous missionary novel, widely read and required in many American high schools. Buck came from a missionary family, grew up in China, and was cared for by Chinese nursemaids. She studied in Chinese schools, spoke fluent Chinese, and, as historian Jonathan Spence remarks, "knew more about [China's] land and rhythms of work than almost any previous American observer . . ." (Spence 1998, 180). *The Good Earth*, which sold over a million copies and in its film version reached twenty million viewers (Spence 1998) traces the rise to prosperity of a downtrodden peasant, Wang Lung. In the opening scene, he marries a slave from the house of wealthy landowners. His wife, O-lan, is a perfect example of the backward, dependent, downtrodden woman that Chinese Communist and Republican reformers, as well as American missionaries, saw as an icon of the feudal past. Stoic through her suffering, patient, enduring, O-lan works unceasingly, bears Wang Lung's children, and helps him make his fortune. When, through a twist of fate, he gains great wealth, he takes a concubine, Lotus. With her, as Spence puts it, he plunges "into the imagined realms of Oriental sensuality" (182), for Lotus is the exotic Chinese seductress so familiar to Westerners. In the 1937 film version, a soap-operatic vehicle for the actress Luise Rainer as the long-suffering wife O-lan, the concubine Lotus looks very much like Turandot as portrayed by Winslow Pels, striking exotic poses and draped with pearls. *The Good Earth* is strangely divorced from the history of its time. When Wang Lung cuts off his queue, Buck never mentions that the long braid is a symbol of oppression forced on ethnic Chinese by their hated Manchu conquerors. Wang Lung simply cuts it off to please Lotus. Buck never identifies the wars that temporarily drive Wang Lung from his beloved land. As Spence notes, missionaries were terrified by the violent Chinese insurgents at the end of the nineteenth century, "but rarely paused to inquire into the root causes of their rage" (187). Representing the missionary point of view, Buck depicts two stereotypes of women very familiar to Westerners, the suffering victim and the exotic seductress. Chinese find the book or film version of *The Good Earth* a well-meaning but simplistic portrait of their country, about as Chinese as the actors chosen for the major roles of the film, Europeans or Americans all.

The novelist Sue Miller's remark, which serves as the epigraph for my chapter, encapsulates the problem inherent in many modern stories depicting girls (and boys) in China's past. Here in America, I believe that, in trying to further an admirable feminist cause, many teachers, writers, and publishers—intellectual descendants of the missionaries, who hope to leave children a better world—recoil from stories depicting outmoded customs and beliefs, whether in historical novels or in folktales, those stories called by the Australian writer Patricia Wrightson "dreams that matter to us all" (1991, 165). Yet those customs, those dreams, have a kind of permanence, for they spring from people like ourselves. Serious writers must try to understand Ko's "experienced realities" and so portray women who lived under traditional rules as full, rounded human beings. As readers we must realize that stories from the past tell us more about who we are as human beings than what we might wish we could become in an ideal future. Too often we teachers want stories that will change hearts and minds, but not those that explore complexities of the past we wish to jettison. To use Ko's terminology, we wish to substitute "normative prescriptions" for "experienced realities." Some specific examples may serve to illuminate the problems and possibilities of depicting women from China's past.

We know that before 1911, Chinese women had relatively little control over many aspects of their lives. Over and over, Chinese stories dramatize the influence of fate on the lives of both men and women. One such traditional story is told in Ed Young's picture book *Red Thread* (1993), set in ancient China. Young's title refers to the red thread that binds the ankles of a couple during a traditional marriage ceremony. When a mysterious old man tells young Wei that his fated wife is a three-year-old girl carried by a ragged beggar-woman, Wei is so enraged that he sends a servant to kill the child. Fourteen years later, after many attempts to marry, he finally weds a governor's kind and beautiful niece. Discovering a scar on her forehead, he learns that when she was three, orphaned and temporarily in the care of her impoverished wet nurse, a madman stabbed her in the marketplace. Wei then recounts his story, concluding, "'It is a wonder, isn't it, that our lives and our fortune are known so well in heaven" (27). After that, Young tells ". . . the couple grew even closer" (28). I am sure my mother-in-law, Li Jú-fun, would have understood the couple's awe at the inevitability of their match, but it was all too much for the reviewer in *School Library Journal*, who admitted her Western bias when she wrote "Young's art is irresistible, but the theme of fatalism of the folktale is less appealing . . . and the gratuitous—and unrepented—violence toward the innocent child is truly disturbing" (Dooley 1993). The story, printed in Chinese on the endpapers, shows us a woman who understands and forgives violence done to her, an act which she believes does not deserve repentance, a woman who welcomes the accomplished husband fate has given her. Listening to the story on its own terms gives us imaginative insight into the mind of a woman from China's past.

The one-dimensional image of Chinese women as submissive victims begins to look more complicated when we consider the different ways Americans and Chinese regard gender roles. In a perceptive afterword to her book on American women missionaries in China at the turn of the century, Jane Hunter writes:

American evangelicals, perhaps Westerners in general, considered sex not as a function of role, which in extreme circumstances could be shed, but as the essence of identity itself, which must permeate self and determine a person's entire temperament. (1984, 261)

Hunter and other observers have maintained that Chinese see gender identity as a role, which may be changed or shed in extreme circumstances. The legendary woman warrior, Mu Lan, is the prime "role model" for these kinds of gender switches. Chinese American artist Jeanne M. Lee translated and illustrated *The Song of Mu Lan* (1995), crafting the most accurate version of the poem available to the children's book community, with illustrations drawing on the aesthetics of Chinese painting. Mu Lan's elderly father is conscripted to serve in the Emperor's army. Because she has no elder brother to take his place, Mu Lan dresses as a soldier and fights among men for twelve years. When the emperor seeks to reward her for her bravery, she asks only to go home. Once there, she puts on woman's clothes and greets her astonished comrades.

Legendary Mu Lan, who shed her role to save her father and resumed it when his need was over, inspired many Chinese women over the centuries. A few seventeenth-century women from aristocratic families were educated as men, and a story from that period tells of a woman who dressed as a man and illegally took the civil service examinations. Still wearing men's clothing, she went on to a distinguished career as a scholar and magistrate. Like Mu Lan, she eventually resumed her role as a woman (Pu Songling 1989). Emily Arnold McCully's *Beautiful Warrior* (1998), a picture book also set in the seventeenth century, dramatizes the life of the legendary woman kung fu master Wu Mei. Born an aristocrat and educated as if she were a boy, Wu Mei lost her family and position when the Ming Dynasty fell in 1644. Because she excelled at martial arts, she made her way to the famous Shaolin monastery, became a nun, and taught both boys and girls the lifelong disciplines and skills of kung fu. McCully steeped herself in Chinese painting, then developed her own fresh interpretation of classic Chinese art, creating vigorous, lively heroines, unusual but consistent with their time.

Hunter tells us that American women missionaries knew (and frequently deplored) Chinese girls who had been educated like boys and sometimes dressed as boys (259–60). In the twentieth century, women assumed men's roles to become Republican or Communist revolutionaries. Molly Bang knew this when she retold and illustrated *Tye May and the Magic Brush* (1981), a folktale shaped by Chinese communist storytellers from elements of traditional Chinese folk literature and first published in English in 1957 by the Foreign Languages Press in Beijing. The original translation into English and subsequent retellings published in the West featured a boy, Ma Liang. Molly Bang made the child whose magic brush enabled paintings to come to life a sturdy little girl of great integrity, a gender role switch in the tradition of Mu Lan, and one that does not violate the story's main theme, that an artist should help the common people. Tye May firmly resists threats, harassment, and bribes from a wicked landlord and a greedy emperor. Bang's illustrations, painted in black and white in a style reminiscent of Chinese brush painting, show Tye May wearing a red jacket "to imply the Communist aspect" (Bang 1998).

Though Mu Lan was well known to Chinese Americans, she was hardly a household word in the United States until Disney Studios decided that a feisty multicultural heroine could mightily improve its bottom line. The Disney version of "The Song of Mu Lan," released in June 1998, will, like the other Disney versions of classic tales, from *Snow White* to *The Hunchback of Notre Dame*, remain forever in American consciousness. It is so comfortably familiar that even the cross-dressing depicted at the end comes off as cutely quirky, not challenging in its strangeness, as was the violence in *Red Thread*. When Mulan looks in her mirror and sings plaintively, "When will my reflection show who I am inside?" (*Mulan* 1998), she is expressing what Hunter calls "a Protestant culture of feeling" rather than "a Chinese culture of role" (261). In the ancient Chinese poem, Mu Lan acted appropriately by assuming a role and then discarding it when she had saved her father's life and her family's position. While modern Western women might want Mu Lan to hold on to her sword, generations of Chinese who learned the story from opera and itinerant storytellers would have believed that she acted appropriately. Disney's Mulan wants her true feelings to be the essence of her identity, and known to the world, a sentiment missionary women tried, without much success, to teach their Chinese converts.

The wish to impose modern feminist values on traditional Chinese stories lies at the heart of Barbara Ann Porte's engaging romp through Chinese legend and history, *Hearsay: Strange Tales from the Middle Kingdom* (1998). In Porte's text for an earlier picture book, *"Leave That Cricket Be, Alan Lee"* (1993), a Chinese American boy catches a cricket, but lets it go at his mother's request. While we may applaud this lesson in animal rights, we must remember that keeping crickets and causing them to fight is a venerable Chinese custom, one Porte summarily dismisses. Porte says *Hearsay* grew out of her fascination with Chinese literature and history. Her careful notes detail the sources of her material and can lead readers back to the original tales. Though she makes clear what she is doing, for she is a serious writer, she places the values we want to pass on to our daughters at the end of the twentieth century firmly in the foreground, rejecting customs and ideas unpalatable to modern tastes. Her "feel-good" interpretation speaks in a contemporary Western voice, drowning out the voices of traditional Chinese storytellers, and so avoiding the strangeness that so disturbed the reviewer of *Red Thread*.

Footbinding heads the list of "old evils" both Chinese and Western reformers sought to eliminate. Porte tells of a Chinese mother who, in a gratuitous and unlikely sacrifice, cuts off her right foot to prevent her daughter's footbinding (Porte 1998, 78). When that does not work, she sends the daughter out into the night alone—a fate more horrifying to traditional Chinese women than footbinding. Dorothy Ko, after careful research into the lives of privileged women in seventeenth-century China writes:

To a modern critic, the gentrywomen's enchantment with bound feet, to the point of defining their femininity by it and devising rituals around it, is a profound statement of their victimization. However valid this critique is from hindsight, it does not accord with the self-perceptions of these women. When they appreciated their bound feet, these gentrywomen were, in fact, celebrating three elements crucial to their identities as women: their agency as individuals, their gentility as members of the leisure class, and their handiwork as women. (1994, 170–71)

Horrible as footbinding seems now, it persisted for hundreds of years. We may learn more about ourselves by imagining why women cooperated than by depicting the rare resistance. It is easy to blame Chinese women for complicity in their victimization. It is not quite so easy to see body-damaging practices in our own culture, and wonder why we participate. Why did Victorian women, living at the same time as Chinese women were binding their feet, wear corsets so tight that fainting was a regular occurrence? Why do women today wear shoes with four-inch heels, which do permanent damage to the feet and spine, and cosmetically enlarge their breasts with a substance that might just compromise the immune system? Why do so many girls of this generation suffer from eating disorders? Footbinding is no longer practiced in China, but today in America, emaciated supermodels set the standard for beauty.

Having turned three Chinese folktales into picture books aimed at American children, I know how difficult it is to take a traditional story entirely out of its context and retain any of its core values and themes. Some would argue that the mere act of translation robs a story of its essence. Since Chinese stories published in America are already far out of context, why should anachronisms matter? These are questions that bedevil any writer who deals with Chinese material. They are questions that are better answered with balance and compromise than with absolutes, questions each writer must answer for herself as she works with different stories. It is important to recognize Western stereotypes of Chinese women—the stoic peasant wife, the pearl-draped seductress—and realize that Chinese women from the past were individuals, like my mother-in-law, shaped as I am by the interaction of circumstance and character. While a few might have dressed as men to be soldiers or scholars, or shaved their heads to become nuns, most wanted to follow the path Confucius and Pan Chao had laid out for them, as did the wife in *Red Thread*.

Ann Scott MacLeod, in a 1998 article on recently published European and American historical fiction for children, writes that "authors want to give their heroines freer choices than their cultures would in fact have offered" (31). Dorothy Ko concludes that the aristocratic women she studied gained a surprising degree of power and fulfillment by complying with "the official gender system" (1994, 292). These real women did not openly rebel, as do the women portrayed in Porte's stories, but staked out positions for themselves within the boundaries drawn by their society. The consequences for transgressing those boundaries were harsh, and I am not sure most of us would want to incur them. Wu Mei, the "Beautiful Warrior" in Emily Arnold McCully's picture book, represents one woman who did not comply. But as a nun she gave up the rewards of husband, children, a home and life of her own, a sacrifice few women of her time would have been willing to make.

MacLeod decries setting "aside the social mores of the past as though they were minor afflictions, small obstacles, easy—and painless—for an independent mind to overcome" (31). I feel strongly that ignoring the historical realities that governed my mother-in-law's life, and the lives of women who went before her, women who found many outlets for self-expression and community even as they swayed gracefully on their bound feet, obviates the courage and intelligence they used to negotiate the terrain they were born to. It is important to look at the past as clearly as we can, and find empathy and understanding for Chinese women who created rewarding lives despite the restrictions of Confucian society, as well as for those who suffered under those restrictions. Denying the restrictions, which women themselves internalized, denies their creativeness and courage as well as their suffering.

If girls and young women are presented a version of the past that conforms to modern ideals, they could easily undervalue, or take for granted, the variety of choices open to them at the end of the twentieth century. I believe my daughter has more freedom than either of her grandmothers knew. Reading historical fiction that recognizes what MacLeod calls "known historical realities" (27) or traditional literature that stays close to its roots can give my daughter a context in which to place her own life, just as my imaginative attempt to understand Li Jú-fen, my husband's mother, gave me a clearer picture of my own inner landscape. Any reader who leaps into the unknown with a story that describes strange events, strange customs, is vigorously exercising her imagination. And imagination is the faculty all young women most need to envision a world better than the one we have left them.

References

BANG, M. 1998. Letter postmarked February 24.

BIRKERTS, S. 1993. "The Good Writer" [an interview with Sue Miller]. *Mirabella* April, 84–86.

DOOLEY, P. 1993. Review of *Red Thread* by Ed Young. *School Library Journal.* 39 (3): 195.

ELLEMAN, B. 1996. Letter dated April 8.

The Good Earth. 1937. Directed by S. Franklin. 2 hours, 18 minutes. Distributed by Metro-Goldwyn-Mayer, Inc. Videocassette.

GUISSO, R. W., & S. JOHANNESEN. 1981. *Women in China: Current Directions in Historical Scholarship.* Youngstown, NY: Philo Press.

HONOUR, H. 1961. *Chinoiserie: The Vision of Cathay.* London: John Murray.

HUNTER, J. 1984. *The Gospel of Gentility: American Women Missionaries in Turn-of-the-Century China.* New Haven: Yale University Press.

KO, D. 1994. *Teachers of the Inner Chambers: Women and Culture in Seventeenth-Century China.* Stanford: Stanford University Press.

MacLeod, A. S. 1998. "Writing Backward: Modern Models in Historical Fiction." *The Horn Book Magazine* 74 (1): 26–33.

Mulan. 1998. Directed by B. Cook and T. Bancroft. 88 minutes. Distributed by Disney Enterprises, Inc. Videocassette.

Pu Songling. 1989. "Miss Yan." In *Strange Tales from a Make-Do Studio.* Bejing: Foreign Languages Press, 205–11.

Spence, J. D. 1998. *The Chan's Great Continent: China in Western Minds.* New York: W. W. Norton.

Scales, Pat. 1996. "Laurence Yep's *Child of the Owl.*" *Book Links* 5 (3): 36–41.

Wrightson, P. 1991. "Deeper Than You Think." *The Horn Book Magazine* 67 (2): 162–70.

Children's Literature

Bang, M. G. 1981. *Tye May and the Magic Brush.* New York: Greenwillow.

Buck, P. 1931. *The Good Earth.* New York: Collier.

Chang, M., & R. Chang. 1990. *In the Eye of War.* New York: Margaret K. McElderry/Simon & Schuster.

The Frog Rider—Folk Tales from China (First Series). 1957. Beijing: Foreign Languages Press.

Lee, J. M. 1995. *The Song of Mu Lan.* Arden, NC: Front Street.

Mayer, M. 1995. *Turandot.* Illustrated by W. Pels. New York: Morrow Junior Books.

McCully, E. A. 1998. *Beautiful Warrior: The Legend of the Nun's Kung Fu.* New York: Arthur A. Levine/Scholastic.

Porte, B. A. 1993. *"Leave That Cricket Be, Alan Lee."* New York: Greenwillow.

———. 1998. *Hearsay: Strange Tales from the Middle Kingdom.* Illustrated by R. F. Covey. New York: Greenwillow.

Young, E. 1993. *Red Thread.* New York: Philomel Books.

Illustrator Profile

PAUL O. ZELINSKY

People have sometimes thought that I specialize in illustrating folktales. I don't, though I very much like the genre, and I have taken on three Grimms' tales so far, all for fairly personal reasons. Folktales do tend to be good stories. By definition, they're narratives that bear repetition and stick in the memory. With repeated telling over generations, inessential elements must get stripped away, strong elements bolstered and simplified, so that folktales are among the most powerful and essential of stories. Which I think is why they can be so meaningful and accessible to children.

Hansel and Gretel (Lesser 1984), my first folktale project, was inspired by a painting my great-grandmother made of a nighttime landscape showing the witch's house. In my early childhood it produced a feeling in me—I remember it clearly—that I never felt in any Hansel and Gretel book I knew, then or since. Eventually I thought that it would be worthwhile to try to evoke it with a *Hansel and Gretel* of my own. My translator friend, Rika Lesser, agreed to provide the text, and she began an investigation into the background of the tale.

Rika found that in the first published edition of the Grimms' tale it was a mother who left her children in the woods, though I had only known it as a stepmother. This was one of innumerable instances, we discovered, where the Grimms substantially revised the stories in their classic collection, *Kinder- und Hausmärchen (Children's and Household Tales)*, from one edition to the next. It seems that the first edition was published as an ethnographic document for adults—but Jacob and Wilhelm Grimm soon found that the public was eagerly buying the book for reading to children. It wasn't long before the Grimms produced a special edition of selected stories specifically for children, but it also seems clear to me that the many changes they made in the great two-volume collection over the next forty years were driven by their idea of a child audience and its perceived needs. In the book's second edition Hansel and Gretel are already living with their father and stepmother. Rika wrote the mother back in. I think that if children can't handle the story with a mother in this role, they probably shouldn't be listening to it with a stepmother, either. In my pictures I tried to make the mother look stern and practical, concerned about herself more than others, but not ugly. I thought someone like that would try to take care of her looks. The parents are morally ambiguous at best; they are faced with starvation, after all, which can force people to do terrible things. But really the mother in this story is somewhat peripheral; it seems to me that the subject is really the children and their adventure.

My central vision of the story was an image of tiny children alone in the huge woods. It wasn't even the wonderful scene of the witch and her house. You asked about the woods—why they weren't haunted, full of trees with faces, and so on. If the trees had faces, the woods would have been too personal. When you are really lost and alone, there is nobody looking at you. I painted the woods as over-sized but realistic when Hansel and Gretel were brought there the first time. I took pictures of some old woods in Connecticut and looked at them as I painted. The children's second trip into the woods was getting creepier and a little fantastic, a place where you might find a house made of bread and cakes. The text said the roof was made of cakes, which I presumed to mean pancake shingles, though I also put in some whipped cream roofing over the dormer, inspired by a lemon meringue pie in the dessert case of a diner I ate in one day. I painted that from memory, but to help me with the shingles I bought pancake mix at the grocery store, made pancakes and laid them out on a tray alongside some wafer cookies for shutters and Twinkies for bricks (I could not find ladyfingers locally). It was a pleasure to paint these materials and then to eat my models.

I had no models for the children, who eventually found their way, uneaten, out of captivity. I don't know if the story has a moral; I'm not really concerned with that. I know that I feel that the story is meaningful; it has weight. But different people may find different meanings. Art has this quality of carrying meaning in its own way; you can't quite pin it down. And if you look at a story like this as a coded message, or as a vehicle to drive home a moral, you're really missing something.

With *Rumpelstiltskin* (1986), as with *Rapunzel* (1997), I did the research and the retelling myself. My special relation to Rumpelstiltskin is that I played him in the Wilmette (Ill.) Children's Theater production of the play when I was about eleven. So I've always felt for the little man. But even for people who haven't played him, Rumpelstiltskin is probably the most sympathetic villain among the Grimm tales. He can be seen as a victim himself. He keeps his word—and what does he get for it? A bloody death, in the later Grimm versions. In the first edition of the collection, though, he goes off angry and doesn't come back; by the third edition he stamps his foot into the ground in a rage, grabs his other foot and tears himself in half. The Grimms were interested in moral lessons: given the opportunity, they gave their villain a worse and worse fate. But I prefer the more ambiguous ending, which happens to be how the story was told to Wilhelm Grimm in the first place. And in my book I used an alternate version he described in his footnotes, the most picturesque one, in which an aggrieved Rumpelstiltskin flies out the window on his cooking spoon.

The young girl in *Rumpelstiltskin* is quite powerless, though less so in the first edition, where she directs her own servant to find the little man, than in later ones, where the king takes this initiative. I am most uncomfortable with the aspect of her relationship to the king. He could be seen as an embodiment of greed, interested only in gold. Yet she marries him; she has little or no choice. But the marriage is not portrayed as a bad thing, and it even has its role in the happily-ever-after ending. I won't claim that stories do not tell lessons, and there is enough material here for an interpretation of blatant sexism. The best case I can make is that the king was not a large part of the girl's story, except to insist that she make good on her initial promise, to spin straw into gold. I see the story of Rumpelstiltskin as the story of a lie and its consequences. In the end, when Rumpelstiltskin is literally out of the picture, I thought there was an opportunity for the king to reenter, to start from scratch, to become a part of a family. I painted him coming down a staircase behind the relieved mother, making an open gesture with his hand. We don't necessarily know this king. Let's believe that he evolved.

Swamp Angel (Isaacs 1994) was an unsolicited manuscript picked up by my editor at Dutton, Donna Brooks (you see, this can actually happen to unpublished authors!), who showed it to me. So it's a tall tale but it isn't a folktale. Of course, the Paul Bunyan stories aren't folktales, either. They were the marketing creation of a lumber company, I believe. But Paul Bunyan has taken on the luster of a folk hero, and it would be fine with me if Swamp Angel did, too. The story was great fun; it made me laugh, and was a pleasure to illustrate.

Angelica Longrider, a.k.a. Swamp Angel, is a powerful young woman who fights and vanquishes an enormous bear. I noticed, though, when beginning the pictures, that the text didn't describe or mention her size except once, to say that at birth she was scarcely taller than her mother. Though I went on to make Angelica bigger than tree-size, the author's relative silence on the point of her size registered the importance of careful reading. Had there been no size reference, I would have felt free to make Swamp Angel any size I wanted: it might have been funnier or more intriguing in some way if her spectacular feats had been accomplished without that size advantage. I decided, though, to let her tower over Tennessee. An important part of the process of growing from infant to adult is learning the limits of yourself. As an infant, you are the universe. Maturing means unlearning this. There is something very comfortable, familiar and reassuring about a story where the protagonist is completely huge, fills the world, and has virtually no limits.

A big Angelica actually made the pictures harder to compose, because with a huge girl fighting a huge bear, the large scale of one cancels out the visual effect of the large scale of the other. I had to think hard to find more indirect ways to express a sense of monumental size. But with Swamp Angel's great height came physical restrictions: the laws of physics would demand enormous feet to support her great weight, and a large head would need a disproportionately stout neck. Of course my pictures aren't slaves to the laws of physics, but I always find that fantasy works best when it remains bound to the rules of the real world.

I didn't have as clear a reason for having taken on *Rapunzel* (1997), only a feeling for the tale that told me it was right. *Rapunzel* is about growing and becoming independent. The story can be read on a sexual level as well, though I don't think it is necessary to think of it in that way.

It begins with an almost independent story, telling of the mother who craves rapunzel the herb, and loses Rapunzel the daughter. This is a prologue for the tale of the girl and the sorceress, her mother-figure, an obsessive parent who won't let go, a woman, in my view, who can't bear her own loss of youth and beauty. Why else would she take Rapunzel away from the world except to subsume her, in a way to become her? So I tried to depict the sorceress as old but having great physical beauty. I'm afraid that she came out less beautiful in the paintings than I had intended; the extreme emotions I planted on her face didn't help to display her glamour, either. But beauty was my intention. The stereotyped image of this character, of course, is an ugly old crone. I tried to contradict this image for reasons central to my understanding of the story and its meaning, but the whole question of audience expectation put me in mind of a large issue that illustration, even of newly written stories, presents: there will always be a culturally understood stereotyped image for almost any character you can imagine. If an illustrator's depiction follows that image it will automatically feel right to most readers, and the communicative power of the illustrations will work to their fullest extent. If an illustrator decides to strike a blow against cultural stereotyping and strays too far from the expected, the effect will tend to be jarring and less communicative emotionally. In the case of Rapunzel's sorceress, the equation between moral turpitude and ugliness of face is a shared subconscious code, and an illustrator ignores it to his or her peril. Luckily for me and my interpretation, I was able to draw a version of the story from a source that didn't vilify the sorceress in this way: the French *conte*, *Persinette*, featured a fairy who placed the girl in a silver tower, a magical isolation chamber that nevertheless supplied its occupant with fashionable clothes, jewels, even bags of money. My Rapunzel's "mother" gave her everything she could need or want, everything except a life of her own. And so she found a prince to run away with. You don't need to see a moral or even consciously to form an interpretation to understand when a folktale is telling you a big truth.

Children's Literature

ISAACS, A. 1994. *Swamp Angel*. Illustrated by P. O. Zelinsky. New York: Dutton.

LESSER, R. 1984. *Hansel and Gretel*. Illustrated by P. O. Zalinsky. New York: Dodd, Mead and Company.

ZELINSKY, P. O. 1986. *Rumpelstiltskin*. New York: Dutton.

———. 1997. *Rapunzel*. New York: Dutton.

7

Truth as Patchwork: Developing Female Characters in Historical Fiction

Janet Hickman

It is common wisdom that fiction gives us the opportunity to try on other lives, to have thrills without risk and suffering without undue consequence. These are the virtual reality games that readers play, and a prime source of our reading pleasure. If the act of reading involved nothing but this, stories could be judged solely on their power to arouse feeling. But of course reading is far more complex. Deliberately or not, in fiction as well as in nonfiction, readers are always collecting information about the world and its possibilities, always learning. Practiced readers are able to sort out which information is the most reliable; but inexperienced or naïve readers of any age, particularly children, are more likely to accept questionable information right along with the good. So, while there is plenty of room for exaggeration and fractured facts in fantasy and comedy, it still makes sense to insist on an obligation to truth in any children's book that claims to portray the world as it is or as it was.

In reading stories of contemporary life, children can bring much of their own experience to the page to help them judge the integrity of what they are reading. With stories of the past, readers often have little or no prior knowledge about a particular setting; they are at the mercy of the author. Thus, historical fiction in particular demands truth; according to Cai (1992), it is one of the defining variables of the genre and serves as a basic standard. In fact, there is such wide agreement among scholars and critics and writers about the need for truth, or accuracy, or authenticity, that the point is beyond argument. The problem comes not in naming truth as a standard but in attempting to define it in practice, a task that requires the piecing together of many perspectives and a great deal of material from disparate sources.

Finding Young Women in History

To a writer, the requirement of truth in historical fiction brings on a whole set of challenges. For any story-to-be, history's record of relevant events and circumstances, such as battles, blizzards, or medical knowledge, must be located and verified to establish a basic frame. A variety of contemporaneous responses to the events must be considered in an attempt to understand prevailing attitudes and beliefs of the time. All along the way, from very early in the planning and thinking stages, choices must be made about meshing background information with the personalized story that will carry the reader through the book. Choices also have to be made about the course of fictional lives that must fit within their frame of real history. And then all of this literal and figurative truth must be made to seem not only credible, but compelling. Luckily, the actual process is more enjoyable than this description makes it sound; digging for facts can be a fascinating activity in spite of the inevitable dead ends and frustrations.

Gender is only one of the aspects of truth in fictional lives, but it creates more than its share of complexities, beginning with the relative scarcity of specific information about real girls and young women. It is hard enough for an author to reconstruct the lives of famous men, whose words and deeds are part of the public record, and about whom much has already been written. It is harder still to capture the facts about everyday people, whose records, such as they may have been, are less likely to have survived. As subjects of historical research, women are more problematic than men, for in most times prior to our own, they appeared far less frequently than men in reference books and published records. For example, my copy of the *History of Delaware County and Ohio*, from 1880, presents many biographical sketches of prominent residents; in the first section alone I count 118 men but only four women, all widows, whose entries are devoted more to their late husbands than to themselves.

If women are all but absent from such sources, children are even less in evidence. It seems to follow that female children would be the most difficult of all to tease out of conventional historical records, a conclusion borne out in my own attempts at research.

Authors have to rely mostly on alternative sources to discern what girls of the past were like, to explore what might have been "true" for a young female character in a particular place and time. The voices and images of women and children aren't really missing from history, they are just less obvious. They are in letters and diaries, journals and cookbooks, paintings and photographs; they are in the margins of school texts, or mentioned here and there in newspaper accounts of social events and ceremonies. The stance is frequently personal, having to do with family and the tasks and activities of everyday life. Fortunately, that is just the kind of detail a novel needs. Unfortunately, it is not always easy to find the right bits and pieces, the ones that will help to develop a specific character.

Creating Characters Piece by Piece

I have struggled several times with the process of finding young women in history, most recently in the writing of *Susannah* (Hickman 1998). The first pieces of that story came directly from the chance reading of a bit of history. A quick follow-up established a basic foundation of events. In 1810, just a few years after Shakers from New England had sent missionaries to the Ohio frontier, a certain Colonel James Smith helped organize an uprising against the Shaker community that had begun to form northeast of Cincinnati at Turtle Creek (later known as Union Village). Smith's complaint against the Shakers was that they were holding his grandchildren hostage. His son had embraced the Shakers' faith, but the son's wife refused to do so and left the community. The predictable accusation that she had abandoned her husband was more interpretation than fact, since the two could not have cohabited in any case. A major tenet of the Shaker belief was strict celibacy; husbands and wives who came to the community together were soon separated from one another, and from their children as well.

The younger Smiths did have children, and their mother wanted to take them away with her. According to the law of the time, however, children were always subject to the control of their fathers, and this father insisted his children should stay with the Shakers. Colonel Smith, their grandfather, agreed with his daughter-in-law. He visited Turtle Creek and was not favorably impressed. Being a man of action with quite a colorful personality of his own, he began to agitate for the children's release. Ultimately the Colonel and others with similar grievances against the Shakers—absent wives, missing children, contract disputes—raised a force of hundreds of men armed with real and makeshift weapons, and marched against the Turtle Creek Shakers. The expedition turned out to be no more than a show of force, ended by negotiation and without significant injury. Nevertheless, my initial reaction was outrage that anyone should have threatened violence against such a peaceable people.

Over the course of several years, I did a lot of additional research on these real events. My searching took me to the Case Western Reserve Library in Cleveland, with its wonderful microfilm collection of Shaker records; to the Warren County Historical Society and Museum in Lebanon, Ohio; to the Archives of the Ohio State Historical Society in Columbus; and to several restored Shaker villages in Massachusetts, New York, and Kentucky. I discovered a great many interesting things about the Shakers, but as my reading and research shifted from general secondary sources to primary-source materials, I found my interpretation of the events at Turtle Creek shifting as well. Bad behavior against the Shakers still seemed outrageous to me, and I learned they had endured considerable harassment. Yet more and more of my sympathy came to rest with the families, like the Smiths, that had been broken or abandoned as the Shaker communities were, in their own word, "gathered." Choices made by family members who joined had a profound impact, both emotional and economic, on those who did not.

In the long run, I was never able to answer all the questions that intrigued me or to piece together all the facts about the Smith family. Thus these real people slipped out of my plans for a book, making way for invented characters. Only the Smiths' various and very real dilemmas remained to haunt me. I wondered if that father had been smug about his legal right to insist on a particular upbringing for his children.

I wondered what it meant to that mother to leave her children behind. Wouldn't there have been practical consequences as she grew older with no family to turn to? Was the grandfather a despicable meddler, or was he truly desperate? But most of all, I wondered about the children and what had happened to them. I didn't have any satisfactory answers. I didn't know their ages or their names, or even whether they were boys or girls.

The big question, then, was whose story it would be. Since the historical record had not provided a particular young person as a model, I needed to make my own narrator. If I were a man, I suppose I might have chosen a boy. But as a woman, I defaulted to a female character. When there is little to go on, it helps to begin where something, at least, is familiar—in this case, the emotional geography of my own gender. I decided to use the voice of Susannah, a girl in her fourteenth year who has been among the Shakers only a short time. Still, that was only the barest of beginnings. I had to explore what Susannah might have been like, how she might have spent her time, and what, given her circumstances, she might have thought and dared to do.

Even the Shakers, who were excellent record-keepers, wasted little paper and ink on young people. There are a few memoirs of childhood published by men and women brought up as Shakers, but most of these reflect later time periods. Moreover, they are filtered through multiple layers of life experience and through memories that may not be entirely dependable. Information about children in the early days of the Turtle Creek community is very hard to come by, even though the record suggests that dozens and dozens of youngsters were connected to the group. I read from archival documents that the Brethren had been at work building a sawmill of such and such dimensions and that the Sisters had fed twenty visitors at dinner on a particular date, but never did I read what chores had been set for the children on a given day, or any definitive primary-source description of children's activities. If such sources exist, I didn't find them.

Maybe the record simply reflects the reality of the Shakers. In their eyes, it was gender, not age, that became the defining issue. The Shakers were founded by a woman, Mother Ann Lee, who was viewed by her followers as God incarnate in female form. The principle of celibacy by which the Shakers lived was meant to protect women from the stresses of marriage and motherhood and make it possible for both sexes to focus on the life of the spirit. Shaker women shared responsibility with men as spiritual leaders and also as managers of other affairs. Although daily work was organized along traditional gender lines, every community had eldresses in charge as well as elders. Because these ideas were such a radical departure from their time and earned such public attention, Shaker women were somewhat better situated than their worldly sisters to become part of recorded history.

Still, the record of the Shakers' early years says relatively little about the role of women and children. It was a challenge to try to make Susannah and the story's other fictional women, young and old, true to the terms of their Shaker circumstances as well as their historical period. As characters, they were patched together from several sources. For whatever truth is reflected in their lives, I am indebted to recent historians who have ferreted out the voices of real women of the time and published them in resources that were nonexistent when I first began my research.

Among the books most important to me was one by women's studies scholar Jean Humez. In *Mother's First-Born Daughters* (1993), I found letters from the very first Shaker women who came from New England to Ohio. Although their topics were often spiritual, they returned over and over again to the rigors of their frontier life:

> In the whole we have nearly twenty to cook for in general, and in harvest time we had upwards of twenty and sometimes thirty, and continual comers and goers daily; there is no cessation. . . But we have all our washing to do outdoors, only a shelter of bushes over us, and we do all our ironing in the room where we all live, which makes it very uncomfortable. . . We used to think that we knew what hardship was, and truly we did, but we knew nothing about it to what we know now. (Humez 1993, 149)

One letter made it clear that the Western Shakers had not attained the same level of decorum in their dance-based worship as their mentors from the East: "'We have great meetings, public meeting [sic] twice a week, when the young sisters [new converts] are under exercise. Sometimes they get us into their arms and make us hardly fit to be seen . . .'" (Humez, 154)

In *The Reshaping of Everyday Life: 1790–1840* by historian Jack Larkin (1988), I found anonymous phrases by which contemporaries had described the general conditions of their time. The "sickly months" were August and September, when intestinal diseases flourished, but the risk of death from respiratory infection was highest in late winter and early spring. Women reported the monotony of spinning and sewing: "My fingers are worn out." Horses traveled over the "rich mud roads of Ohio," but most poorer Americans covered long distances on foot "without thinking it a trouble."

One of the most useful sources in piecing together my characterization of Susannah herself was Mary Beth Norton's *Liberty's Daughters: The Revolutionary Experience of American Women, 1750–1800* (1980). Although the period seems wrong for a story set in 1810, this book suggested to me what life might have been like for Susannah's mother, and thus what precepts she might have passed on to her daughter. A young person in Susannah's position would be shut off from her own time in two ways, first by the relative isolation of frontier life, and even more by the restrictions of the Shaker community. It seems logical that such a child would rely even more than usual on the values of a beloved parent. Many of Susannah's memories of her mother, which frequently guide her actions, reflect items about education, finances, or family bonds quoted in Norton's book. Even Susannah's moderately independent spirit is modeled in part on Norton's description of that minority of colonial women who were "as independent as circumstances will admit."

Liberty's Daughters also gave me a term that was invaluable but potentially problematic: *notable housewife*. According to Norton (4–5), the concept of notability refers to a woman's capacity to run her household, large or small, with skill and efficiency.

At the end of the eighteenth century, the notable housewife was a widely held ideal, a male expectation, and the goal of a great many young women in spite of their complaints about the drudgery of household work. For a woman of that time, becoming a notable housewife was a mark, perhaps *the* mark, of success. That is one of the problems Susannah has with the Shakers; being part of a communal group of females will not save her from household drudgery, but it will prevent her from ever assuming the responsibility of managing her own family's domestic affairs. She can grow up exhausted by housework, but she can never grow up to be notable.

Alternate Perspectives

From my view as Susannah's creator, her feelings about being a notable housewife are part of the emotional truth of the story, a likely response in terms of her personality and the circumscribed choices her life would offer. Yet this is an example of the kind of instance in which other views might differ from the author's. For a generation now, both the professional and popular press have been discussing the attributes of female characters that girls (and boys) should be meeting in their reading. Needless to say, notable housewifery is not high on the list. As a matter of fact, such a concept is more likely to be viewed negatively, like the role of June Cleaver on *Leave It to Beaver,* as almost toxic in its limitations.

In constructing a character, an author selects from all the pieces of information available, which are always more numerous than space will allow, and sometimes contradictory. The author makes choices based on her own sense of what is important, what is engaging, what is dramatically powerful, and what serves the logistics of the story at hand. When that work is on the page, readers of all sorts go through a related process in piecing together the character for themselves. Readers also select from the information available to them, which includes what the author has offered plus other facts and beliefs they may hold. They also make choices based on their sense of what is important and engaging and dramatic. Even if every single piece of information available to authors and readers were absolutely accurate, the pool of information would be different for each one; their valuing of one fact over another would be different; their patterns of choice would be different. Author and readers alike could be creating "truthful" images, yet no two would be alike. It's little wonder there is so much disagreement about interpreting the standard of authenticity.

When I am reading in my critical-theory mode, I might look for a character who is not only true to the record but who embodies qualities that would be useful against the injustices of our time as well as her own. I might even second-guess my own choices about Susannah's yearning for domesticity. Couldn't she have longed for a more autonomous adult life? Had higher aspirations? As a writer, I would not dismiss these questions, but I would argue that it is equally legitimate to focus elsewhere—in this case on the dilemmas arising from Susannah's "care orientation" (Gilligan and Wiggins 1988), her desire for attachment to others, and her tendency to make decisions based on those relationships, a circumstance that is also pertinent to her gender.

When I am reading and thinking in terms of the classroom teacher I once was, I put more attention on the representativeness of characters in historical fiction. While I want to see a good story that will involve students on many levels, I hope for a character who can be somehow typical of her setting, who can help students understand and remember the historical particulars of her time. Representativeness in historical fiction serves curriculum well, and I am still happy to recommend books whose protagonists seem to speak for a host of young people who may have led similar lives. But yet, when I am writing, it is uniqueness of character that becomes my goal. I know that a girl from the past will not be memorable if she is only generic, if she fits too neatly into her context without a distinct personality of her own.

The multiple perspectives from which we read, and write, bring richness to literature and to our conversations about books, just as a patchwork of sources brings texture and dimension to individual characterizations, female or male. When we offer a variety of good books to children, this is one of the things we give them—a chance to piece together their own larger version of truth.

References

Cai, M. 1992. "Variables and Values in Historical Fiction for Children." *The New Advocate* 5 (Fall): 279–91.

Gilligan, C., & Wiggins, G. 1988. "The Origins of Morality in Early Childhood Relationships." In *Mapping the Moral Domain*, ed. C. Gilligan, J. V. Ward, J. M. Taylor, 111–38. Cambridge, MA: Harvard University Press.

History of Delaware County and Ohio. 1880. Chicago: O. L. Baskin and Company.

Humez, J. 1993. *Mother's First-Born Daughters: Early Shaker Writings on Women and Religion*. Bloomington, IN: Indiana University Press.

Larkin, J. 1988. *The Reshaping of Everyday Life: 1790–1840*. New York: HarperCollins.

Norton, M. B. 1980. *Liberty's Daughters: The Revolutionary Experience of American Women, 1750–1800*. New York: HarperCollins.

Children's Literature

Hickman, J. 1998. *Susannah*. New York: Greenwillow.

Author Profile

Karen Cushman

I have always been interested in the Middle Ages avocationally: the music, costumes, Renaissance fairs, medieval fairs. I had written a grant proposal to the NIH, on children's material culture—that is, objects made or used by children over the ages. I started thinking about what life was like for children in other time periods, when they had less power and less value than they do now. What if there was this independent spirit who was at odds with her family and her society's desire to control her and use her for economic gain? The story of Catherine came to me one morning. What if there was this girl, and most of my stories start "what if," and that's what got me started on *Catherine, Called Birdy* (1994). I think that the second one, *The Midwife's Apprentice* (1995), came from knowing that period and the people so well, and having another image of another child with a different kind of life in the same time.

Women of the Middle Ages were not all the same. They were not all passive, easily frightened, and dreadfully dull; there was a spectrum of people, including women, and their responses and their attitudes and their willingness to knuckle under. We have Eleanor of Aquitaine as a great example of a very independent, powerful woman who knew how to say no when she didn't want to do something. She knew how to get what she wanted. Even with ordinary people there was a range, so I thought it would make a much more interesting story to have somebody who was at odds with her world, rather than someone who was just happily sitting and embroidering.

What I like best about Birdy is that she is me the way I would have liked to have been. I wasn't a tomboy. I wanted to be a saint. I never wanted to be a nun, but sometimes I wanted to be a saint. I was very obedient as a child, a good girl. As I was creating Birdy I kept thinking this is the way I would have liked to have responded. I would have liked to stand up for myself. I really like that about her, which is why a lot of people, including Anne MacLeod in her *Horn Book* article (1998), criticized the character and the book's ending. I was not about to marry Birdy off to Shaggy Beard, because I cared about her and lived with her so intimately for years. It was *my* story, and having her marry Shaggy Beard and live with him is another story, a different story, not the story I was telling. For example, if she had married Shaggy Beard, I couldn't have told the story without a lot of attention paid to her sex life. That wasn't the story I wanted to tell to a ten- or eleven-year-old.

I know there are quite a few documented cases of women agreeing to marry the first time out of duty, like Birdy's friend, Aislinn, if they could then have the right to choose their second husband. The sister of Henry VIII did that, when she married Sir Charles Brandon. You also see a lot of cases of widows, who chose to remain unmarried once they were older, who had made these arrangements when they were young unmarried women. Marjorie Paxton married a family servant. Her family complained and hollered but it was done and she was married. Within the same family one of the daughters was locked away until she agreed to marry as directed and, one generation removed maybe, there was a woman who married whom she wanted.

When I first started writing about the Middle Ages, especially the British High Middle Ages, it occurred to me that the Middle Ages were turning into the Renaissance, very much like a child growing into adolescence. There were many parallels. For example, there was the development of books of etiquette, which was a new phenomenon. Suddenly there was this realization of "me" as opposed to other people and how do I look to them? There was a new emphasis on privacy, the development of the solar, where the lord of the manor and his family could withdraw from the communal. There was a new appreciation for the works of individual people as opposed to the community. I thought Birdy was almost moving into the Renaissance, leaving all these other people behind her.

I disagree with MacLeod's (1998) conclusions. *The True Confessions of Charlotte Doyle* (1990) by Avi is almost fantasy, similar to Tamora Pierce's *Alanna* (1983) books about a girl who dresses like a man and becomes a knight. In that time and place it would be impossible for a young girl living so intimately with people to pass herself off as a knight or a sailor. But *Catherine, Called Birdy* and *Sarah, Plain and Tall* (1985) are not fantasy; what happens to them is something that could happen. It's certainly something that did happen in the case of *Sarah, Plain and Tall*. We have the letters of Elinore Pruitt Stewart, the female homesteader, who placed an advertisement and went across the country to be housekeeper to a man she did not know. In her letters and in other accounts of pioneers there are many examples of hardships and a lot of work, but there were also picnics and parties.

In the case of Birdy, I tried extremely hard not to make her modern. Sometimes Birdy's reactions are different from the ordinary reaction. When she goes to see the public hanging she is sickened by it, because I wanted young people to be able to identify with her. I tried not to give her modern choices, because that would evade the common realities of her time and society. Birdy does have a clear understanding of her limitations, though she throws herself against the bars of her cage; she sees them there and figures out which ones she can live with and which ones she can't.

Children tend to react positively to *Catherine, Called Birdy* because they really like the character of Birdy. A lot of children have complaints about why the father is so mean, and ask how he could force her to marry. I tried hard to make kids realize that they're seeing her father through Birdy's eyes. I put hints in there of how he was different, how he acted with her mother, that he wasn't completely how Birdy saw him. That's the point of the diary form: we're seeing it all through her eyes, and she could be exaggerating or leaving some things out. They ask why she didn't just run away and work in a boutique in London or something. When I write back to them I talk about how the times were so different and how there weren't the same options we have now. Birdy was the one who was considered wrong, because she was rebelling against the established order. Her father was not unusual. She was the one refusing to do what she was supposed to do. Kids ask, "Why couldn't she just go out on her own?" and I tell them she wouldn't have survived. Let's talk about that. It is impossible. She would have been raped and murdered.

I think Birdy's mother is probably pretty content living in her cage. One thing I talk about with kids is how young Birdy's mother is. She got married at fifteen and her oldest son is twenty, so she's probably thirty-five years old. She's not an old lady at the end of her life. She's a young woman who sees a completely different husband than Birdy sees and is happy with her children. Birdy's mother says that "patience, gentleness and a willing heart make the most of any union," and then asks, "Why not cease your fearful pounding against the bars of your cage and be content?" I think her mother, for all her good qualities, does not understand Birdy at all.

The people of the past are not just us in odd clothing, as I wrote in the author's notes. I mentioned that there were very real differences in people. We have to look at Birdy through medieval eyes and see that she's the rebel, that she's the different one, and that she's struggling to create something that didn't really exist.

I received a letter from a librarian in a town in Texas who wouldn't put my books on her shelves, because Birdy said "piss" and "privy," and *The Midwife's Apprentice's* theme of childbirth was not a suitable topic for young people. At the bottom of each page she wrote, "The community speaks. Censorship is good." That's an extreme reaction. I also got a letter from a twelve-year-old girl who was appalled at the way I treated the holy saints in *Birdy* and made fun of them. She said that it's better that someone be cast into darkness than to lead a child into sin. Her letter was really disturbing, because it came from a child. Some teachers want to put Birdy on their required reading list, and some parents object because of the words *piss* and *privy*, yet they are the same people who really like the book because it's historically authentic. They should see the words that I left out! Back then *piss* was the accepted term, the polite term.

There was a whole constellation of working women in the Middle Ages. Most of the people who were brewers were women. Most of the spinners were women. Sometimes women could be members of guilds, mostly through a husband. There were a lot of apothecaries run by a man and a woman. Women in the villages worked all the time. They had occupations as farmers and laborers. Women in the towns worked in the inns or spun silk or worked in a tannery. The noblewomen who did not have an occupation worked all of the time, too, running the household.

In *The Midwife's Apprentice* I made Jane sour and bitter to combat the stereotype of the midwife, who was usually either a great wonderful goodhearted beautiful woman who invented forceps or a drunken slattern who spread disease and passed out on the birthbed. In fiction there are these two different images and that's about all we have, so I wanted to put somebody in the middle who was competent. It wasn't Jane's good heart or her friendliness or her willingness to help or her dedication to Alyce that caused Alyce to learn what she needed to know. Alyce got what she needed from somebody who was cold, removed, and even hostile, regardless of Jane's willingness to participate.

I think that personal satisfaction and contentment was not as big an issue then as now. I don't think people, men or women, sat down and said, "Am I making the most of my potential, do I really feel happy, does this really satisfy me?" The times were so different. They more likely asked, "Is this good for my family or my country?" Or "Will this help me get to heaven or save my soul?" Self-fulfillment was a topic that didn't come up much.

Lucy Whipple's (*The Ballad of Lucy Whipple*, 1996) world was rough too. In many ways she's like Catherine and Alyce. All three books are coming-of-age stories. I think girls today are faced with sexual choices at a younger age, do I go to college, do I get married right now, do I get a job, how do I support myself? I can see my daughter, who's twenty-five, becoming really involved or really devastated by what's going on in Serbia or South America; we try to make sense of the world, which I don't think they were asked to do historically. Issues of life and death, war and starvation, were at that time much more prevalent, but I think that issues now are more complicated.

Most of the women who came across the country followed their men and weren't the ones who instigated the move, but there were a number of women who were the ones who wanted to move west, who had the itchy feet. I pay tribute to them in the character of Lucy's mother.

I read a number of diaries and different kinds of composite biographies. The woman would arrive in her wagon and pull in at four o'clock in the afternoon in some gold rush town, and break the wagon down and build a table, light a fire, and make a sign that said "restaurant." Some women chose to do this.

Death was such a commonplace part of life at that time, especially in the wilds of this country. Women died in childbirth, miners died of pneumonia or injuries, or freezing to death. People died from eating bad food, children died frequently, doctors were far away, good medicine was not available, there were no hospitals. They could fall in the river or get hit by a falling tree. Death was really commonplace and I thought that I could not ignore it.

I read an account of the first library in California, which was started in a Gold Rush town in 1848. We forget that people who came in the Gold Rush were not just frontiersmen. People kept moving a little bit west and a little bit west all along from one frontier to the next. But that was not true in California, especially at the time of the Gold Rush. People came from Boston, New York, London, Paris, South America, China, Russia, from all over the world. People came not only from small towns and villages but also from big cities, people who wanted what they were used to, like theatres and newspapers and libraries. One of the great entertainments was the Shakespearean troupe. Originally I had a whole chapter about a Shakespearean troupe that came to town. *Richard III* and *Romeo and Juliet* were two favorite plays. People really participated. They threw rotten fruit and yelled. Newspapers developed very early and people wanted books. They wanted some of the amenities of life, so these things developed very early and once I discovered that, it was obvious what Lucy was going to do.

People often ask me who was a great influence on my life when it comes to writing, or who were my mentors. I pretty much made it on my own. I made a lot of mistakes and took a really long time and stumbled into things. I suppose that's what I wanted for these three girls, not to have somebody make it easy for them and give them all the answers, but to have them struggle and make a life that was meaningful to them.

Matilda Bone (2000) took about four years to write and is about a girl who was raised by a priest, so she knows all about heaven and hell but nothing about this world. She comes to a town to be the assistant to a bonesetter, like an early chiropractor, in the medical quarter of the town. She's surrounded by bloodletters and bonesetters and barber surgeons and all of the blood-and-guts things of life, so different from where she's been. She has to learn to cope. I had a hard time with this novel, because I always try something different and this character is more passive and obedient before she grows. I keep thinking, "But will children like her?"

Lucy Whipple was much easier for me because she was so much like me. When I was ten my parents moved from Chicago to California and left behind my grandparents and my dog and my apple tree and my public library, so I felt very close to her and her experience and that was easier. Lucy Whipple is a lot of me.

References

MacLeod, A. S. 1998. "Writing Backward: Modern Models in Historical Fiction." *The Horn Book Magazine* 74 (1): 26–33.

Children's Literature

Avi. 1990. *The True Confessions of Charlotte Doyle*. New York: Orchard.

Cushman, K. 1994. *Catherine, Called Birdy*. New York: Clarion.

———. 1995. *The Midwife's Apprentice*. New York: Clarion.

———. 1996. *The Ballad of Lucy Whipple*. New York: Clarion.

———. 2000. *Matilda Bone*. New York: Clarion.

MacLachlan, P. 1985. *Sarah, Plain and Tall*. New York: HarperCollins.

Pierce, T. 1983. *Alanna: The First Adventure*. New York: Atheneum.

Author Profile in Two Voices

PATRICIA AND FREDRICK MCKISSACK

Patricia: When we were growing up we didn't have African American heroes in our history books. Quite often we learned about them in church clubs or some source other than school. At church, I had a wonderful Sunday school teacher who was also a professor at Meharry Medical College. At the same time he was teaching us about Daniel and the lion's den he talked to us about Sojourner Truth. That's how I got to know her. Even so, I had no clue that she was one of the earliest feminists.

When I was asked to write a book about Sojourner Truth, I wondered why another book about Sojourner Truth was necessary. My editor said that she had not seen a book that approached Truth as a feminist, rather than an abolitionist. The structure of our book shows Truth's voice as a feminist as well as in the abolitionist movement. Truth was a woman who did not fit the nineteenth-century woman's mold. Truth was a big woman, well over six feet tall, and she could work as hard, as she says in her own words, as hard as any man, "no man could head me." I think she spoke out of that voice. So that's why we decided we would write about her.

What I've found inspiring about Sojourner Truth is her complete abandonment of fear; she would walk into a totally hostile environment, but she remained fearless. Sojourner was a traveler, and she said, "Now that I'm no longer a slave, I will not take my slave master's last name. Another name for God is Truth and therefore I will call myself Truth, because I am God's child." With total abandonment she traveled into terrible situations where her life was in danger. She didn't seem to worry about her own safety. Wherever she went, she spoke the truth.

She was so strong, so large, that one antislavery advocate, a doctor, demanded that she take her shirt off to prove she was a woman. "I will do so. It's not my shame, it's yours for asking." She was quick-witted. Her opponents would say, "If God had intended for women to have a place among men, He would have made Jesus a woman, but Jesus was a man." To which she retorted, "Where do you think Jesus came from? He came from a woman, and God. Man had nothing to do with it."

Fredrick: When we do research we first see what others have written. We write about slavery and the struggle for freedom, so we read a lot about that subject. We've not only read about people like Sojourner Truth and Frederick Douglass, we've done extensive research on the Underground Railroad, we've studied the Civil War, and many other sources over the years. And we travel. We've gone to Charleston and other places where Sojourner lived; we visited Battle Creek, where she lived and is buried. It's like a kaleidoscope; the more you know, the more it changes.

Sojourner Truth's role as a suffragette is left out of history and it's deliberate. We do not need to mince words, or say they forgot it, but those who wrote it, those who published it, those who do the editing, the scholars who did the research, deliberately left her out. The public was saying we don't want this, so the publishers went along because they want to sell books. As soon as there was a cry among the public, demanding that African Americans' and women's voices be included, the publishers and writers got busy. Now their stories are included in anthologies, history books, and so on.

In our biographies we to try to show children the importance of universal truths, as well as courage and fortitude, determination, and love. Those are the tools that they'll need to get through their lives. Other men and women have come through some of the darkest hours, some of the roughest of times, yet they have achieved against all odds. Our fall as humans begins not when we are at the bottom, but when we are at the top. We must be watchful when everything is alright and times are very good. We want kids to have heroes instead of the negative types of characters, the victims. The world needs heroes.

Patricia: It is extremely painful to read some of these tragic stories from African American history. But it is also uplifting. The people we have written about were able to succeed in spite of adversity. What would African Americans have been able to do, if they had just been given opportunity? What could we have done if we had been turned loose, to fulfill all of our potential? If we have done this well with a foot in our backs, what could we have done with proper education and encouragement?

It puts a block in the pathway of learning when people insist that we don't need to talk about slavery, we don't need to talk about war, we don't need to talk about the civil rights movement, we don't need to talk about what's happening in the inner city today. We must talk about these things or we will never get a full understanding of what really happened, and without understanding there can be no healing. All we can achieve is a negative peace.

Bitterness is destructive. It has a tendency to destroy the person who is bitter, not the person that is causing it. You destroy yourself with bitterness. The story of Sodom and Gomorrah expresses it best. When you look back over your shoulder the cities turn to a pillar of salt. We want to look ahead, move ahead, and that's why we write for children. Children are vessels ready to be filled. We love getting the letters they write.

In *A Picture of Freedom: The Diary of Clotee, a Slave Girl* (1997a), the reader lives through Clotee's experiences as a slave, hopefully without being overwhelmed. Slavery is a very difficult concept for both black and white children to comprehend. Being black is trying to realize that someone in your family at one time was owned, like you own a dog or a cat, or horse, or a car or house, that a person was property.

It is very difficult for children to understand owning another human being. It is repulsive to both black and white children. Both of them look at the situation and say that is horrible. I would never want to own anybody, and the other person says, I wouldn't want to be owned. What I want them to come away with is an understanding of the slave experience and the only way to do that is to find a character who's a lot like them. Clotee has the same hopes and dreams as any child. She loves her mother. She loves Hence. She loves where she lives. She is a child of her environment, but that doesn't mean she is void of being a child, or growing up. She likes dancing and looking pretty and wearing ribbons in her hair. Any little girl can recognize that.

Clotee knows her world and knows that her world is limited, but she does not limit herself. By learning to read, she is able to go beyond the situation. Many literate slaves knew that they had to go along with the situation, because they couldn't get out of it, but that didn't mean that they had to acquiesce; that didn't mean that they gave over their minds and hearts to the situation as they were sometimes misunderstood to do.

All three of our books about slavery, *Christmas in the Big House, Christmas in the Quarters* (1994), *Rebels Against Slavery* (1996), and *Clotee* are based on the same research. All of it is just leftover material, leftover research material.

Fredrick: *Christmas* (1994) was the book that started it all. It's like a river from which come many tributaries. In the Civil War, 700,000 people died directly from the war and several hundred thousand more died afterward from cholera and other diseases. We wondered if there were any special signs that people expected the war to come. Did they have any idea of the horror that was getting ready to happen? We began to research to find out. We began to look at houses of that period, stories of the period, art, music, and seasonal celebrations.

Patricia: It was amazing to us how oblivious people seemed to be about the coming Civil War. The average citizen didn't realize that the politicians had talked up on a horrific war.

The literature of that time period contains a lot of heated and angry talk about states' rights, the right of property, the right of the private citizen to do with his property what he wills. It had a lot to do with the westward expansion and whether slavery would be allowed to go there. The South had stripped the land and the cotton crops were not yielding as they had in the past. Farmers didn't practice rotation of crops, so planting cotton year after year had depleted the soil. They were looking for new ground in Kansas and Nebraska with its rich black soil. Southerners wanted to take slavery to the West. If they had known that a war was imminent, could they, would they have negotiated to bring the debate to an end? France, England, and other countries, except Spain, had ended slavery. It was just a matter of time before it would end.

We found in our research that the governor of Virginia wrote in his personal papers that he would support a gradual abolishment of slavery in Virginia, much the way New York had. It worked like this: An arbitrary date would have been chosen, like

1870. Then Virginia would have worked toward that date to free all slaves as they turned twenty-five.

I think if Virginia, the mother colony, had led the way through a process of gradual emancipation, a few of the other states might have followed. If that had happened it would have eased the tension. No one was willing to back down. Our book, *Christmas in the Big House, Christmas in the Quarters*, looks at these issues as they were in 1859. We show what the attitudes of that time were, what the white and black families talked about that Christmas. What was the dance at the time? What was the food? But more important, Christmas would never be celebrated that way again.

Fredrick: In the slave trade itself, millions died. It's a bane not only in the United States and the Americas, but on the West coast of Africa. Until we get familiar with slavery, there can be no healing. What good is this knowledge? Children should begin to know as soon as they go to school about these things. In small doses, they should learn some of the bad things that mankind has done at the same time that we tell them about the good things that mankind has done. Balance is the key.

Patricia: What Martin Luther King said will come to pass, that we are going to have to deal with people by the content of their character and we're going to have to group people along those lines. Racism is at the core of many of the problems that we have in this country. Until we deal with that issue one on one, talk about it honestly and openly, then we aren't ready to judge by the content of character, not yet. That's a perfect world.

When *Christmas* first came out there were teachers who didn't know what to do with it. I always use this analogy: If you try to put the puzzle of American history together and you don't know my story, there are missing pieces. The picture is not clear. This book fills in the blanks for those who have been studying history and looking at the Civil War and looking at that part of our history and wondering, "Oh, I didn't know that, oh, that's what was going on." One of the scenes that children really enjoy about *Clotee* is when the child up in the big house writes in her diary that the slave who is singing a carol is happy because he is singing. But the children in the quarters know that it is their father. He has made contact with a conductor on the Underground Railroad. Music was used very often by slaves to communicate thoughts and ideas and to send messages. Kids love knowing and learning these kinds of details.

Slaves weren't passive; they were empowering themselves and one another to take control of their lives. We often get questions like, "What is a pit school?" A pit school was a hole that slaves dug large enough for two or three people to gather in. There, one of the slaves who could read taught the others to read and write.

Do we see accounts of rebellions reflected in the texts of social studies curricula? Absolutely not. Educators have said that it was too violent, but then they teach the Revolutionary War. Was it any different? The struggle for freedom is often violent. What could have been more bloody and violent than the Russian Revolution or the French Revolution, or the Thirty Years War in Germany, where they wiped out 30 percent of the population? In *Rebels Against Slavery*, we tried to do the right thing for our young readers. We told them the truth without emphasizing the violence. We tried to do an honest job.

Fredrick: When you look at the history of the American labor movement, and the resistance that free people have put up against tyranny, how in the world could one conclude that slaves, who made no wage and were tied to a plantation all of their days, and had no health care, could be happy? In our books about slavery, we tried to show children what slavery was really like and help them to feel what they would have felt in the same situation.

It is absolutely ludicrous to even suggest that African American people were happy in the situation that they were in; that does not mean, however, that they did not have happy times. That's a difficult concept. Yes, slaves had happy times; they told funny stories; they made the best out of what they had to work with. But they were never happy in their condition.

Patricia: There were incredible women in the nineteenth century. Ida B. Wells was a suffragist, born free in Mississippi, attended Russ College in Mississippi, went to Memphis, and started a newspaper. During Reconstruction, blacks were losing their rights as fast as they had gained them after the Civil War. Wells was forced to ride in a separate streetcar and she protested to the point where she had to be removed kicking and screaming; she sued the company and won her case. But the momentum was against African American equality. She began using her newspaper to speak out against discrimination.

A lot of the accomplishments that were made in the 1880s and 1890s were done by newly freed African Americans. They started insurance companies, banks, small businesses. What if they had been left alone to grow and develop? Instead their homes and businesses were burned down, there was constant interference by racist organizations, such as the Ku Klux Klan. Ida B. Wells spoke out against such injustice. In return, she also had to run. A mob came for her, burned a cross, and burned her newspaper building. She got out just in time and fled to New York and later to Chicago where she was one of the early founders of the NAACP. She later became the founder of the Ida B. Wells Women's Club, who were suffragists. She started the antilynching movement, because the Klan had reorganized in Georgia after WWI. An average of eighty or ninety people were lynched every year. Wells tried to make lynching a federal crime and eventually legislation was passed. Ida B. Wells was an extraordinary woman.

So were other women, such as Mary McCleod Bethune, who started a school with one dollar and fifty cents. Madame C. J. Walker rose from poverty to become one of the first black self-made millionaires in the country. Rebecca Cole was a pioneer in the medical profession. She was the first black female doctor to graduate from medical school.

Name a profession and I can name you a woman who stepped out on faith or hope and achieved her goals. It takes a lot of spirit and a belief in oneself to succeed.

You mean to tell me that you won't treat a child who is sick and you call yourself a doctor? Well, I know what I'll do, instead of getting angry, instead of being bitter, I'll just become a doctor. That's how so many African American greats have dealt with racism and discrimination. They just jumped over it, ran around it, catapulted over it, went over, under, through, and beyond it, do what they had to do. And of course encouragement and family support. A lot of famous people had parents, grandmothers and grandfathers, uncles and aunts, who were always at their backs saying, *you can do better, you can do whatever if you try.*

Unfortunately, our young people today don't have that generational support system. They are not linked to anything. Visualize a chain. Somewhere along the line it has been broken. I think in families the chain is broken because our grandmothers are only thirty, our parents are fourteen. The wisdom is not substantial enough to hold it together.

Flossie and Mirandy and Nettie Jo are my daughters. We never had daughters—we have three sons—so my fiction characters are my three daughters. They are a combination of all the women that I've read about, all the strong women in my family, and a bit of myself. I do have a legacy of strong women upon whose shoulders I stand. I've got a whole lot of women at my back, my mother, sister, sister-in-law, stepmother, my mother-in-law, my grandmothers, and my aunts. I mean I've got them as close as a phone call. Every last one of them has been encouraging to both Fred and me, even though they didn't always understand what we were doing many times. When we stepped out on faith to begin our careers as writers, they were supportive of our efforts. They are very proud of us, even though I'll call and say, "Mom, I won a Newbery, aren't you proud?" And my mother replies, "Yes, daughter, but what is a Newbery?"

Every time I pick up *Ma Dear's Apron* (1997b), it gives me such a warm and wonderful feeling. The way Floyd Cooper captured the love between the mother and son. The tight shot of David Earl in his mother's arms is my favorite. I like the calmness of the boy asleep on the floor covered with the yellow apron. The scenes he chose to illustrate were up close and personal. When I saw the layout, I was floored. It was so beautiful! The words and the pictures are a 50 percent collaboration. Without the words, the pictures still talk, and that's what a good picture book is supposed to do.

My paternal family is from Clayton, Alabama. My great-grandmother's name was Leanna Crossley Bowens. She had three children and made her living as a laundress, washing and ironing, cleaning for other people; she also made pies and sold them around town. I can remember bits and pieces of my grandmother talking about her grandmother, whose name was Georgia Ann Crossley, who also was a laundress. I've been told she was a very loving and caring woman, a very big woman, who held her family together and raised them with little or no money. Doing laundry didn't pay a whole lot back then.

My brother, sister, and I finished college because we were expected to do so. There was never any question about it. My grandparents on both sides were people of limited educational backgrounds, but they were determined that their children and grandchildren were going to do better. All of that pride, determination, conviction, and dedication to excellence is in *Ma Dear's Apron.*

Runaway Home (1997c) is a very important book for me because it's a continuation of my search for family and my own identity. The difficulty of writing out of one's culture is very problematic. If it had not been for an Apache consultant, I would have never tackled the project. Michael B. was very helpful in getting me through not just the facts, and getting the dates straight, but the subtleties that only an Apache child would know. It was challenging, so much so that I won't do it again. I won't write outside my culture again. It's a little bit too difficult for me, and it made me too nervous. I wondered, every time I wrote, "Am I on target here?" When I write about African Americans, I know what I'm writing about, because I'm black. I know, for example, what a black child would or wouldn't say or do. I can pick up a book and know if it's authentic or not, if the writer has been true to the African American experience. I know if the voice is authentic, if the setting is right, if the responses are right. I came very close to making an error when writing *Runaway Home*, because I was not familiar enough with the culture to know that no Apache child would have done or said what I had written.

Yet, with all the problems, *Runaway Home* had to be written. I had to get the story out of me. It started as a nonfiction book about my Apache ancestors, but without documents and records, nonfiction didn't work. So, I had to fictionalize the story. But I got a lot of family history in the introduction, for my children and grandchildren.

Fredrick: I'm optimistic about the future of children's books. There's plenty of work to do; in fact, there are more ideas than people to write about them. Pat and I hope to continue to write about those ideas, even though they're hurtful to think about.

When we started out, there were so few faces of African Americans in books. We set a goal to write one or two books, never believing that we could actually make a living writing books for children. We were willing and foolish enough to take a chance in writing one or two. Then we would move on. At the same time, the Coretta Scott King award committee honored a few of our books and this brought about a greater awareness of books for, by, and about African Americans. That was eighty books ago, and we are still writing . . . trying to fill the void.

Patricia: We try to look at things realistically. If you go into any inner-city school or neighborhood, you will recognize that we are a troubled people and our young people are in trouble. But there are young people who are writing letters who tell us, "I'm going to go to college, because I read your book, about the woman who started the college with a dollar and fifty cents. That makes me say, wow!" We frame letters like that. Another young girl said, "I like Clotee, I like her a lot. She reminds me of me. If I had been a slave, I would have been just like her." This is a white child writing from a small town in Connecticut.

Bitterness is not in my mental capacity. It has no place in our life. We are realistic in the way we look at the world. We're very realistic about the way we see it, but we will not relinquish our dream or our hope for a better world. And that's why we write for children.

Children's Literature

McKissack, P. 1986. *Flossie and the Fox*. Illustrated by R. Isadora. New York: Dial.

———. 1988. *Mirandy and Brother Wind*. Illustrated by J. Pinkney. New York: Knopf.

———. 1989. *Nettie Jo's Friends*. Illustrated by S. Cook. New York: Knopf.

———. 1997a. *A Picture of Freedom: Clotee, a Slave Girl*. New York: Scholastic.

———. 1997b. *Ma Dear's Apron*. Illustrated by F. Cooper. New York: Simon & Schuster.

———. 1997c. *Runaway Home*. New York: Scholastic.

McKissack, P., & McKissack, F. 1992. *Sojourner Truth: Ain't I a Woman?* New York: Scholastic.

———. 1994. *Christmas in the Big House, Christmas in the Quarters*. Illustrated by J. Thompson. New York: Scholastic.

———. 1996. *Rebels Against Slavery*. New York: Scholastic.

8

Separating the Men from the Boys: Coming of Age in Recent Historical Fiction for Children

Daniel P. Woolsey

Listen to the voices of some of the characters who inhabit historical fiction for children published since 1985:

> You're not a child. You may do as you wish.
>
> *Father to Star Boy, in* Morning Girl, *57*

> Men like war. It makes 'em feel big. There's nothin' so bad it can't be talked out without fightin'. But some do dote on fightin'.
>
> *Granny Bent, in* Charley Skedaddle, *127*

> Around these parts, a man takes pride in doing things for himself.
>
> *Uncle Jed, in* Shades of Gray, *39*

> Honor yourself, Tomi, and you honor us all.
>
> *Papa, in* Under the Blood-Red Sun, *228*

> It's your time, Sorry. When you become fourteen, you must use your mind as well as your muscles.
>
> *Mother, in* The Bomb, *36*

The novels in which these characters live, and five others analyzed in this chapter, have all received the Scott O'Dell Historical Fiction Award, which honors a distinguished work of historical fiction set in the New World. As such, these books provide a representative sampling of contemporary historical fiction for children. Since my focus here is on the ways that boys in historical fiction novels experience the process of coming of age, I will include only the award-winning books that feature

1999 — Harriette Gillem Robinet, *Forty Acres and Maybe a Mule*

1997 — Katherine Paterson, *Jip: His Story*

1996 — Theodore Taylor, *The Bomb*

1995 — Graham Salisbury, *Under the Blood-Red Sun*

1993 — Michael Dorris, *Morning Girl*

1991 — Pieter Van Raven, *A Time of Trouble*

1990 — Carolyn Reeder, *Shades of Gray*

1988 — Patricia Beatty, *Charley Skedaddle*

1985 — Avi, *The Fighting Ground*

1984 — Elizabeth George Speare, *The Sign of the Beaver*

Figure 8–1. *Ten Scott O'Dell Award Winners Featuring A Male Protagonist*

male protagonists. These books are listed in Figure 8–1. These ten books provide images of boys in the course of becoming men in various historical eras and in geographical locations around the world. They also present clues about the conceptions of mature masculinity held by their contemporary authors.

Coming of age has been defined as the "transition from immature individual to mature member of society" (Attebury 1996, 288). It requires "coming to terms with the realities of the adult world" (Agee 1973), and usually involves the assumption of new roles, rights, and responsibilities. All of the protagonists in these books struggle to leave behind their childish näiveté, lack of experience, and immaturity, and move toward maturity by assuming more responsibility for themselves and their families. Coming of age also implies a search for self-definition and an exploration of several critical questions: Who am I? Where am I going? What is my place in this world? This aspect of coming of age is most clearly represented by Jip's anguished cry, "Whatever I am or am not, I got to be somebody's lost boy. I wasn't born on the West Hill Road. I jest fell off a wagon there. Whose wagon? And why didn't no one come back looking for me?" (*Jip: His Story*, 47).

My decision to focus on this subset of the winners of the Scott O'Dell award creates certain limits on the conclusions I can draw. For example, I cannot explore how modern conceptions of masculinity and male rites of passage compare with those presented in children's books published earlier in the century, since the first winner of the award, *The Sign of the Beaver*, was published in 1983. Nor can I compare the male experience of coming of age with that of their female counterparts. However, these books offer considerable range and variety in other ways. Though the award is given to a book published in America, the writers of the selected novels represent a multitonal chorus, including Jewish American, African American, Native American, and

	1492		1768	ca. 1780	1855	1863–1865	ca. 1930	1941	1946
Morning Girl	●								
The Sign of the Beaver			●						
The Fighting Ground				●					
Jip: His Story					●				
Charley Skedaddle						●			
Shades of Gray						●			
Forty Acres and Maybe a Mule						●			
A Time of Trouble							●		
Under the Blood-Red Sun								●	
The Bomb									●

Figure 8–2. *Range of Historical Settings*

Hawaiian voices. The protagonists are all male, but half of them were created by female authors, so these novels present both male and female perspectives. Finally, as seen on the time line in Figure 8–2, the time settings of the books cover over 450 years. They extend from 1492 and Morning Girl's sighting of Columbus, all the way to 1946, when Sorry Rinamu defies the orders of the U.S. military by sailing his outrigger into a nuclear test site in *The Bomb*. The geographic settings of the books also stretch across a wide territory. They range from Sorry's village in Micronesia, to Tomi's Hawaiian island home in *Under the Blood-Red Sun*, to the Caribbean island village of Morning Girl and Star Boy. In the United States, they range from the California orange groves of *A Time of Trouble* to southern Maine, where Matt and his father build a cabin in *The Sign of the Beaver*.

Male Coming of Age: Multiple Lenses

The process of male coming of age has been depicted many times in literature for children and for adults (cf. Agee 1973; Johnson 1959). It has also been a focus of special interest to scholars in other fields, most notably anthropology, sociology, and developmental psychology. A review of the literature in such diverse disciplines is beyond the scope of this chapter. However, a brief excursion through some of the most pertinent research and theories should illuminate our understanding of the literary depictions of the road from boyhood to manhood that are found in the ten children's novels under consideration.

The term "rites of passage" is generally attributed to anthropologist Arnold van Gennep. In 1908 he published *Les Rites de Passage*, in which he concludes that

"The life of an individual in any society is a series of passages from one age to another and from one occupation to another" (2), and that "A man's life comes to be made up of a succession of stages with similar ends and beginnings: birth, social puberty, marriage, fatherhood, advancement to a higher class, occupational specialization and death" (3). He sees these experiences as universal human "life crises" and notes that all of the cultures he studied had developed certain rites and rituals around these events. Further, these rituals followed a particular pattern of three phases. **Separation** from the world of women and children is the essential first step on the path to manhood. This disconnection allows for the **transition** phase, which might last just a few days, but could take months or years. This period is spent in seclusion, often in sex-segregated groups, and during this time boys are tutored in the ways of men. Expanding upon the work of van Gennep, Turner (1987) emphasizes the importance of this second stage, which he calls the liminal stage (from the Latin *limen*, "threshold"), describing it as a "psychological and spiritual threshold between what one was and what one will become" (5). Van Gennep concludes that after initiates have participated fully in separation and transition, they enter the third stage of **incorporation** into the world of the adults of the tribe. At this point the transition is complete and the community accepts the initiates as individuals with a new identity, and often a new name, and assumes that they are able to fulfill adult roles in the community.

Commentators on contemporary society have identified a similar threefold pattern, including severance (leaving home and family), threshold (taking on new challenges, testing limits, and learning new roles in these settings), and an eventual return to family and friends (Allan and Dyck 1987; Christopher 1996). Examples of modern-day rites of passage that fit this pattern include activities as diverse as earning a driver's license, graduating from high school or college, getting married, starting a job, being inducted into the military, or being initiated into a gang. Christopher (1996) notes that all of these activities include many of the same elements: a changed setting, new relationships, and new challenges. The transition period is critical in that successfully facing these challenges requires access to privileged knowledge and/or skills. Fulfilling these new roles and responsibilities tends to lead to an expanded sense of power and autonomy, which may bring about a new perception of self, and often a recognition by others of that new status.

Further evidence of the universality of the process of coming of age is found in *The Hero with a Thousand Faces*, Joseph Campbell's (1949) description of the classic journey of the hero found in the mythologies of various cultures around the world. Campbell argues that all literature tells one or another aspect of the same story, which he called the monomyth. According to his analysis, the heroic journey begins at home, where the hero is unaware of his own heroic potential and may be perceived by others as unlikely to succeed. This changes with the call to adventure, in which the hero is summoned from home to an unknown place. He sets off on a quest and proceeds despite uncertainty about whether or how he will succeed. The hero moves across a threshold into a dangerous, dreamlike landscape where he must survive a succession of trials. These trials bring him face to face with his own confusion and inadequacies, but the hero is often assisted by a mentor. Through these experiences he learns valuable lessons that are necessary for full participation in the adult life of his world. Having survived and grown through these trials, the hero returns home, bringing the knowledge gained in his adventures and generally enjoying recognition by others for his growth and development.

Obviously, the pattern of the hero's journey is in accord with van Gennep's anthropological findings. In Campbell's terms, "the standard path of the mythological adventure of the hero is . . . separation—initiation—return" (1949, 30). Some critics of children's literature have noted the ways this mythic pattern is played out in modern fantasy stories for children (e.g., Attebury 1996; Lehr 1995), and others have explored this pattern in contemporary realistic fiction (e.g., Bell 1985; Yoder 1976). Campbell sees these mythical stories as parables of the individual's search for identity and the quest for self-realization (1988). The heroic quest is a metaphor for an interior journey as well as an external reality. Thus, the pattern may be applied to the development of characters in realistic fiction, whether they live and move in contemporary or in historical settings.

The quest for identity is of great interest to psychologists as well. Developmental psychologists see adolescence—the broad age range encompassing all of the protagonists in the stories under consideration—as a particularly critical period in the process of identity formation. Erikson (1950) argues that the primary task of adolescence is to resolve the "crisis" of personality by defining the self, that is, how we see ourselves and how we see others. This forms the foundation of our adult identity, which depends upon the "external development of autonomy and responsibility and the internal development of increasing differentiation between self and parents, greater psychological distance from family and reduced emotional dependency on parental support and authority" (Schofield 1993, 62).

Some psychologists have posited that males and females experience growth and maturation differently. Boys and men have been described as discovering identity through achievement and autonomy, whereas girls and women are seen as more focused on interpersonal awareness and attachment (e.g., Chodorow 1978; Gilligan 1982). According to Gilligan (1982), women's early sense of interpersonal awareness leads them to continue to strive for intimacy and to find their identity through a network of relationships. In contrast, men tend to focus first and foremost on creating a strong and separate sense of identity, often at the cost of relationships. In later life and with greater maturity, they may be able to achieve a more comfortable capacity for intimacy. Betcher and Pollack claim that this is necessary for healthy, mature masculinity, arguing that men need to see their "precious autonomy as perhaps necessary, but limiting," and that they need to accept "their need for other people as neither shameful or weak" (1993, 22).

I will now turn to an analysis of these ten historical fiction novels to explore answers to several questions: Who are the male protagonists in these novels? How is their process of coming of age depicted? How is mature masculinity portrayed in these stories? How are these coming-of-age patterns and images of mature masculinity molded and shaped by the social, cultural, and historical settings?

Who Are the Male Protagonists?

A number of common strands are woven through all of these novels, providing a fairly universal depiction of a boy who is becoming a man. Except for Star Boy (whose age is not identified, though we know he is younger than his twelve-year-old sister), these boys are on the cusp or in the middle of adolescence. Ranging in age from twelve to sixteen, but mostly clustered around the age of thirteen, they are looking back upon childhood but have some distance ahead before they reach adult status.

Although they are referred to and perceived as boys by the adults in their lives, in most of these stories they take on what contemporary readers might see as a man's work. Most of these boys live in a preindustrialized, agrarian society. Thus, their daily lives and those of their family members tend to be consumed with meeting basic needs: hunting and gathering food, caring for livestock, and tending to shelter and safety from wild animals and the elements. These boys are comfortable using weapons to protect themselves and their loved ones. Much of their time is spent out-of-doors and engaging in hard work. With the exception of Jip, and of Tomi in *Under the Blood-Red Sun*, they spend little time in school in comparison to contemporary early adolescents. Even in their infrequent moments of relaxation and play they tend to engage in physical activity outside the home.

The three books set in the twentieth century also include protagonists who assume more than the responsibilities that most contemporary readers would expect for boys. In the early pages of *The Bomb* Sorry Rinamu turns fourteen, the traditional starting point of manhood in his clan. Thus, he officially becomes head of the household and represents his family in the village council. However, Sorry has been the primary provider of food for his family ever since his father's death four years earlier. Before his fourteenth birthday Sorry goes to school three mornings a week like the other village children, but he does not return after this milestone birthday. Similarly, school, play, and freedom from responsibility are not part of fourteen-year-old Roy Purdy's life in *A Time for Trouble*. Instead he works at a boat-building shop in Maryland, takes primary responsibility for getting his father and himself to California, and then works in the orange groves. In the first half of *Under the Blood-Red Sun* Tomi leads the life of a fairly typical modern American youngster; he is responsible for a few light chores, but mostly concerned with playing baseball with his friends, dealing with a neighborhood bully, and completing school assignments. However, in the days after the bombing of Pearl Harbor, school is closed for months and Tomi and his friends are absorbed in the work of rebuilding and in tending to the daily needs of their families. After his father is unfairly incarcerated, Tomi assumes even more responsibility for the family.

Like Tomi, most of these protagonists have been forced to take on responsibilities beyond those normally expected of boys by circumstances beyond their control. These external forces serve to separate these boys from their families so that they are forced to be self-sufficient and to fend for themselves. This is even true for Star Boy, the youngest protagonist; he lives within a very tight-knit clan and spends most of his days and nights in the company of family, but he is temporarily separated from all of them by a ferocious hurricane. In *The Sign of the Beaver* Matt plans to stay alone for a brief period in the new cabin he and his father have built, but his family is long delayed by sickness and bad weather and he ends up spending many months away from them. Jonathan is separated from his family for only two days in *The Fighting Ground*, but it becomes two days of sheer terror and physical effort when he is taken prisoner by Hessian soldiers.

It is noteworthy that in five of the ten books, the male protagonists are entirely separated from one or both parents by death, abandonment, or imprisonment. Four of these boys are essentially orphans. Will's entire family has been destroyed by the ravages of war in *Shades of Gray*; Charley "Skedaddle's" father has not been heard from since he went west to work on the canals, and his mother died of consumption. Pascal, the freed slave in *Forty Acres and Maybe a Mule*, and Jip have never known their fathers. Pascal's beloved mother is killed by an overseer just before his story begins, and Jip's mother is separated from his mother by her enslavement. As noted above, Sorry Rimanu lost his father at the age of ten, and Tomi is separated from his father for most of *Under the Blood-Red Sun*, first due to his father's career as a fisherman and then by his brutal internment. In *A Time of Trouble* Roy has been abandoned by his biological mother, and his father, Harlow Purdy, is an alcoholic and an irresponsible and negligent father; their relationship is clearly one in which the roles of caregiver and dependent are reversed.

Beyond the turmoil and trouble in their personal family lives, all of these boys are caught up in societal, cultural, and political upheavals and conflicts that require them to take on new roles and responsibilities that most would consider to be adult rather than childlike. Three of these boys become embroiled in military battles and conflicts. Jonathan clumsily participates in a brief and chaotic battle between a handful of militiamen and a battalion of Hessian troops. Planning to avenge the death of his older brother, Charley "Skedaddle" runs away to become a drummer with the Union troops and ultimately finds himself in the hellish "Battle of the Wilderness." Sorry Rimanu doesn't engage in a battle, but he faces the awesome power of the American military in his courageous efforts to prevent the testing of an atom bomb in his ancestral homeland.

Though they do not personally engage in battle, five other protagonists find their lives powerfully affected by the tensions and sufferings inflicted upon ordinary citizens in a time of war. In *Jip: His Story* the title character is forced to run away from his Vermont home and the people he loves when his origins as the child of a runaway slave are discovered. Will loses his entire family during the Civil War, with his father and older brother dying from battle wounds, his sisters from an epidemic, and his mother from grief. Pascal, the crippled protagonist in *Forty Acres and Maybe a Mule*, is still reeling from the death of his beloved mother when he is reunited with his older brother, Gideon, and they set off with high hopes of claiming the land promised to black soldiers by General Sherman. However, the promised freedom and land on which they can build a better life prove to be elusive in the difficult years directly following the Civil War. In *Under the Blood-Red Sun*, Tomi, a Hawaiian American of Japanese descent, finds his life turned upside down in a matter of hours when the Japanese attack Pearl Harbor and his friends and neighbors look upon him and his family as dangerous enemies.

Patterns in Coming of Age

This overview of the situations of our ten male protagonists hints at the fact that most of these boys experience their progress toward manhood in a manner that follows the classic heroic pattern of separation, initiation, and incorporation described by Joseph Campbell and observed by anthropologists and sociologists. All of these boys are separated from the safety of home and the comforting support of parents, at least during most of the time period described by the storytellers. Thus, all are thrust into the demanding challenges of new roles, relationships, and responsibilities. The result of these trials and stretching experiences is sometimes-painful but always results in growth. All of these protagonists do not finally achieve incorporation by the end of their initiatory experiences, but in every case it is clear that they are well on the way to manhood.

As discussed above, in most cases the initial separation is brought about by circumstances beyond the protagonists' control: life-threatening weather, sickness and death of family members, societal prejudice, or the unwanted presence of more powerful others, as in the case of Sorry Rimanu. In other instances, this separation is instigated by poor judgments on the part of the boys, missteps often resulting from their boyish näiveté and inexperience. For example, Matt suffers unexpected difficulties in finding food when his rifle is stolen by a trapper to whom he has given his misplaced trust, and a hungry bear devours most of his precious provisions when he fails to latch the cabin door before going hunting. The final mistake, one that leads to serious injury, is his foolish attempt to raid a beehive high in a tree. Jonathan and Charley display another kind of näiveté. They both have a false sense of their own abilities; this coupled with their delusions about the glories of soldiering lead to run away to join fighting troops long before they are ready to assume such responsibilities.

Once separated from home and the support of their families, all of these male characters engage in a time of intense experience and learning, a time of initiation whereby they gradually learn and grow into more mature ideas, actions, and attitudes. As indicated above, in almost every case these boys experience initiation and begin to assume the skills and knowledge and attitudes and responsibilities of men, without the presence and guidance of their parents. Although these boys have little help from parents, they are not without guidance and support. In every case, there is a mentor and guide who assists them in navigating the tricky and often life-threatening waters in which they find themselves. These tend to be adults and older peers whose lives intersect with those of the boys during their time of trial and growth.

Sometimes, the mentor is a family member. For example, in *Shades of Gray* Will is sent to live with his mother's sister and his Uncle Jed, a man he believes to be a traitor for his refusal to fight in the Civil War. Much of the internal and external conflict in the novel arises from the struggles that Will and the other villagers have in understanding and accepting Uncle Jed's pacifist position. However, over the course of the summer Will grows reluctantly to understand and follow the example of his hardworking and morally courageous Uncle Jed. Sorry's life is powerfully affected by the presence of his Uncle Abram, though he is only present in his village for a couple of years. Sorry admires his young uncle for his skills as a fisherman and because he has done what Sorry yearns to do, having left the confines of the Bikini atoll to travel the world with the merchant marine. Abram tells him of the beautiful places he has been, but he also warns that "I've seen all I want of the other world. They work too hard doing stupid things. They hurt each other" (69), and he is the first villager to see through the heinous plan of the American military to remove these peaceful villagers from their prosperous island so that it can be used as a military test site. And after Abram's untimely death, Sorry adopts his desperate plan to bring the world's attention to the plight of his people.

Grandfathers play an important role in these stories as well. This is particularly true for Tomi in *Under the Blood-Red Sun*, who gradually comes to honor and to emulate his grandfather for the way he has proudly upheld the family's honor and clung to his loyalty to their Japanese heritage. Tomi discovers his own identity apart from his grandfather's and proudly insists upon his dual heritage as an American of Japanese origins. When he is accosted and verbally abused by a stranger who yells, "Hey, Buddahead—you got a lot of nerve coming out in the open after what you people did," he proudly asserts, "You got it wrong, Mister. I was born here. I live here, just like you do. And I'm an American" (240–41). Still, he also treasures the *katana*, the ceremonial sword passed on to him by his grandfather, and in the last scene of the novel he imagines how he will introduce his little sister to this powerful symbol of their heritage:

> I decided that tonight I would take out the *katana* and . . . let Kimi hold it. I would tell her where it came from, and why we needed to protect it and keep it clean and what it stood for. I would tell her that Papa and Grandpa would be so proud of her when they came home and found out that she knew all about why we still had it after all these years. (244)

In a mystical scene from *Morning Girl*, Star Boy's dead grandfather speaks to him. As he is lashed by the terrifying winds and rain of a powerful hurricane, Star Boy clings desperately to the roots of a tree that is revered by his people as a place where they could find "the faces of all the people who have ever died, if you needed to talk to them once more." Through the howling, angry winds Star Boy senses his grandfather's voice saying, "It's all right, Star Boy. Stay with us, and you will be safe. I'll stay with you as long as this storm lasts" (43).

Some of these boys also come under the influence of mentors outside their family circle. Matt is assisted by the wise chief Saknis, and also by Saknis's grandson. Attean is Matt's peer, but far more knowledgeable about self-sufficiency in living off the land. Since he has no known family, Jip benefits immeasurably from friendships with several mentors, especially Put, the so-called lunatic, who between his manic seizures is a wealth of wisdom and a key source of Jip's growing self-respect. When Jip is able to go to school he comes under the powerful influence and loving guidance of his teacher and her fiancé. These two play a crucial role in the ultimate battle of Jip's preadult life, the dark moment when he must overcome his despair and self-recrimination over the death of Put in order to flee north to freedom to escape the slave-catcher.

Several figures serve as guides for small parts of Charley's journey from the New York Bowery to the maturity he finds in the Blue Ridge Mountains. Silas is an older boy who teaches him the routines and skills of a Union drummer boy. And Jem Miller is a Union soldier who provides fatherly nurture and advice as Charley trains and anxiously waits for their first battle, explaining that war is "four parts waiting, four parts blundering about, and three parts marching and fighting" (67). But Charley watches in horror as both of these friends are killed in the Battle of the Wilderness and this along with his belief that he has killed an enemy soldier leads him to desert his duties and to make his desperate flight away from the battlefield. He doesn't meet his true mentor, Granny Bent, until he wanders up to her isolated cabin in the foothills of West Virginia when he is at his point of greatest confusion and despair. Her character is the most archetypal mentor of any in this particular group of books. There is an air of mystery about this woman who is part Creek Indian, a "yarb" woman and a midwife. Though Charley only gradually learns of her history and her generous spirit, he gradually forms a strong bond with this no-nonsense and knowledgeable mountain woman. She offers a place of refuge and teaches him the basics of farming. Even more important, she helps to heal his wounded heart and mind as she guides him to discover that he does indeed possess courage and goodness.

In many of these stories the process of coming of age is completed with some sort of victory and a glad reunion with friends and family. With this victory and reunion comes an acknowledgment of new status and enhanced respect. This is very explicit in some of these stories. At a feast following their survival in the hurricane, Star Boy's accomplishment in surviving the storm by clinging to the ancestor tree is celebrated, and the heightened respect of his family and kinsmen is signified by the acknowledgment of a new name. As Morning Girl explains, "No one would forget that my brother had once been Hungry, but today they would listen for who he had become. And Star Boy, too, would remember that he was now older, that he could no longer behave as a child" (53).

Matt's wisdom and growth is acknowledged by Saknis when he chooses to stay at the cabin to await his father rather than traveling north with the Beaver clan: "White boy good son but better you come. Saknis glad for white boy be *nkweniss*," using the clan's word for grandson. Despite the appeal of staying with Attean and his people whom he has come to love and respect, Matt stays on his own in the steadfast hope that his family will return. A few weeks later he is rewarded with a joyous reunion with his family. This is the occasion on which his father acknowledges, "You've done a grown man's job, son. I'm right proud of you," and his mother exclaims, "You look different, Matt. You're almost as tall as your pa" (133–34).

At the end of *Shades of Gray* Will has made his peace with his Uncle Jed and decided that his uncle's farm is where he belongs, writing "Now I understand that there were good men fighting on both sides—and that some good men didn't fight. I also understand now that people have to decide for themselves what is right and then stand up for what they believe in" (164). Thus Will has integrated the conflicted feelings he has struggled with throughout the novel, and he is truly united with the only family he has left. He's home.

In some of these stories there is not a physical return home or an actual reunion, but there is a recognition of growth and accomplishment, and a literal movement on to the next phase of life. Perhaps the clearest example is the martyrdom of Sorry Rimanu, who gives his life in a courageous but vain attempt to prevent the imperialistic U.S. military from destroying his homeland. However, there are other examples as well. Jip takes ownership of his heritage as the child of black slaves by making the perilous trip north on the Underground Railroad after escaping his jail cell. His ongoing growth is clear in the letter from his refuge in Canada. Here he expresses his gratitude to the Freedmans who "have given me the family and the name I was long denied" and have helped him to "learn the art of living as a man both black and free" (179). He also tells of his dangerous plans to return to fight for the freedom of his brothers and sisters. At the end of his story Charley Skedaddle is ready to launch off from Granny Bent's hollow, for as she assures him, "Nobody'd dare call ya a coward after the brave things ya done today. Ya killed the critter and ya saved me with nary a soul to see what ya did, and that makes 'em deeds even braver. Ya got the grit to make yer way in the world jest fine. Ya could leave here tommorer and go over the hills to the west if ya had a mind to" (170). Though Charley is planning to head west, he promises Granny that "I reckon when I get to be as tall as I'll ever be, I'll be back. This ain't so bad a place for a man to settle" (180), hinting at a reunion to come. At the end of *Forty Acres and Maybe a Mule*, Pascal and his surrogate family have been forced off the land that they worked so hard to cultivate. Still, they have stood up to the hateful night riders and are planning to travel further east and buy some land, for "Ain't nobody taking away our next farm!" (126).

Several of these adolescent heroes achieve reunion and incorporation in more subtle or in less fully developed ways. Jonathan in *The Fighting Ground* is the protagonist who most clearly does not achieve manhood at the end of his story. At the end of the novel it is clear that he is still perceived as a boy by others, including the tavern keeper whose gun he borrowed and lost: "You gave me your word, boy. The honor of your word. I'll be after your pa!" (150). When they are reunited Jonathan's father asks if he was hurt and breathes a prayer of thanks when Jonathan shakes his head no:

"Praise God. I'm so glad, so glad, boy." While there is some sense of heightened mutual understanding and disclosure, this scene suggests the continuation of a father/son relationship rather than the conversation of two men.

It is interesting to consider some possible reasons for Jonathan's failure to complete the transitional stage and to be incorporated into the adult community. One of these is the rather brief period of his separation and trials, just two days. However, Star Boy's separation is even shorter. A more compelling explanation is the fact that Jonathan is left without a true mentor during his transitional period. He comes to develop some sympathy for his captors, but the language barrier and the hardened ways of these professional soldiers contributes to the Hessians' harsh treatment of Jonathan. The American colonel who leads Jonathan into battle plays an even more ambiguous role in Jonathan's life. Though he tells him that "Soldiers do what they're told to do. And you're a soldier. You're needed." (131), he is a less-than-trustworthy character and his motives are far from altruistic. Still, even in Jonathan's case with a very brief initiation period and a lack of worthy mentors, the story ends with the suggestion of growth and the hope for continued development in the years ahead. He returns home a different person, coming to a new understanding of his father's emotional life and realizing that he is lucky to have been spared and to be able to look ahead to manhood.

The stunning conclusion to *A Time of Trouble* is similar to that of *The Fighting Ground*. Roy Purdy's trials are hardly over at the end of the book. Walt Landon, the gentle Kansas farmer who has become like a father to Roy, is killed by a security vehicle in which Harlow Purdy is a passenger, and Harlow will be tried as an accomplice to murder. There are many unanswered questions and uncertainties at this point, but Roy comforts Walt's wife and articulates what he has learned about perseverance even in the face of terrible adversity and grief:

> You lost your husband and Mary lost her dad, and it looks like I lost my dad too. There's no help for it now, so we just have to keep on going. Mr. Landon got us this far, looking after us. We have to keep on going without him, and someday we'll be all right again. I just know it's so. We'll be all right. (180)

Here we have a sense of hope for continued development in the years ahead, and it is not difficult to project that Roy will continue his involvement with the Landon family as well as his efforts to fight for the rights of migrant workers.

Conclusions: Images of Mature Masculinity

With the exception of Sorry, the boys in these works of historical fiction have not yet reached their final destination on the road from boyhood to manhood. Yet all of them have made significant progress toward that goal, and in most cases the reader is left with the sense that mature masculinity is within reach. How is this mature masculinity pictured? In every case, these young boys have struggled to find some level of achievement in fulfilling the responsibilities of young men in their historical and social context. Whether that work involves chores around the home, providing food and shelter, or taking a job to earn income for the family, they have learned to conduct that work with increased skill and independence. They have learned to accept one of the realities of the adult world: These responsibilities must be fulfilled even when it would be easier to deny them and when they come into conflict with personal wishes.

They have not only gained independence in dealing with life's daily challenges. They have also started to address long-term personal problems and begun to attend to social problems in the larger world around them. The discoveries and lessons learned by these protagonists are as varied as the boys themselves. Star Boy discovers the importance of kinship ties within his family and tribe and his need to control his own impulses for the good of the clan. Matt learns to fend for himself in the woods; even more important, he learns to be responsible for his own actions and to care for others. Jonathan learns to value the life that he has and realizes his need to gain more experience and growth before assuming adult responsibilities. Jip learns to accept himself and his identity. Charley learns of resources and courage that he didn't know he had, as well as the importance of making right moral choices even when others don't know or notice. Will comes to understand the courage it takes for his Uncle Jed to live by his pacifist principles, and by the end of the story he is taking his own moral stands. Pascal has discovered inner strength and the personal dignity of freedom. Tomi has learned to celebrate his dual heritage and is beginning to consolidate his self-respect as he acknowledges his Japanese heritage even while practicing his father's nonaggressive response to racism. Both Pascal and Tomi learn to persevere even in the face of powerful aggression, crushing oppression, and racial prejudice. And all of these boys make progress toward taming the beast within, whether that involves uncovering the dangers of false and unrealistic dreams, dealing with guilt, fear, and shame, or struggling with selfishness and pride, and learning to accept the help of others.

For each of these boys the road toward mature masculinity involves some degree of self-discovery and self-acceptance. Even more striking in these novels is the extent to which mature masculinity is described as a balance of independence and interdependence with others in the family and the community. Like Campbell's hero, these boys learn that a true man is not simply a loner. Most of them are assisted by guides and mentors, and their ultimate goal is reunion with home and loved ones. Thus, as they make their way toward mature masculinity, they choose to reach out to this community in loyalty and solidarity, having understood their need for others and having overcome the fear of asking and receiving help. Thus, at the end of his story each of these young men stands poised for what is truly a new beginning.

References

Agee, H. 1973. "Adolescent Initiation: A Thematic Study in the Secondary School." In *Literature for Adolescents: Selection and Use*, ed. R. Meade and R. Small, 132-37. Columbus: Merrill.

ALLAN, J., & P. DYCK. 1987. "Transition from Childhood to Adolescence." In *Betwixt and Between: Patterns of Masculine and Feminine Initiation*, ed. L. Mahdi, S. Foster, & M. Little, 24–43. LaSalle: Open Court.

ATTEBURY, B. 1996. "Women's Coming of Age in Fantasy." In *Only Connect: Readings on Children's Literature*, 3rd ed., ed. S. Egoff, G. Stubbs, R. Ashley, & W. Sutton, 288–300. Toronto: Oxford University Press.

BELL, A. 1985. "Adolescent Initiation in Cormier's *After the First Death*." *The ALAN Review*, 12 (2): 19, 37–38.

BETCHER, W., & W. POLLACK. 1993. *In a Time of Fallen Heroes: The Re-Creation of Masculinity*. New York: Atheneum.

CAMPBELL, J. 1949. *The Hero with a Thousand Faces*. Princeton: Princeton University Press.

———. 1988. *The Power of Myth with Bill Moyers*. New York: Doubleday.

CHODOROW, N. 1978. *The Reproduction of Mothering: Psychoanalysis and the Sociology of Gender*. Berkeley: University of California Press.

CHRISTOPHER, N. G. 1996. *Right of Passage: The Heroic Journey to Adulthood*. Washington, D.C.: Cornell Press.

ERIKSON, E. 1950. *Childhood and Society*. New York: W. W. Norton.

GILLIGAN, C. 1982. *In a Different Voice: Psychological Theory and Women's Development*. Cambridge, MA: Harvard University Press.

JOHNSON, J. W. 1959. "The Adolescent Hero: A Trend in Modern Fiction." *Twentieth Century Literature* 5 (1): 3–11.

LEHR, S. 1995. "Wise Women and Warriors." In *Battling Dragons: Issues and Controversy in Children's Literature*, ed. S. Lehr, 194–211. Portsmouth, NH: Heinemann.

SCHOFIELD, R. 1993. "Ritualistic Initiation and the Development of Male Identity." *Progress: Family Systems Research and Therapy* 2: 61–74.

TURNER, V. 1987. "Betwixt and Between: The Liminal Period in Rites of Passage" In *Betwixt and Between: Patterns of Masculine and Feminine Initiation*, ed. L. Mahdi, S. Foster, & M. Little, 3–19. LaSalle: Open Court.

VAN GENNEP, A. [1908] 1960. *Les Rites de Passage*, trans. by M. B. Vizedom & G. L. Chafee. Introduction by S. T. Kimball. Chicago: The University of Chicago Press.

YODER, J. M. 1976. "The Rites of Passage: A Study of the Adolescent Girl." *News from ALAN* (Fall): 3–5.

Children's Literature

AVI. 1984. *The Fighting Ground*. New York: Lippincott.

BEATTY, P. 1987. *Charley Skedaddle*. New York: Morrow Junior Books.

DORRIS, M. 1992. *Morning Girl*. New York: Hyperion.

PATERSON, K. 1996. *Jip: His Story*. New York: Lodestar/Dutton.

REEDER, C. 1989. *Shades of Gray*. New York: Macmillan.

ROBINET, H. G. 1998. *Forty Acres and Maybe a Mule*. New York: Jean Karl/Atheneum.

SALISBURY, G. 1994. *Under the Blood-Red Sun*. New York: Delacorte.

SPEARE, E. G. 1983. *The Sign of the Beaver*. Boston: Houghton Mifflin.

TAYLOR, T. 1995. *The Bomb*. San Diego: Harcourt Brace.

VAN RAVEN, P. 1990. *A Time of Trouble*. New York: Scribner.

9

Representations of Native American Women and Girls in Children's Historical Fiction

Debbie A. Reese

. . . so little is known about the women.

From *Completing the Circle*, by Virginia Driving Hawk Sneve

Native Women: Past and Present

Native women are largely absent from history textbooks and literature. When they are present, it is as "anonymous figures who prepare food, haul wood, tan hides, and take care of children" (Green 1992, 14). Generally, the Europeans who first described Native culture were men who were interested in war and diplomatic relations. As men, their writings focused on Indian men and their roles as hunters, chiefs, warriors, medicine men, and diplomats. Rarely did European men take note of Native women's roles and their responsibilities to the community and family. Women worked hard, planting, harvesting, tanning hides, and cooking, but their work was respected; it was not considered demeaning or unimportant. Throughout North America, men and women valued and appreciated each other's contributions. Complementary roles offered community stability and mutual satisfaction (Medicine 1996; Bataille and Sands 1984; Green 1992; Sneve 1995).

Most Americans are familiar with a few Native women. Pocahontas, for example, and Sacajawea. Sneve suggests these women's lives are noted in history texts because they served to help the white man. For some, they are considered traitors. Recently, however, Pewewardy (1996/97) and Medicine (1996) have put forward counterarguments that suggest these women were sophisticated in their ability to function as diplomats who were successful intermediaries between contending powers and cultural traditions.

Beatrice Medicine (1996) writes that Native women are the "hidden half" (685) in the writings of traders, trappers, missionaries, and pioneering anthropologists. Yet, in traditional Native societies, women were and are significant—perhaps more so than men. Jaimes and Halsey (1992) write that women are the backbone of indigenous nations on this continent. Traditionally, women made key decisions directing the course of events for their tribes and exercised considerable control and influence. For example, among the Haudenosaunee (Six Nations Iroquois Confederacy) women selected the males who formed the council charged with making decisions on behalf of the confederacy's interests. If one of the men took a position contrary to the people's best interests, the woman who selected him could replace him (Jaimes and Halsey 1992; Allen 1986). Moreover, across the United States, many tribes attribute the origin of their culture to a female (in contrast to Judeo-Christian theology), who is the source of life and who provides sustenance and protection for her people (Green 1992).

Regardless of the complementary roles of men and women, the status and respect accorded to women, and the power they wielded in some tribes, women are for the most part missing from the historical record and missing from history textbooks.

Native Women in Acclaimed Children's Historical Fiction

In some acclaimed children's books, Native women are missing, barely present, or presented as the hardworking drudge with little status. The ways the women are characterized go unnoticed and unquestioned in children's literature textbooks designed for students in teacher education programs. Examples from noted titles follow.

In Edmonds' celebrated *Matchlock Gun* (1941), a white family (mother, ten-year-old boy, younger girl) fear they will be killed by Indians and their home burned. In the climax of the book, the boy fires the matchlock gun, killing three Indians who are about to enter their home. There are no Indian women in the story. While it may be argued that the plot does not allow for the inclusion of women, the story presents the Indian people as vicious men. Nowhere is it suggested that the Indians are fighting to defend their land and protect their own families.

Elizabeth George Speare's 1957 book *Calico Captive* and the 1983 *Sign of the Beaver* are both engaging stories. In each, however, Native women are shown only as hard workers and are called "squaw." In *The Sign of the Beaver*, women are referred to as "squaw" by the white protagonist, Matt, but also by Attean, the Native American character, and other men in the tribe. It is highly improbable that Attean would have feelings of disdain for the women in his tribe, and it is highly unlikely that he would use the white man's word *squaw* to refer to them. Matt, perhaps, but probably not Attean.

In *The Courage of Sarah Noble* (Dalgliesh 1954), Tall John's wife is introduced on page thirty-six, not as an individual with a name, but as Tall John's "squaw." We never learn what her name is or much about her. We do know she cooks and sews. (For an informative discussion of other problems with this book, see Slapin and Seale's review of the book in *Through Indian Eyes* [1998].)

128

In her 1999 article in *Booklist*, Joyce Saricks writes, "Historical fiction makes a point of conveying a serious respect for historical accuracy and detail, and its intention, beyond providing reading pleasure, is to enhance the reader's knowledge of past events, lives, and customs" (1392). In all the aforementioned books, Native women are inaccurately portrayed. While some might argue that the portrayal of the white settlers is accurate, the portrayals of Native women and culture are flawed and do nothing to enhance the reader's knowledge of Native Americans.

"Squaws" and "Princesses"

The word *squaw* is ubiquitous. Ski enthusiasts visit "Squaw Valley," students at Stanford cast their eyes on "Squaw Mountain," bakers search for the recipe for "squaw bread," and hikers learn the differences between poison ivy and "squaw bush." The entry for *squaw* in *The Encyclopedia of North American Indians* (Hoxie 1996) states that its origins are with the northeastern tribes; in Massachusett, *squa* referred to a younger woman; in Narrangansett, *sunksquaw* meant "queen" or "lady."

Yet there have been numerous protests against its use. Many Native American women argue that the word is offensive. According to Henrietta Mann, a Northern Cheyenne woman from Missoula, Montana, the word *squaw* is a shortened form of the Mohawk word *tsikwaw,* which means "female genitalia." Fur traders who traveled the region in the late 1700s and early 1800s corrupted the word and shortened it to *squaw*. Katsi Cook (1997), a Mohawk woman, writes:

> One word which has been used since colonial times to denigrate Indian women is the word "squaw." It wasn't until I was having children myself and began practicing midwifery that I began to ask the old people about Mohawk words used to describe female anatomy and physiology. It was then that I learned that the word "squaw" comes from the Mohawk word *otsiskwah* (oh-gee-squaw), which means "it's slippery," describing the vagina. (44)

Some protests against the use of the word have been successful. In Montana, mountain peaks, hills, streams, and trails that include the word are being renamed. At Clyde A. Erwin High School in Buncombe County, North Carolina, the U.S. Department of Justice ordered the school to stop using "squaw" to refer to their women's athletic team (Molin 1999).

Although scholars are loath to engage in debate over the etymology of the word, there is general agreement that *the term is currently regarded as highly derogatory* (Hoxie 1996; Green 1992; Molin 1999; Bataille and Sands 1984).

The word *squaw* is negative. At the other extreme is the "Indian Princess." Some might identify the "Indian Princess" as a positive stereotype. The phrase in and of itself is intriguing. Pewewardy (1996/97) writes that the "Indian Princess" stereotype has its roots in the legend of Pocahontas. Early on, Europeans wrongly assumed their own traditions of royalty existed among the Native people. Thus, Matowa (commonly known as Pocahontas) was called a princess.

An Indian Princess is typically characterized as a maidenly, demure young woman who is deeply committed to a white man. "Romantics," says Beatrice Medicine (1996) "wrote of the duskily alluring Indian 'princess' who was free from the restraints of 'civilized' society" (686). In the Disney movie *Pocahontas* we see both: she is a maiden committed to a white man (John Smith), and her movements are free from restraint as she revels in the feel of the wind blowing her hair across her face, neck, and shoulders.

Many young American girls who aspire to be an Indian Princess can do so by joining the YMCA Indian Princess program for fathers and their young daughters. The activities they engage in can create confusion about Native culture. Each YMCA chapter chooses a tribal name by which they will be known. The choice is arbitrary. It has nothing to do with location and can result in some rather strange configurations. In Florida, for example, there is the "Hopi YMCA Indian Princess Tribe of Coral Springs, Florida" which is "part of the Mandan Federation." This arbitrary use of tribal names may prove confusing to any child who has just learned in school that the Hopi tribe is in Arizona and the Mandans are in North Dakota.

Rounding out popular culture images of the Indian Princess are the "Native American Princess Barbie" and numerous pornographic sites on the World Wide Web that feature dusky Indian maidens engaged in various sexual acts.

Although squaws and princesses figure prominently in popular culture and literature, they do little to inform our understanding of Native women, past or present.

Authentic Characterization of Native Females

Children's literature textbooks typically include guidelines on how to evaluate historical fiction. A story should include a wealth of accurate historical detail about the characters, events, setting, customs, beliefs, culture, society, and habits, and there should be authenticity in portrayal of characters. This means avoiding anachronisms of language and behavior. But it also means avoiding what Joseph Bruchac calls "the dangers of cultural ventriloquism." Speaking at the 1999 "Windows to the Past" children's historical literature conference in Madison, Wisconsin, Bruchac noted that this can occur when an author fails to do the kind of research necessary to write a book about a culture they don't know much about. Such books fail on many levels when examined from a Native American perspective, and are problematic because readers often assume the work to be an accurate and authentic portrayal of the culture. At that same conference, Anne Scott MacLeod spoke about accuracy of characterization in works of historical fiction. She was specifically critical of authors whose female characters think and behave like women of the 1990s. Indeed, she stated that books with female characters that don't reflect the values and attributes of women of their time period are more aptly described as adventure stories than historical fiction.

More so now than in the past, critics, teachers, librarians, and parents look carefully at the illustrations of Native Americans in children's books. Many have gained awareness and have become adept at recognizing a stereotyped illustration. In our evaluation of Native female characters in historical fiction, we must develop the same awareness and skill in recognizing stereotyped characterizations. Do the actions, behaviors, attitudes, and private thoughts of the Native characters seem similar to those we expect in white characters? If they do, the characterizations may be flawed. Native people are not dark-haired, dark-skinned people who think and behave just like white people. While that is possible in a story about contemporary Native people, it is not likely in a historical context, especially in a time period prior to European contact, or one with little contact with white people.

Although it must be remembered that there are over five hundred tribes in the United States, and that each tribe is in some way distinct from others to varying degrees, there are some generalizations that apply across tribes. Critics, teachers, and librarians can consult various sources (listed in the resource portion of this chapter) to determine distinctions such as the roles of women in patrilineal/matrilineal societies. The following set of characteristics of Native women in historical periods has been gleaned from a number of sources, including Rayna Green's 1992 book *Women in American Indian Society*, Bataille's and Sands's 1984 book *American Indian Women, Telling Their Lives*, and Beverly Hungry Wolf's 1982 book, *The Ways of My Grandmothers.*

- Humor is an important central characteristic that tempers the burden of responsibility women bear individually and collectively.
- Native women are modest in dress, demeanor, and attitude, in a way that is self-respectful and brings honor to the individual and her family. Women are guarded in emotion and in private aspects of their lives.
- Native women are the repositories of tradition and concern for spiritual ideals. By sharing their knowledge with children, they stabilize the tribe.
- Native women tend to defer but not forgo their immediate personal goals for the well-being of family members.
- Native women are especially skilled in creating a support network of other women who share responsibility and pleasure in day-to-day work.
- In most tribal groups, a woman's marriage was arranged by her father, brothers, or uncles. The woman, however, retained control over her body and behavior, her children, and the property she held prior to the marriage or that she produced during the marriage.
- Women held authority over property and its uses, and over the distribution of material goods they or their men produced.
- Divisions in men's and women's work were complementary and egalitarian, with neither accorded a greater status. Women's work (e.g., planting, harvesting, tanning, sewing) was not looked down upon by men.

- Though women did not usually take part in combat, there are several instances in which a woman led her people in warfare (Jaimes and Halsey 1992) identify some of these women: Cousaponakeesa—a.k.a. Creek Mary in Dee Brown's 1980 novel *Creek Mary's Blood: A Novel*, and the Cherokee woman Da'nawa-gasta, Cheyenne Buffalo Calf Road).

- Grandparents had a larger role in rearing children than did parents. They cooked and prepared food, did household chores, and cared for the children while the parents were tending to the needs of hunting, farming, and other economic activities. They passed on cultural knowledge and wisdom through instruction and stories.

- Grandmothers and mothers taught girls how to make moccasins, clothing, and lodge coverings, and to participate in daily chores such as preparing food and carrying water. This instruction was cooperative, primarily through observation and example, rather than by didactic methods.

- Girls were responsible for the care of younger siblings. Strong emotional attachment characterized their relationships.

- Among some tribes (e.g., Blackfeet and Crows), men developed strong relationships with their daughters, often taking them along on hunting and raiding forays. These girls became proficient in male activities, becoming noted warriors and leaders.

- Strong, nurturing, positive relationships between siblings were encouraged.

Two Recent Books That Are Problematic

Occasionally, books are written and published that tell a story from the perspective of a Native female. In these books, the women take center stage; they are not missing or marginally present. They must be examined, however, for the ways in which the author has chosen to depict the female characters.

My Heart Is on the Ground: The Diary of Nannie Little Rose, a Sioux Girl, by Ann Rinaldi (1999), is part of the Dear America series of historical fiction diaries published by Scholastic. Set in 1880, the book is fraught with factual errors, but the focus of this discussion will be on the characterization of Nannie and other women (to read an in-depth review, go to http://www.oyate.org and click on "Books to Avoid"). The protagonist, Nannie Little Rose, is a Sioux girl who goes to Carlisle Industrial Indian School, one of the first off-reservation boarding schools established by the U.S. government. Carlisle was run by Captain Richard Henry Pratt, who is well known for his philosophy: "Kill the Indian and save the man." Agents of the government used many tactics to coerce parents into sending their children to these boarding schools. Yet as depicted in this book, the schools were a step in the right direction. Nannie embraces the school and what it signifies. In the end, she agrees to be a Pilgrim woman in the Thanksgiving play. The book fails to convey the harsh realities children experienced: punishment for speaking their language, death from exposure to elements when the children ran away from the school, and death from illness. The abuses that occurred there are whitewashed. In addition to this distorted picture of the boarding school experience, the characterization of the females is inconsistent with Native culture, specifically the Lakota and Hopi, both of which are featured in the story.

Among their people, Lakota children were taught to be deferential, cooperative, and respectful to their elders. They were also taught to care for their siblings even more than spouses. However, throughout Nannie's diary, she writes disparagingly about her elders, her mother, and her brother. On page five, she writes "our chiefs have made large mistake in giving over our lands." Of her brother, she writes on page ten: "He much time acts like a fool." Of her mother, she writes on page eleven: "My mother is jealous of Red Road because she is so young and pretty." In addition, it is important to note that concepts of "young and pretty" were not found in Lakota culture. The Lakota people cherished their children, treated them with respect, and did not talk down to them. They marked a young girl's passage into womanhood with a sacred ceremony. Yet, Nannie writes on page four: "Of what worth am I, a girl of twelve winters?" And on page thirty-two, her mother says to her "What will you learn? To be more silly than you are?" The Hopi child, Belle Rain Water, is the antagonist. Her character is not an accurate reflection of a Hopi child of that time period. One example is the scene in which Belle, swimming naked, taunts Nannie to join her. This is contrary to Hopi mores of maidenly modesty in the nineteenth century. *My Heart Is on the Ground* is particularly troublesome because teachers report that students use the Dear America series as though they were primary sources of information about the time period being depicted. So little is available for children that accurately presents the boarding schools for Native Americans that it is unfortunate that this book missed the mark in so many ways, yet will undoubtedly be widely read.

Although not as problematic as *My Heart Is on the Ground*, Jan Hudson's novel *Sweetgrass* (1984) merits a second look. *Sweetgrass* won the Canadian Library Association Book of the Year for Children, and the Canada Council Children's Literature Prize. In the United States, it received starred reviews from *Booklist* and *School Library Journal*. In the story, Sweetgrass, a Blackfoot girl, saves her family from a smallpox epidemic. For the most part, the book is engaging and the story is well told. And in some cases the characterization of the women fits with what we know about Native women in that historical time period. Sweetgrass's grandmother, for example, has a sense of humor that lightens tension. However, throughout the book, Sweetgrass is preoccupied with the question of whom she will marry. This theme dominates and overwhelms the otherwise positive aspects of the story. Although this theme may appeal to young girls who read the book, we should pause to ask just *why* it appeals to this audience. This is, after all, a book about a Blackfoot girl in the 1800s. Critics such as Slapin and Seale (1998) are on target when they point out that the Sweetgrass character and her preoccupation with whom she will marry sounds more like an upper-middle-class American girl than a Blackfoot woman of the 1800s. It might very well be the case that a Blackfoot girl in the 1990s would be preoccupied with that question, but this is not a girl of the 1990s; *Sweetgrass* is set in the 1830s. Later in the story, Sweetgrass goes to a sweathouse. Laden with ceremony, a sweathouse is used for a ritual sweat bath to bring spiritual and physical health. While in the sweat, participants sing, pray, and meditate (Hoxie 1996). The experience Sweetgrass describes sounds more like a modern-day sauna than a traditional sweat, and as she reflects on her time in the sweathouse, Sweetgrass says that she ". . . wished Eagle-Sun could see me flushed rosy pink under my beautiful brown." The expression of that thought runs counter to the modest attitude typical of a Blackfoot girl of that time period. This lack of modesty is also evident in this sentence: "It certainly was not some young Cree or Crow hiding in the rushes, wanting to make love to us" (43).

Returning again to Saricks's definition of historical fiction (1999), both of these books violate the intention of historical fiction. Rather than enhancing the reader's knowledge, the books provide inaccurate and inauthentic information about Native women and Native culture.

Notable Books

In the following books, there aren't any squaws or princesses. There are, however, Native women and girls who are respected by their people, who live meaningful lives within their communities. Some of the women are leaders charged with great responsibility. In these stories, women's lives include hard work and struggle, but they also contain much more: humor and joy, pain and sadness. They are people—not caricatures, not stereotypes. Most are readily available at bookstores, and most school and public libraries probably have copies. Most are published by mainstream publishing houses. What is striking is that there are so few. MacCann (1993) argues that, unlike the case with other ethnic groups, there are *too many* books about Native Americans. But in looking over the possibilities for this chapter, very few historical novels published by mainstream presses include female Native characters. The majority of books published about Native Americans are myths and legends, biographies, and stories of cultural conflict that invariably present a Euro-American perspective that stereotypes, marginalizes, or omits Native females. Some of the books discussed below are from small publishers or university presses, neither of whom typically send books to the major children's literature review journals.

The Birchbark House by Louise Erdrich, 1999, Hyperion

The opening pages of *The Birchbark House* describe quietly, without dramatic overtones, the infant days of Omakayas's life. Her people were devastated by smallpox. She is the only survivor. In the first chapter, Erdrich introduces seven-year-old Omakayas. She's Ojibwa, and in the pages to come, we meet her family, and we come to know and care about this child with "shining brown eyes" who wonders when her front teeth will come in. Through Neebin (Summer), Dagwaging (Fall), Biboon (Winter), and Zeegwun (Spring), we also come to know the women in Omakayas's life. All the women are strong. All work hard. First we meet Nokomis, Omakayas's grandmother when they are out gathering the bark, Omakayas, Nokomis, Yellow Kettle, and Angeline (Omakayas's mother and sister) will use to build their summer home. Throughout the story, the relationships between the women and children demonstrate the deep commitment the women have to the children as Yellow Kettle parents her children and Nokomis tells them stories, passing on the information she holds within her. The special bond between Nokomis and Omakayas strengthens as the seasons pass and it becomes clear that Omakayas will, like Nokomis, be a healer. A character who figures prominently in the story is Old Tallow, a rather intimidating woman who lives alone with her dogs and is a skilled hunter. It is she who rescued the infant Omakayas from the island, and it is her rabbit soup that pulls Omakayas out of despair after smallpox strikes her family, killing Neewo, the baby brother Omakayas adores. And it is Old Tallow who tells Omakayas why she was not struck with the disease. Erdrich's descriptions of the lives of the women in this story provide the rich detail necessary in a work of historical fiction, and her characterization of the women is exceptional.

Daughter of Suqua *by Diane Johnston Hamm, 1997, Albert Whitman*

Daughter of Suqua is a deeply moving story set in 1905, on the Northwest Coast. The protagonist is Ida, a ten-year-old girl living through a particularly difficult time. Her people, the Suquamish, are losing their land and with it, the access to resources necessary to maintain some of their traditions. They are also experiencing the harsh educational policies of the U.S. government that pressured parents to send their children away to distant boarding schools. Ida's relationship with her grandmother is central to the story. The first chapter opens with Ida and her grandmother leaving together for fish camp. Once a yearly occurrence, canneries have reduced the number of fish in Puget Sound, so fewer and fewer people set up camp. Throughout the story, Ida's grandmother strives to teach her the traditional ways of their people, while Ida's mother and father try to help her understand the government's decisions to turn them from fishermen and loggers who live in villages to farmers on allotments out of sight from one another.

Children of the Longhouse *by Joseph Bruchac, 1996, Penguin*

In *Children of the Longhouse* chapters alternate between the voices of Ohkwa'ri and his twin sister, Otsi:stia. Through them, we learn a great deal about Mohawk life in the 1490s, but *if the readers pay attention*, we also come to understand the important roles women held. On page eleven, Bruchac (through Ohkwa'ri's voice) deftly describes the political structure of the Mohawk people: "Their grandmother, She Opens the Sky, was the oldest of the three Clan Mothers of the big longhouse . . . it was her job to help everyone follow the right path . . . Everyone respected her . . . she was one of those who chose the clan's leaders . . ." Later, on page twenty-two in Otsi:stia's voice, we learn about the responsibilities of women: "We are the ones who carry life . . . care for the earth . . . keep the families together . . ." When Ohkwa'ri decides to build a small lodge for himself, Otsi:stia gathers a basket of strawberries for him and places it where he will find it the morning after his first night alone. The twins' grandmother has told them many stories, and Otsi:stia repeats these stories to herself as she works. As she walks in the forest, she recalls to herself the roots and herbs her grandmother has told her about. Through her grandmother's teachings, Otsi:stia is becoming a repository of the traditions and knowledge that will help the tribe maintain its stability in the years to come.

Sees Behind Trees *by Michael Dorris, 1996, Hyperion*

The mothers in *Sees Behind Trees* are responsible for teaching their sons to shoot a bow and arrow. But Walnut cannot see well and his mother's efforts to teach him to shoot fail. When she realizes his vision is poor, she abandons the shooting lessons in favor of long hours during which they sit quietly while Walnut describes to her what he hears. In this way, his acute listening skills are strengthened. At an end-of-summer feast, boys who are ready to become men demonstrate their skills with the bow and arrow. Walnut dreads the feast because of his inability to shoot. The coming-of-age ceremony is presided over by a woman named Otter, who is the tribe's weroance. She issues a challenge to the boys who are gathered, asking them to tell her what they see behind the trees. Walnut wins this contest and she gives him the name Sees Behind Trees. While the story focuses on Walnut, Dorris's characterization of Otter merits attention. She is the weroance for the tribe; in addition to being an expert hunter, she controls the comings and goings of the people and presides over important events, yet she is a caring woman who is deeply attached to her twin brother.

Two Old Women *by Velma Wallis, 1994, HarperPerennial*

At first glance, the abandonment of two older women in this story may appear to run counter to the respect for elders that is significant in Native American societies. However, during particularly harsh conditions such as famine, some tribes left the elderly who were near death on their own when the tribe had to move quickly to survive. In Velma Wallis's story, Ch'idzigyaak and Sa'—two older Athabascan women—are surprised when the chief of their band announces that they will be left behind when the band moves on to their next camp. Although Ch'idzigyaak is eighty years old and Sa' is seventy-nine, neither woman is feeble or near death, but they are constantly complaining about their aches and pains and feign helplessness so the younger ones in the band will take care of all their needs. Finally, the council has decided they will be left. The band leaves; the women sit, stunned. After a while, Sa' says, ". . . if we are going to die, my friend, let us die trying, not sitting." They decide they cannot stay in this camp, so they make snowshoes, pack their things, and set out on an arduous journey to establish a winter camp. The journey exhausts them, yet builds their confidence, strength, and determination. In the new camp, they laugh as they remember how helpless they seemed when they were with the band, they cry when they think about family members in the band, but through the winter, spring, fall, and summer, they grow stronger. Their food stores grow and they sew far more clothing than they can ever use. Meanwhile, the band has continued to experience hardship and guilt over having left the women. It is winter again, and they return to the old camp, look-ing for Ch'idzigyaak and Sa'. *Two Old Women* is a beautiful story, rich with detail about life in Alaska, laced with the strength of the women and their eventual contribution to the survival of their people.

Waterlily, *by Ella C. Deloria, 1988, University of Nebraska Press*

Ella Deloria's *Waterlily* follows the female Teton Sioux protagonist from birth to old age. Deloria was a Yankton Sioux woman who worked and studied with Franz Boas, Ruth Benedict, and Margaret Mead. For Boas, she translated material, and Benedict encouraged her to study the roles of women and children (Demallie 1988). From these experiences she went on to write a superb novel that records traditional Sioux ways from a woman's perspective. Seamlessly, Deloria shares fundamental aspects of women's lives. For example, Waterlily recalls what her mother told her about the responsibilities of a woman: "When you marry, my daughter, remember that your chil-dren are more important than you. Always the new life comes first. Your duty to your children must be in accordance to this rule" (180). The book is published by the University of Nebraska press and is available in paperback. Other Native women have written about how their people struggled to maintain their ways during devastating periods of their history. Some examples are Ignatia Broker's *Night Flying Woman* (1983, Minnesota Historical Society Press) and Maria Campbell's *Halfbreed* (1973, University of Nebraska Press). Hopi author Polingaysi Quoyawayma's autobiography, *No Turning Back* (1964, University of New Mexico Press), is especially poignant as she recounts her decision to leave home to go to school, while maintaining her traditions.

Native Women: Survival and Endurance

In the twenty-first century, it is disheartening to learn that far too many children in the United States think all the Indians are dead and gone, and if they learn anything at all about Native women, they learn to view them as squaws or princesses. It is important that we all spend time reflecting on these images, their history, and the steps that are necessary to correct them. It is vitally important that children learn about contemporary Native women who have attained recognition for their achieve-ments. Some of these women are Ada Deer, Wilma Mankiller, LaDonna Harris, Annie Wauneka, and Suzan Shown Harjo in politics; Joy Harjo, Buffy Sainte-Marie, and Helen Hardin in the arts.

Finally, it has been interesting to go through this exercise, this writing of a chap-ter about Native women in a book about gender. Some of the books and articles I read as I wrote this chapter address the feminist movement and the criticism Native women receive for not taking a larger role in that movement (Bataille and Sands 1984). To that criticism, Native women reply that their struggle, right now, is not one of gaining equality with men. Their struggle focuses on aspects of community survival, such as treaty rights, protection of Native resources, and child welfare (Medicine

1996). This struggle is not without consequence. Anna Mae Aquash and Tina Trudell lost their lives by taking a stand for the rights of Native people (Jaimes and Halsey 1992).

Prior to contact, Native women were on equal footing with men. The impact of contact led to an eventual demise of the status of women within Native culture. Today, Native women are regaining their status and asserting their voices. We need more children's books that provide us with accurate and authentic portrayals of women prior to contact and in the early periods of contact. We need more books about modern Native women, or with characters like them, because Native women, like Native American culture, are not "vanishing."

I opened this chapter with a quote from Sneve, who said, "so little is known about the women." I close with a traditional Cheyenne saying (printed in the preface to Bataille's *American Indian Women, Telling Their Lives*, 1984) that reflects the very real fact that Native women are not squaws and princesses. They survive and endure, and because they do, Native people survive and endure.

> A Nation is not conquered
> Until the hearts of its women
> Are on the ground.
> Then it is done, no matter
> How brave its warriors
> Nor how strong its weapons.

References

ALLEN, P. G. 1986. *The Sacred Hoop: Recovering the Feminine in American Indian Traditions.* Boston: Beacon Press.

BATAILLE, G., & K. M. SANDS. 1984. *American Indian Women, Telling Their Lives.* Lincoln: University of Nebraska Press.

BERKHOFFER, R. F. 1978. *The White Man's Indian: Images of the American Indian from Columbus to the Present.* New York: Random House.

BRUCHAC, J. 1999. "Windows to the Past." Children's Historical Literature Conference. University of Wisconsin.

COOK, K. 1997. "The Coming of Anontaks." In *Reinventing the Enemy's Language*, ed. J. Harjo and G. Bird. New York: W. W. Norton.

DEMALLIE, R. J. 1998. "Foreword." In *Waterlily* by E. C. Deloria, 233–34. Lincoln: University of Nebraska Press.

GREEN, R. 1992. *Women in American Indian Society.* In the series Indians of North America, ed. F. W. Porter. New York: Chelsea House.

HOXIE, F. E., ed. 1996. *Enclopedia of North American Indians.* Boston: Houghton Mifflin.

HUNGRY WOLF, B. 1982. *The Ways of My Grandmothers.* New York: Quill.

JAIMES, M. A., & T. HALSEY. 1992. "American Indian Women at the Center of Indigenous Resistance in Contemporary North America." In *The State of Native America*, ed. M. A. Jaimes. Boston: South End Press.

MACCANN, D. 1993. "Native Americans in Books for the Young." In *Teaching Multicultural Literature in Grades K–8*, ed. V. J. Harris, 139–69. Norwood, MA: Christopher-Gordon.

MEDICINE, B. 1996. "Women." In *Encyclopedia of North American Indians*, ed. F. Hoxie. Boston: Houghton Mifflin.

MOLIN, P. F. 1999. "Eliminating the 'S' Word." In *American Indian Stereotypes in the World of Children*, ed. A. B. Hirschfelder, P. F. Molin, & Y. Wakim. Lanham, MD: Scarecrow Press.

PEWEWARDY, C. 1996/97. "The Pocahontas Paradox: A Cautionary Tale for Educators." *Journal of Navajo Education* 14 (1/2): 20–25.

SARICKS, J. 1999. "Historical Fiction—Rules of the Game." *Booklist* 95 (15): 1392.

SLAPIN, B., & D. SEALE. 1998. *Through Indian Eyes: The Native Experience in Books for Children*. Berkeley: University of California American Indian Studies Center.

SNEVE, V. D. H. 1995. *Completing the Circle*. Lincoln: University of Nebraska Press.

Children's Literature

BROKER, I. 1983. *Night Flying Woman*. St. Paul: Minnesota Historical Society Press.

BRUCHAC, J. 1996. *Children of the Longhouse*. New York: Penguin.

CAMPBELL, M. 1973. *Halfbreed*. Lincoln: University of Nebraska Press.

DELORIA, E. 1988. *Waterlily*. Lincoln: University of Nebraska Press.

DORRIS, M. 1996. *Sees Behind Trees*. New York: Hyperion.

ERDRICH, L. 1999. *The Birchbark House*. New York: Hyperion.

HAMM, D. J. 1997. *Daughter of Suqua*. Morton Grove, IL: Albert Whitman.

QUOYAWAYMA, P. 1964. *No Turning Back*. Albuquerque: University of New Mexico Press.

WALLIS, V. 1994. *Two Old Women*. New York: HarperPerennial.

Problematic Children's Literature

*Note: This is a list of books cited. For a list of *recommended* books, see the list above.

DALGLIESH, A. 1954. *The Courage of Sarah Noble*. New York: Scribner.

EDMONDS, W. 1941. *Matchlock Gun*. New York: Dodd, Mead.

HUDSON, J. 1984. *Sweetgrass*. Edmonton: Tree Frog Press.

RINALDI, A. 1999. *My Heart Is on the Ground: The Diary of Nannie Little Rose, A Sioux Girl*. In the series Dear America. New York: Scholastic.

SPEARE, E. G. 1957. *Calico Captive*. Boston: Houghton Mifflin.

———. 1983. *The Sign of the Beaver*. Boston: Houghton Mifflin.

Recommended Professional Resources

Books, articles, and websites listed here can help teachers and librarians locate books, do fact checking, and gain insight and awareness of issues related to Native culture and Native perspectives.

APERTURE. 1995. *Strong Hearts: Native American Visions and Voices*. New York: Aperture.

BERKHOFER, R. E. 1978. *The White Man's Indian*. New York: Vintage.

BIGELOW, B. 1998. *Rethinking Columbus: The Next 500 Years*. Milwaukee: Rethinking Schools.

DAVIS, M. B. 1996. *Native America in the Twentieth Century: An Encyclopedia*. New York: Garland Publishing.

HIRSCHFELDER, A., P. F. MOLIN, and Y. WAKIM. 1999. *American Indian Stereotypes in the World of Children*. Lanham, MD: Scarecrow Press.

HOXIE, F. E. 1996. *Encyclopedia of North American Indians*. New York: Houghton Mifflin.

KUIPERS, B. 1991. *American Indian Reference Books for Children and Young Adults*. Englewood, CO: Libraries Unlimited.

REESE, D. 1998. "Look Mom! It's George! He's a TV Indian!" *Horn Book Magazine*, 74 (5): 636–41.

———. 1999. "Authenticity and Sensitivity: Goals for Writing and Reviewing Books with Native American Themes." *School Library Journal*, 45 (11): 36–37.

REESE, D. A., and N. CALDWELL-WOOD. 1997. "Native Americans in Children's Literature." In *Using Multiethnic Literature in the K–8 Classroom*, ed. V. J. Harris. Norwood, MA: Christopher-Gordon.

SEALE, D., B. SLAPIN, and C. SILVERMAN. 1998. *Thanksgiving: A Native Perspective*. Berkeley: Oyate.

SLAPIN, B., and D. SEALE. 1998. *Through Indian Eyes: The Native Experience in Books for Children*. Berkeley: University of California American Indian Studies Center.

STEDMAN, R. W. 1982. *Shadows of the Indian*. Norman: University of Oklahoma Press.

Internet Resources

A Critical Bibliography of North American Indians, for K–12
> http://www.mnh.si.edu/anthro/outreach/Indbiblindx.html
> This annotated bibliography of children's literature was developed for the Smithsonian Institution's outreach program and is quite extensive in scope. Downloaded, it numbers nearly three hundred pages—a great resource—categorized by geographical area.

"I" Is Not for Indian: The Portrayal of Native Americans in Books for Young People
> http://www.pitt.edu/~lmitten/ailabib.htm
> Written in 1991 by Naomi Caldwell-Wood and Lisa A. Mitten, this online article includes discussion of problematic portrayals as well as several book reviews.

Internet Public Library: Native American Authors
> http://www.ipl.org/ref/native
> This site provides a list of Native American authors. There is a short biography for each author and a list of published works. Some also include links to other sites with information about the author.

Native American Indian Resources

http://indy4.fdl.cc.mn.us/~isk/mainmenu.html#mainmenutop
One of the larger Native American sites on the Web, the site has a Native books section that is especially useful.

Native American Resources on the Internet

http://www.hanksville.org/NAresources/
An extensive site, it is divided into many categories, such as Culture, Language, History, Education, Music, Art, and Books.

Native American Sites on the World Wide Web

http://www.pitt.edu/~lmitten/indians.html
This site has the most extensive set of Internet links to tribal home pages, many of which are maintained by the tribe itself or a Native American of that tribe (noted by a drum icon).

North American Native Authors Catalog

http://nativeauthors.com/
This site is useful for finding literature about Native Americans written by Native Americans. It includes biographical information, lists of books, and links to other sites with information about the author and his or her books.

Native Americans: Recommended Books and Resources

http://ericeece.org/pubs/reslist/native99.html
This site contains a list of children's books about contemporary Native American people, grouped into fiction and nonfiction.

Oyate

http://www.oyate.org
Oyate is a Native organization highly regarded for the quality of its teacher workshops and books, tapes, posters, and curriculum materials. The website includes critical reviews of "Books to Avoid."

10

Why Gender Stereotypes Still Persist in Contemporary Children's Literature

BELINDA Y. LOUIE

In the early 1970s, research on gender bias in children's literature emerged as a result of the women's movement. Since then men have added their voices to the ongoing dialogue, recognizing that gender stereotypes are harmful to everyone, not just women (Rudman 1995). Research in developmental psychology indicates that children's knowledge of gender begins at an early age (Jacklin and Maccoby 1978). The development of gender role identity is shaped by shared beliefs of society, usually by oversimplified gender role stereotypes (Beall 1993). The acquisition of such stereotypes is a continuing process, a gradual increase in the amount and complexity of information as the child grows (Deaux and Kite 1993; Dellmann-Jenkins, Florjancic, and Swadener 1993).

Children's literature is one mechanism through which society exerts its influence on young minds: "Texts are important influences that shape us by reflecting the politics and values of our society" (Fox 1993a, 656). They present images of ourselves, molding and shaping our definitions and expectations of how we should behave, think, and feel as male and female in our world. Stories open "a map of possible roles and of possible worlds in which action, thought, and self-definition are permissible (or desirable)" (Bruner 1986, 66). Many have advocated that in order to develop the fullness of human potential in our children, we have to examine the gender-related messages embedded in books for them.

After three decades of studies in gender issues in children's literature, there is strong consensus in the following areas:

- Males have been represented more than females in books. While the numbers have varied over the years with different samples of books using different categories of analysis, the imbalances still persist (Crabb and Bielawski 1994; Ernst 1995; Rudman 1995).
- Although the number of females in books has increased over the years, they are portrayed with similar stereotypical behaviors. Boys have been generally

known as powerful, independent, problem solvers, active, and in charge of situations, while girls are often portrayed as demure, weak, dependent, problem causers, passive, and followers (Tetenbaum and Pearson 1989; Kortenhaus and Demarest 1993; Crabb and Bielawski 1994; Ernst 1995; Turner-Bowker 1996).

- The agents of change to reduce gender biases should be authors, illustrators, publishers, and teachers (Fox 1993a; Ernst 1995; Rudman 1995; St. Pierre 1999).

Despite the strong evidence that many have reported on gender biases in children's literature, little improvement has taken place. In order to challenge the perpetuation of gender stereotypes in books, we have to understand the forces undermining the effort to present a balanced portrayal of gender identities.

Belief vs. Implementation

Authors have an undeniable responsibility in creating gender balance since they are the creators of images in text. Most authors will agree with Jane Yolen's comment on gender representation in children's books: "I feel to overemphasize one gender in favor of the other does damage to where we as a (human) race want to be at the end of time: where boys and girls are equal. Where men and women are both heroes. Where there is an androgeneity of terms of success" (Enciso et al. 1999). I believe that authors do share Yolen's commitment and belief to create a better world in their books for the young readers.

If authors indeed believe in the empowerment of both boys and girls, how do they continue to support the imbalance of gender representation (Ernst 1995)? The problem is not a matter of the heart. Difficulty occurs when deep-seated socialized thinking becomes a barrier as authors attempt to put their beliefs in action. Mem Fox is a powerful voice in the fight to eliminate gender stereotypes in children's literature (Fox 1993a, 1993b). Even Fox laments that she can still be easily "tricked into writing badly" regarding sexist portrayal when she does not consciously monitor her story development (Fox 1993a). In an earlier version of *With Love, at Christmas*, a woman cries over the loss of her husband's job, saying, "How shall we live?" Fox abhors the sexist assumption that women are helpless and require support. She later changes the story. In the new version, it is the woman who loses the job; and it is the husband who cries for the difficult time ahead.

Achieving balance in gender is more easily said than done. It is unrealistic to expect authors to write their stories with gender restrictions placed on them. They set out to write good stories. Constant monitoring of gender balance may inhibit the creative process. However, I would like to see more authors such as Mem Fox, who has taken a conscious effort to present more balanced images during different stages of the writing process. With increased awareness of gender issues, authors can become their first and best critics to ensure that their beliefs are implemented in their work.

Motivating Reluctant Male Readers vs. Empowering Female Readers

Children learn the gender norms through storytelling and book-sharing experiences at an early age. In order to help children develop their full potential as human beings, it is only logical to introduce balanced gender roles in their reading materials. Therefore, some educators have urged the publication of more books with strong and positive portrayals of female characters (Maher, Wade, and Moore 1997; Enciso et al. 1999). However, many parents and teachers are concerned with reluctant male readers who need much enticement and encouragement to get them to read. They keep requesting more adventurous books for boys to motivate these reluctant readers. Temple (1993) wonders "how much is the cause of girls' empowerment being forfeited for the sake of stimulating reluctant boys to read?" (90).

Motivating male readers and empowering female readers are not mutually exclusive acts. I believe that we can accomplish both goals by selecting books that boys and girls enjoy reading. They like stories in which the characters are powerful, resourceful, and active. There is little indication that boys will reject the books if the female protagonists are the ones who possess such qualities, provided that the male characters are not portrayed in a negative way. In order to empower female readers and to motivate male readers, the key is to look for stories with dynamic female characters and action-packed plots. Here are a few good examples:

- In Philip Pullman's *The Firework-Maker's Daughter* (1999), Lila is determined to seek the royal sulfur from the sacred volcano so that she will become a master in firework just like her father. She overcomes pirates, demons, and severe hardship in her journey. Intermediate readers will be enticed by the suspenseful plot and find delight in Pullman's lively descriptions of innovative firework arrangements. Lila's passion and courage will inspire all, and the female readers will be empowered to see that a girl can rank among the masters in a nontraditional career choice.

- Louise Erdrich fills her first novel for young readers, *The Birchbark House* (1999), with daily activities in a traditional Ojibwa tribe in the 1850s. Omakayas is a mischievous and spirited girl who talks to bears and keeps a black crow as a pet. She is independent and resourceful, and eventually takes care of her family during a smallpox epidemic. Omakayas's strong and powerful father also suffers from the illness. Erdrich shows that even a male leader of the family has moments of weakness in times of trouble. This proud figure is also capable of gratitude and appreciation when he openly acknowledges the achievement of his daughter. Omakayas is both nourishing and fearless in her nature. Her father reveals the coexistence of humility and pride in a man. Erdrich's sensitive portrayal of human characters will speak to both female and male readers.

- Young readers love mysteries with unpredictable plots. *Who Are You?* (1999) is Joan Lowery Nixon's latest novel in her mystery series for young adults.

Kristi Evans is involved in an attempted murder whose victim keeps a file of her pictures and artworks. The fast-paced novel with its unexpected plot will capture the attention of readers throughout the book. Reluctant male readers will love Nixon's thrillers, whose female protagonists will empower female readers because of the active, problem-solving, and adventurous qualities these women possess.

- In *A Blizzard Year* (1999) by Gretel Ehrlich, thirteen-year-old Timmy helps her family run their cattle ranch. Although the ranch life is harsh and physically demanding, the author never suggests that Timmy is held back from certain tasks due to her gender. The ongoing activities in the ranch appeal to both male and female readers. The ending will especially delight young people who work with computers, showing how technology saves the ranch from its economic trouble.

- Patricia Polacco's *Mrs. Mack* (1998) is an action-filled picture book about young Patricia's summer horse-riding lessons. Many young readers can identify with Patricia's love of animals. Mrs. Mack, the competent teacher, is a hero in the story. She is strong and caring, in control and passionate, providing a well-balanced role model for young people.

Very often, classroom instruction reinforces stereotypes in books. Although teachers have the power to change "gender-appropriate" behavior and attitudes, many seem blind to the opportunity (Fox 1993a). Male and female teachers alike have been conditioned to see and read literature in certain unquestioned ways. In literature discussion, teachers tend to perpetuate "the privileging and naturalizing of a male perspective," leaving many questions unexamined (Page and Townsend 1999, 48). Teachers who introduce literature by trailblazing women and/or with female protagonists usually encounter opposition from colleagues and students (Slack 1999).

In order to challenge gender stereotypes in children's literature, we must change classroom instruction that allows such notions to prevail. McCracken (1992) observes that boys read as boys and girls read as boys in the current literature curriculum. "No one, not even girls, gets much practice reading as girls" (55). She suggests that teachers should teach girls and boys to read as girls. One way is to provide students with different stories in which girls have space to express their feelings. There are thought-provoking books that teachers can use to stimulate class discussion to combat gender stereotypes. For young readers, Kathryn Cristaldi's *Baseball Ballerina* (1992) is about a girl who prefers baseball to ballet. In Leslea Newman's *Heather Has Two Mommies* (1989), Heather has two caring mothers who are lesbians. Judith Vigna's *I Live with Daddy* (1997) portrays a divorced couple with the father being the caretaker. For readers in the intermediate grades, the unconventional grandmother in Nina Bawden's *Granny the Pag* (1996) is an inspiration to her granddaughter. Carol Coman's *What Jamie Saw* (1995) shows both the fear and the strength of Jamie and his mother in an abusive relationship. Ntozake Shange's *White Wash* (1997) deals with hate crime suffered by an African American girl. For older readers, Laurie Halse

Anderson's *Speak* (1999) is a powerful book on the numbing and guilt-ridden year of a thirteen-year-old rape victim. Francesca Lia Block's *I Was a Teenage Fairy* (1998) opens up the world of teenage supermodels with its sexual exploitations behind the glitter and glamour. Sharon Flake's *The Skin I'm In* (1998) tells how a girl's self-esteem is tied with her skin color. Marie Lee's *Finding My Own Voice* (1992) reveals the struggle of a Korean American girl to be her own person. Jackie Woodson's *If You Come Softly* (1998) deals with the tension of an interracial courtship, portraying a African American young man who is gentle and sensitive.

These books reflect both the gender biases in our society and the ability of individuals to conquer such barriers. Louise Rosenblatt (1938) offers advice on overcoming gender stereotypes with teacher guidance. "By helping to focus the student's attention upon the actual emotions through which he has entered into the lives of others, the teacher can reinforce the power of literature to develop social imagination" (187). In the classroom, students can create a chart mapping the ups and downs of the protagonists' emotions. How does societal pressure influence the emotional life of the characters? How will the characters react if they are of a different gender? How will people treat them if they are of a different gender? What will happen to these characters if they behave in ways against other people's expectations? I believe that these open-ended questions will shape students' mental framework to comprehend the gender battle raging in characters' lives.

Then vs. Now

The portrayal of androgyny appears to be a predominant dimension of the recent award-winning picture books (Dellmann-Jenkins, Florjancic, and Swadener 1993). Females have received more positive evaluation than males in Caldecott Medal and Honor books with no difference in the number of central roles (Turner-Bowker 1996). Turner-Bowker (1996) considers these progressions in gender representation as forms of modern discrimination: "In modern discrimination, the overt behaviors expressed through feelings of prejudice toward a certain group have changed, but the underlying problem remains" (474). Is it true progression when award-winning books present female characters handling household-oriented artifacts similar to their counterparts fifty years ago (Crabb and Bielawski 1994)? Is there real improvement when female characters are described more positively because they fulfill stereotyped roles? Although women all over the world are breaking traditional stereotypes, this is clearly not reflected in children's literature. Children do not receive an accurate picture of contemporary life in award-winning books. There is an overgeneralization of historically based gender bias to contemporary children's literature.

Despite the fact that there are contemporary stories written by female authors with strong female characters, teachers still select books consistent with their ideology. Most of them may not consider gender factors when they select books for their students (Luke, Cooke, and Luke 1986). When Mem Fox (1993a) gave her college students a chance to write the beginning of a children's book, most of them chose to make their main character male. Fox (1993a) concludes that men and women are greatly conditioned in gender constraints. Many teachers accept the traditional gender roles in historical fiction. They enjoy the comfort in dwelling on the well-defined gender roles in books such as Laura Ingalls Wilder's Little House series. Such acceptance extends to their reading of similar roles in contemporary work.

Teachers can easily combat gender stereotypes by comparing historical fiction and contemporary stories with their students. The first goal is for them to discuss the presentation of gender identities and roles. They might consider presenting Laura Ingalls Wilder with Maria Kunstadter's *Women Working A to Z* (1994), which depicts women of different ages and ethnicity holding traditional and unusual jobs. Caroline Bauer's *My Mom Travels a Lot* (1981) provides another useful contrast. Alice Mead's *Soldier Mom* (1999) will further the discussion of the work of today's mothers. A second objective is for teachers to examine how traditional presentations have conditioned students' expectations of gender-related behaviors and the values they attribute to those behaviors. Teachers can introduce historical accounts focusing on the women's experience to challenge students to reevaluate their expectations. *Women of the West* (1988) by Rick Steber for students in elementary school and *Women of the West* (1982) by Cathy Luchetti and Carol Olwell for older students are good examples to use. Both books portray women who "cooked, sewed, complained, and nurtured—all the while living their lives under unbelievably hard circumstances" (Luchetti and Olwell 1982, 14). These women were a spirited lot, loving and caring, strong and independent, active and resourceful. They stepped away from the strictly established social boundaries. The westward migration allowed them more freedom "to stretch their wings and explore the realm of their experience. And in the process they tamed the wild West" in their own ways (Steber 1988, 1).

Teachers can select historical fiction and biographies to reshape students' understanding of gender roles. Karen Cushman's *The Ballad of Lucy Whipple* (1996) shows the humor and the courage of a young girl who makes a life in California around 1850. Lensey Namioka's young adult novel *Ties That Bind, Ties That Break* (1999) and Paul Yee's picture book *Roses Sing on New Snow* (1992) can extend classroom discussion on gender roles in the Chinese American community as the women struggle to establish themselves in a new world. McKissack and McKissack's *Sojourner Truth: Ain't I a Woman?* (1992) is a mighty biography of a woman rising from slavery into politics, always proud of her identity as a woman and as an African American. Jeri Ferris's *Native American Doctor: The Story of Susan LaFlesche Picotte* (1991) shows the obstacles that women faced if they wanted to become a doctor in 1886. Susan LaFlesche's ethnicity brought her additional challenge in a hostile world.

In reading historical fiction, teachers should emphasize that women played an important role in family, local, and national development no matter whether they held traditional or unusual jobs. Women in the past were creative, capable, and intelligent. They were not lame individuals waiting to be served and rescued. In contrast, as the above literature titles have demonstrated, women of various cultural groups were pioneers in building a new life for their people to turn the uncertain world into a promised land.

There vs. Here

Cultural factors increase the complexity of male and female identities in children's literature. Enciso and her colleagues (1999) comment that many writers try to retell traditional tales to satisfy a call for stronger girls or more sensitive boys. They criticize that although Fa Mulan, the heroine in San Souci's Chinese folktale, goes to war and fights bravely in the Disney's movie, her ultimate goal is still male approval. They regret that although books and films claim to offer "progressive, feminist stories for young audiences, [they] ultimately retain traditional images, metaphors, and narrative structures" (286).

I believe that rewriting traditional tales for strong female roles does not justify the unintended result of onslaught of cultural values within the historical setting. The tale of Fa Mulan is a story of a woman who dares to be different against certain customs of her culture and her time. She defies the image of the passive Oriental female (Lee 1999). She is a woman warrior, a classic character type in Chinese culture and film that is "an independent outsider, resolute and aggressive in her efforts to institute correct order" (Berry 1988, 68). In the original version, Fa Mulan's action receives strong support from her family. Disney's Mulan acts independently against the wishes of her parents. Such individualism in decision making would have violated the Chinese honor code of her time. To the Chinese and Chinese American audience, Disney's eagerness to create a strong-willed female fails to appreciate Mulan's struggle to reconstruct her gender role within the cultural constraints. Ironically, Disney's revised Mulan still falls short of the Western ideals of a strong female to some American audiences (Enciso et al. 1999). However, why should we temper the authenticity of gender portrayals in cross-cultural traditional tales to satisfy today's audience? Young readers will never understand the progress achieved if adults lie to them about situations in the past. Why should we use Western norms to measure cultural values in other parts of the world? Young readers need to realize and accept the diversity of gender roles among cultural groups.

Instead of condemning or accepting the gender roles as portrayed in books on different cultures, we should use literature as a window to explore diversity in gender identities. For example, Omar Castaneda's *Among the Volcanoes* (1991), Judith Ortiz Cofer's *Silent Dancing: A Partial Remembrance of a Puerto Rican Childhood* (1990), Adeline Yen Mah's *Chinese Cinderella* (1999), Suzanne Fisher Staples's *Shabanu: Daughter of the Wind* (1989), and Yoshiko Uchida's *Picture Bride* (1988) provide wonderful materials for students to read and to discuss the culturally engendered self of the female characters.

Conclusions

Gender is both culturally and individually constructed (Beall 1993). It takes great effort for an individual to explore and to question the well-established cultural norms regarding gender. Questioning the values and attitudes associated with one's gender role may threaten a person's identity and worldview. This potential impact may cause indifference and resistance to any effort that brings disturbance to a person's core identity. In order to challenge gender stereotypes in children's literature and in people producing and reading these books, we need to proceed with patience and sensitivity. Future research should focus on cross-cultural gender roles in books for young people. The results will inform us of the universal barriers and the unique difficulties that men and women face when they seek to live beyond the gender-based expectations of their people.

References

BEALL, A. E. 1993. "A Social Constructivist View of Gender." In *The Psychology of Gender*, ed. A. E. Beall & R. J. Sternberg. 127–47. New York: The Guilford Press.

BERRY, C. 1988. "The Sublimate Text: Sex and Revolution in Big Road." *East-West Film Journal* 2: 66–86.

BRUNER, J. 1986. *Actual Minds, Possible Worlds*. Cambridge, MA: Harvard University Press.

CRABB, P. B., & D. BIELAWSKI. 1994. "The Social Representation of Material Culture and Gender in Children's Books." *Sex Roles* 30: 69–79.

DEAUX, K., & M. KITE. 1993. "Gender Stereotypes." In *Psychology of Women: A Handbook of Issues and Theories*, ed. F. L. Denmark & M. A. Paludi, 107–39. Westport, CT: Greenwood.

DELLMANN-JENKINS, M., L. FLORJANCIC, & E. B. SWADENER. 1993. "Sex Roles and Cultural Diversity in Recent Award-Winning Picture Books for Young Children." *Journal of Research in Childhood Education* 7: 74–82.

ENCISO, P., T. ROGERS, E. MARSHALL, C. TYSON, & C. JENKINS. 1999. "Gender Representations: Reaching Beyond the Limits We Make." *The New Advocate* 12: 285–97.

ERNST, S. B. 1995. "Gender Issues in Books for Children and Young Adults. In *Battling Dragons: Issues and Controversy in Children's Literature*, ed. S. Lehr, 66–78. Portsmouth, NH: Heinemann.

FOX, M. 1993a. "Men Who Weep, Boys Who Dance: The Gender Agenda Between the Lines in Children's Literature." *Language Arts* 70: 84–88.

———. 1993b. "Politics and Literature: Chasing the 'isms' from Children's Books." *The Reading Teacher,* 46, 654–58.

JACKLIN, C. N., & E. E. MACCOBY, 1978. "Social Behavior at 33 Months in Same-Sex and Mixed-Sex Dyads. *Child Development* 49: 557–69.

KORTENHAUS, C. J., & J. DEMAREST, 1993. "Gender Role Stereotyping in Children's Literature: An Update." *Sex Roles* 28: 219–32.

LEE, C. 1999. "Mulan: Woman Warrior as Embodied Ambiguity." [Online]. Available FTP: http://www.sshe.murdoch.edu.au/hum/as/intersections/current2/Mulanreview.html

LUKE, A., J. COOKE, & C. LUKE. 1986. "The Selective Tradition in Action: Gender Bias in Student Teachers' Selections of Children's Literature." *English Education* 18: 209–18.

MAHER, A., B. WADE, & M. MOORE. 1997. "Goslob Is a Boy's Name." *English in Education* 31: 24–35.

McCRACKEN, N. M. 1992. "Re-Gendering the Reading of Literature." In *Gender Issues in the Teaching of English*, ed. N. M. McCracken & B. C. Appleby. 55–68. Portsmouth, NH: Heinemann.

PAGE, B. G., & J. S. TOWNSEND. 1999. "Gender Roles: Listening to Classroom Talk About Literary Characters. *Language Arts* 88: 43–49.

ROSENBLATT, L. 1938. *Literature as Exploration*. New York: Noble.

RUDMAN, M. 1995. *Children's Literature: An Issues Approach* (3rd ed.). White Plains, NY: Longman.

ST. PIERRE, E. A. 1999. "A Historical Perspective on Gender." *English Journal* 88: 29–34.

SLACK, D. B. 1999. "Why Do We Need to Genderize? Women's Literature in High School." *English Journal* 88: 91–95.

TEMPLE, C. 1993. "'What if "Beauty" Had Been Ugly?' Reading Against the Grain of Gender Bias in Children's Books." *Language Arts* 70: 89–93.

TETENBAUM, T. J., & J. PEARSON. 1989. "The Voices in Children's Literature: The Impact of Gender in the Moral Decisions of Storybook Characters." *Sex Roles* 20: 381–95.

TURNER-BOWKER, D. M. 1996. "Gender Stereotype Descriptors in Children's Picture Books: Does 'Curious Jane' Exist in Literature?" *Sex Roles* 35 (7/8): 461–88.

Children's Literature

ANDERSON, L. H. 1999. *Speak*. New York: Farrar, Straus & Giroux.

BAUER, C. F. 1981. *My Mom Travels a Lot*. New York: Puffin.

BAWDEN, N. 1996. *Granny the Pag*. New York: Clarion.

BLOCK, F. L. 1998. *I Was a Teenage Fairy*. New York: HarperCollins.

CASTANEDA, O. S. 1991. *Among the Volcanoes*. New York: Bantam Doubleday Dell.

COFER, J. O. 1990. *Silent Dancing: A Partial Remembrance of a Puerto Rican Childhood*. Houston, TX: Arte Público Press.

COMAN, C. 1995. *What Jamie Saw*. Arden, NC: Front Street.

CRISTALDI, K. 1992. *Baseball Ballerina*. New York: Random House.

CUSHMAN, K. 1996. *The Ballad of Lucy Whipple*. New York: Clarion.

EHRLICH, G. 1999. *A Blizzard Year*. New York: Hyperion.

ERDRICH, L. 1999. THE BIRCHBARK HOUSE. NEW YORK: HYPERION.

FERRIS, J. 1991. *Native American Doctor: The Story of Susan LaFlesche Picotte*. New York: Carolrhoda.

FLAKE, S. G. 1998. *The Skin I'm In*. New York: Hyperion.

Fox, M. 1988. *With Love, at Christmas*. Nashville, TN: Abingdon Press.

Kunstadter, M. A. 1994. *Women Working A to Z*. New York: Highsmith.

Lee, M. G. 1992. *Finding My Own Voice*. Boston: Houghton Mifflin.

Luchetti, C., & C. Olwell. 1982. *Women of the West*. New York: Crown.

Mah, A. Y. 1999. *Chinese Cinderella*. New York: Delacorte.

Mead, L. 1999. *Soldier Mom*. New York: Farrar, Straus & Giroux.

McKissack, P. C., & F. McKissack, 1992. *Sojourner Truth: Ain't I a Woman?* New York: Scholastic.

Namioka, L. 1999. *Ties That Bind, Ties That Break*. New York: Delacorte.

Newman, L. 1989. *Heather Has Two Mommies*. New York: Alyson Wonderland.

Nixon, J. L. 1999. *Who Are You?* New York: Bantam.

Polacco, P. 1998. *Mrs. Mack*. New York: Philomel.

Pullman, P. 1999. *The Firework-Maker's Daughter*. New York: Scholastic.

San Souci, R. 1998. *Fa Mulan*. New York: Hyperion.

Shange, N. 1997. *White Wash*. New York: Walker.

Staples, S. F. 1989. *Shabanu: Daughter of the Wind*. New York: Knopf.

Steber, R. 1988. *Women of the West*. Prineville, OR: Bonanza Publishing.

Uchida, Y. 1988. *Picture Bride*. New York: Simon & Schuster.

Vigna, J. 1997. *I Live with Daddy*. Morton Grove, IL: Albert Whitman.

Woodson, J. 1998. *If You Come Softly*. New York: Penguin Putnam.

Yee, P. 1992. *Roses Sing on New Snow*. New York: Macmillan.

Author Profile

Alice Mead

"America has lost its boys!" trumpets an alarmed psychologist on the Oprah Winfrey show, following the school shootings at Littleton, Colorado, and Jonesboro, Arkansas. As we watch the violence unfold on CNN, we cry out as a nation, "How could these boys do this to other children? What are their hearts and souls like? What are their parents like?"

In seeing children who resort to violence as different or "other," we wonder what has happened to their characters. Meanwhile, we carefully maintain our own family myth of comfort, distance, and safety from what we fear are dangerous circumstances. These are kids, without fail, who are in pain, isolated. They don't fit in and are easy to ignore. By failing to acknowledge our connections with them, we don't acknowledge that the excruciating pain and danger that the world's children experience is present everywhere, even in our own well-protected homes. Pain happens. So does joy and silliness. And grief.

To develop a broad capacity for empathy, children need stories with characters that guide them through a variety of startling, wild, and joyous experiences in ways and places they never expected to find themselves. In this way, reading itself is an odyssey and remains a crucial part of our development, timeless and necessary despite rapid advances in electronic communications.

Constantly upgraded, society's fast-paced lifestyle is unavoidable, and by now has had a profound effect on children and their family life. Working parents and full schedules further place a strain on free time. If parents abandon their kids to the maze of information on the computer screen or television screen, family relationships can become eroded. Author Russell Banks writes tellingly of this familial loss of connectedness and the resulting violent consequences in his novel *Continental Drift* (1985).

> Knowledge of the facts [of Bob's life and death] changes nothing in the world. Our celebrating his life and grieving over his death, however, will. Good cheer and mournfulness over lives other than our own, even wholly invented lives, no, especially wholly invented lives, deprive the world as it is of some of the greed it needs to continue to be itself. (366)

Heroes, however, must reach out to others and change the status quo. Heroic characters must pass through the inner feelings and dynamics of family relationships and discover their true personal history, which is the starting point of character. According to James Hillman in his book *The Soul's Code* (1996), a family story is not one of cause and effect, but one of deepening of character, a discovery of increasingly complex, widening, and differentiated feelings and understanding. When we are indifferent to our own egocentricity, we fail to recognize the consequences of our words and actions; we stray toward violence to communicate hurt, fear, and rage.

Feeling is growing, and all children must grow. They have no choice! The true job of a child-hero is to learn to feel and be aware of his or her own personal history as deeply and fully as possible. Eventually this knowledge will lead the child to an awareness that transcends both gender and ethnicity, creating in a moment of recognition a bond of unity.

We are accustomed to think of sensory experience as appropriate for childhood—how a grapefruit tastes, what fuzz feels like. But the other realm of feeling is that of emotional relationship and the basic mythical dynamics within family roles. Repression of these experiences, if they remain unfelt and unvoiced, will result in inappropriate emotions being triggered and interrupting us throughout life, controlling our interactions, as a need projected onto others (Miller 1981). If we force these uncomfortable feelings from our lives, these passions reemerge as insensitivity and violence.

In ancient times, myths told stories of loss or being lost. Through bravery and sacrifice, the hero gradually recognized his flaw and found redemption and wholeness. But this took time. It required heroic voyages to the unknown, to the ends of the earth and even beyond. Odysseus went all the way to Hades to gain wisdom from his dead mother before he could return to earth and regain his proper relationships with his wife, son, and kingdom. Until he went to the depths of hell, faced his past, and returned, his character remained undeveloped.

The overriding myth of the American family in this technological era is one of disconnectedness and rampant consumerism. The "American dream" is of possessing a single-family home, in which each family accrues its own material items year by year. These objects give the family status within the community through a display of ownership. But this dream immediately sets up a situation of "haves" and "have nots." Where will children experience fear, joy, loss, and survival? And how can this dream create the kind of heroism and sense of sacrifice necessary for kids' moral growth, so that one day they will be ready to bravely face fear and mortality, to bridge racial chasms and conflicts, to live in poverty if that's what it takes to bring justice to the far corners of the world or even next door?

The freshness and vitality of children's literature has to do with the fact that children implicitly dwell at the heart of mythology and its differentiation. They are on the verge of discovering new relationships, past and future, that may break or at least confront traditional social roles and thus nudge the world forward just a little. I hoped that Junebug would change the world just a little with his freshness and determination to explore the unknown.

I have always had a fascination with boats and islands, and I gave that sense of longing and hope for discovery to my young male hero. When I wrote *Junebug* (1995),

I hoped one day it would be a trilogy, and that Junebug would emerge as heroic in the classic sense of a young man in search of his father. Junebug is drawn to the water and the unknown. He gets his nickname from the fact that he always asks questions regardless of the consequences as he tries to make sense of his world. The emphasis on the image of shattered glass in windows and along the gutters early in the book gradually shifts as Junebug prepares his flotilla of fifty bottles and corks, each containing his secret wish for sailing lessons. He launches them on his birthday—fifty tiny journeys—floating off to seek connections. He knows instinctively that he must get beyond the Auburn Street projects.

He lives in the isolation of an inner-city housing project, and grows even further isolated when his only guide, an older boy named Darnell, leaves the area to escape from a vengeful drug dealer. Meanwhile, danger visits the family, not from a black male character—as our unexamined cultural mythology would have us believe—but from Junebug's troublesome young aunt, Jolita, who gave up on her dreams years before. Without dreams or a sense of direction, she drifts into increasingly dangerous relationships, ones that are in danger of harming her family.

When I visit schools, I am very gratified to hear third-, fourth-, and fifth-grade students discuss not only Junebug but many of the secondary characters as well—Darnell, whose loss they feel acutely, Jolita and her betrayal of the family for her friends, and the stubborn dignity of little five-year-old Tasha.

Character development and growth is demonstrated in relationships, in how we treat each other. Interactions with each of these secondary characters shows Junebug's increased sense of self, his direction. The McClain family is one where each character's integrity must be explored. In the third book, Junebug's determination will lead him to ask questions about his father, directly challenging his mother's attempt to shield him from this painful knowledge.

The uniquely vital role of children's literature is that the story is all about portraying the essence of the child-hero, whose dignity is honored, observed, and restored. This integrity, then, is the heart of a child's character. In *Junebug*, I wanted Tasha to take a step forward, too. I like Tasha a lot, because even though she's shy, she never lets her dignity be compromised. Near the end, she overcomes her timidity and gives the ferry captain one of Junebug's last bottles with his wish inside.

Characters that live and act in the realm of heroism pass through danger (real or imagined, with or without guides as Odysseus had Athena), loss, and then return to dignity. These characters are not bound by gender or ethnic group; they transcend it. While writers must be mindful of being ethnically sensitive and inclusive, the true tests of character are, like Odysseus's, timeless and universal ones, particularized by a certain place, plot, and setting.

In *Adem's Cross* (1996), set in the western mountains of Kosovo, in the former Yugoslavia, Adem and family live in a harsh, dangerous, and lawless society. Under the rule of a brutal Serb apartheid system, a system entirely without civil rights for Albanians, Fatmira, his older sister, wants to re-create her right to free speech by reading a poem about the power of children and their timeless ability to restore justice.

Standing on an ancient Ottoman bridge in the historic city of Prizren, she acts fearlessly and heroically, but she is gunned down in front of Adem and his little sister.

At her funeral, the Albanians treat her as a martyr, a symbol of their plight. After the funeral, the police arrive in the middle of the night, and beat Adem's father severely. In Kosovo, both the oppressor and the oppressed lose their individuality and are treated as ideological symbols, rather than as characters who can grow, develop, and make meaningful choices of their own. Without the process of individuation, they all, regardless of their ethnic group, live in a society with no future. This becomes the question Adem faces. How will he create a future for himself, and eventually a future for his little sister and his family?

Adem becomes obsessed with wondering what makes the Serb police act the way they do. How can they carelessly and indifferently commit such senseless acts of brutality? He feels compelled to find out and searches their living quarters, trying to locate a diary, a letter, photos of their families, anything that will indicate their inner thoughts and feelings. He finds nothing—only beer, cigarettes, and a deck of cards, things they need to numb themselves from what they are doing, things to help pass the monotony and isolation of their time in Kosovo.

The soldiers discover him searching through their things. In an act meant to destroy his identity as an Albanian, they carve the Serb cross on his chest.

The only heroic choice left to Adem at the end of the novel is for him to ease his family's burdens by sacrificing his own safety and escaping to Albania through the mountains. This selfless voyage, literally into the unknown and marked by the death of his friend Fikel, will eventually lead him to a freer world with restored human rights and dignity. When he achieves this renewed power, he hopes to return and save his family.

As Russell Banks stated, the path to growth and meaningful relationships with others, especially those we do not readily understand, is through caring, not only in the sensory and factual world, but also in the world of the imagination through the act of reading. As librarian Tim Wadham (1999) states, "Despite our leap into the digital age . . . stories still matter . . . Books are a defense against the collapse of literacy in the electronic age" (445).

Young readers need, as they have always needed, to travel this path over and over again, to visit new particulars in time and place. With stories as a guide to light our way, to reduce fear and anxiety, kids and their parents will gain a more profound empathy and understanding of "the other." And that is humanity's most vital and marvelous task.

References

BANKS, R. 1985. *Continental Drift*. New York: HarperCollins.

HILLMAN, J. 1996. *The Soul's Code*. New York: Random House.

HOMER. *The Odyssey*. 1999. Translated by W. H. Rouse. New York: Signet.

MILLER, A. 1981. *Drama of the Gifted Child*. New York: Basic Books.

WADHAM, T. 1999. "Plot Does Matter." *The Horn Book Magazine* (July/August), 445.

Children's Literature

MEAD, A. 1996. *Adem's Cross*. New York: Farrar, Straus & Giroux.

———. 1995. *Junebug*. New York: Farrar, Straus & Giroux.

Author Profile

PAT MORA

Autumn in Northern New Mexico is glorious. The breeze is warm, the sky blue and immense. Prickly pears display their ruby globes, cottonwoods rattle their gold, and the roasting of green chiles scents the air. Not often enough, I push myself away from my computer and sit on a boulder outside, staring into the pond of this rented house. I'm learning from this watery mirror. Like any good writer, the pond waits patiently, accepts what appears. The pond, like the page, helps me notice and reflect, refreshes me, focuses my gaze and releases my imagination. Watching the pale minnows, I begin to construct stories about their underwater lives—bilingual, of course. I peer, hoping for a glimpse of the elusive bullfrog that serenaded us so boldly until a few weeks ago, my summer brush with unrequited love.

I am teaching at the University of New Mexico this fall, trying to breathe deeply, ingest the Southwest landscape that though dry so feeds my spirit, my writing. I began to devote significant time and energy to my writing about twenty years ago in my hometown of El Paso and have learned to move back and forth between writing projects for adults and children. Some days here, I'm writing what I've tentatively titled "Adobe Odes" for an adult book, odes to bullfrogs, a pond, a bumblebee,

> weaving from [his] dark,
> rumpled den into the morning
> light, nodding shamefaced,
> tipping [his] battered hat
> at disapproving neighbors,
> those industrious ants
> who shake their heads,
> skinny limbs akimbo
> at [his] perceived laziness . . .

I learn "delirious dedication" from the Bumble [bumblebee], and I experience the wonder of diversity in the garden around the pond. How the variety enriches my days, the seasonal bloomings, the aromatic unfolding of roses, the abundant, open-faced cosmos, and now the chrysanthemums, autumn wine.

I cherish diversity in the natural world as well as on the canvas, stage, page, the swoop out of my skin-bound self. Books help me cross borders. Until I was an adult reader, the lives and homes I entered on the page didn't include families like mine that spoke English and Spanish. Now all our children and young adults can enjoy the art of Carmen Lomas Garza and Edward González, the photography of George Ancona, the stories of Rudolfo Anaya, Sandra Cisneros, Victor Martínez, and Francisco Jiménez, the poetry of Gary Soto and Francisco Alarcón, among other Mexican American authors. On April 30th we can participate in Día de los niños: Día de los libros, a daylong celebration of a yearlong commitment to linking all children to books, languages, cultures.

Why we write and what I write can be both clear and mysterious. I love the mystery most. Perhaps because I'm thinking about odes, I see that my children's books are praise songs, many to the desert landscape and its resourceful denizens—horned toads, snakes, cactus, people. Family relationships interest me, whether the affection between the grandfather and his adopted grandson in *Pablo's Tree* (1994) or the affection between Carlos and his aunt in *The Gift of the Poinsettia: El Regalo de la Flor de Nochebuena* (1995). My aunt and my youngest daughter star in the first children's book, *A Birthday Basket for Tía* (1992), and my mother and grandmother star in *The Rainbow Tulip* (1999); the young in each are sustained by a devoted relative.

I think about *Tulip* often. How is it being treated in its first months in the world? Do people hold it with care? Is it receiving enough oxygen, i.e., attention, to survive? Will it find a place in people's hearts, for it's that soft yet sturdy home I want for my books. Although I write and speak about the importance of having books by Latinos in libraries, bookstores, and schools, and I do think that is vital in our multicultural society, secretly I want my books not only in public spaces, but also in private places. I want the books to live long lives deep inside the reader.

Most of us like the old stories, myths, legends, all part of our human legacy. How the translator and I struggled with *The Night the Moon Fell* (2000b) (Spanish edition, *La noche que se calló la luna*), a second Mayan myth I've retold, revising the tale for years, initially fascinated by the basic story. Long ago, the Maya say, the moon fell into the sea. The tiniest fish helped her return to the sky and then remained, swimming the sky in their net, the filmy Milky Way.

But how passive should the moon be in a story published in the year 2000? Ah, the play of text and context. I'm a strong feminist and stare with attention at spunky girls, probably because I have a very spunky mom and daughters. I pondered the fine line between what initially interested me, the poetry of the story if you will, and how my work would be interpreted by young readers. The moon had made a mythic journey, I realized over time, and could not only participate in composing her broken self but also return to her sky-home transformed, with new songs to sing. She says to the little fish,

> All you need is part of you,
> Ask yourself what you should do.

And, of course, as friends do, they gently remind her to heed her own words.

The gender of my main characters seems to evolve naturally. Pablo, Carlos, and Tomás in *Tomás and the Library Lady* (1997) all find strength and comfort in family. They are boys I'd like to have around—curious, funny, sensitive, like my son. Tomás, of course, is a praise-song to a Mexican-American academic and intellectual who began life a migrant worker in Texas. The intent for that book included the desire to have people know the name Tomás Rivera, to remind children that leaders don't always come from wealthy families or English-speaking families, and to remind librarians and teachers that they can change a child's life.

Georgia O'Keeffe said she painted those giant blooms to focus our attention, and that's one of my motivations for portraying inventive Mexican American girls, the strength and resilience I encounter and respect, not the stereotypes too often perpetuated. Daily, then, in addition to thinking about *The Rainbow Tulip* and *The Night the Moon Fell*, I'm thinking about the manuscript, recently finished, *A Library for Juana*, on Mexico's most famous woman poet, the amazing Sor Juana Inéz de la Cruz, an icon in Mexico who even appears on thousand-peso bills, revered throughout the Spanish-speaking world, a seventeenth-century nun who wrote plays and songs in addition to complex poetry. How sad that I never heard about her when I was in school and college, but when I did finally discover her brilliant essay on women's right to an intellectual life, I became fascinated by a woman determined to learn to read at the ripe old age of three. I've enjoyed reading a poem about her to high school and college students these last years, telling them about this Mexican woman's delight in learning. The poem, titled "The Young Sor Juana," begins,

> I'm three and cannot play away my days
> to suit my sweet *mamá*. Sleep well, my dolls,
> for I must run to school behind my sister's frowns.
> for I must learn
> to unknit words and letters, to knit them new
> with my own hand.
>
> (Communion, *1991*)

Now I face the challenge of completing a picture book that connects young, contemporary readers with this brilliant, witty woman, who as a child refused to eat cheese because she heard it dulled the wits.

Teachers and librarians sometimes nudge me into a book. Librarians in the Ohio/Kentucky area asked me some years back why I wrote poetry for adults and not for children. *Confetti* (1996) and *This Big Sky* (1998) evolved. Librarians in California asked a few years ago why I didn't write poetry for teens, which prompted me to compile *My Own True Name: New and Selected Poems for Young Adults* (2000a). The volume contains poems from previous collections that I thought young adults might enjoy, and some new poems I wrote for them, including "Ode to Pizza."

Yeast pillow/sailing/through the green/oregano air . . .

The book also includes a letter in which I urge young writers, "Bring your inside voice out and let us hear you on the page. Come, join the serious and sassy family of writers." I tell them that "I became a writer because words give me so much pleasure that I wanted to sink my hands and heart into them too, to see what I could create, what would rise up, what would appear." That curiosity continues. I look into the pond and the page to see what I'll find, and often I find what I cherish, strong women of all ages, like Doña Flor, the heroine of a new tall tale; like Clara, the protagonist of an evolving novella.

Beginning writers often ask me about writer's block. Well, I've encountered blocks, as does any writer who is perceived as representing a particular group, but the blocks aren't inability to write. I have more ideas than time to pursue them and more manuscripts looking for a home than editors ready to welcome them. This will change when our national colors and cultures are represented in all aspects of the world of children's books—publishers, editors, marketing directors, reviewers, scholars, award committees. Although demographers tell us that soon we will all be minorities, we know that reality won't happen soon or easily in power structures, including the publishing world. Our print legacy sadly is often one of exclusion rather than inclusion. Print is a privilege, access to it and presence in it, having our stories and lives recorded and thus remembered.

Following Gandhi's dictum of being the change we wish to see in the world, each of us can nudge the process along. We can ask necessary questions of publishers, purchase books written by diverse voices and train parents on the importance of this practice, and read a broad array of books to young people that enrich their lives, as the garden enriches mine.

Autumn invites us to harvest, and the harvest that most interests writers is the harvest of stories. We are diversity-rich in these United States—our languages and cultures: our common wealth. In the new millennium, may our literature for children shine in its resplendent complexity and variety. Through tragedy and triumph, may our books portray the many phases and faces of our United States, books of bold beauty.

Children's Literature

MORA, P. 1991. *Communion*. Houston: Arte Público Press.

———. 1992. *A Birthday Basket for Tía*. New York: Simon & Schuster.

———. 1994. *Pablo's Tree*. New York: Simon & Schuster.

———. 1996. *Confetti: Poems for Children*. New York: Lee & Low Books.

———. 1997. *Tomás and the Library Lady*. New York: Knopf.

———. 1998. *This Big Sky*. New York: Scholastic.

———. 1999. *The Rainbow Tulip*. New York: Viking.

———. 2000a. *My Own True Name: New and Selected Poems for Young Adults*. Houston: Piñata Books/Arte Público Press.

———. 2000b. *The Night the Moon Fell*. Toronto: Groundwood Books.

MORA, P., & C. RAMÍREZ BERG. 1995. *The Gift of the Poinsettia: El regalo de la flor de nochebuena*. Houston: Piñata Books.

11

Parent Characters in Children's Novels:
Lessons Learned

SYLVIA M. VARDELL

*He was also very wrong about there not being anything like magic
powers or genies or angels. . . . Maybe they were in the way your
father smiled at you even after you'd messed something up real bad.
Maybe they were in the way you understood that your mother wasn't
trying to make you the laughing "sock" of the whole school when she'd
call you over in front of a bunch of your friends and use spit on her
finger to wipe the sleep out of your eyes. Maybe it was magic powers
that let you know she was just being Momma. Maybe they were the
reason that you really didn't care when the kids would say, "Yuck!
You let your momma slob on you?" and you had to say, "Shut up.
That's my momma, we got the same germs."*

(CURTIS 1995, 204–5)

Kenny talks lovingly about his parents in the excerpt above taken from Christopher
Paul Curtis's wonderful novel, *The Watsons Go to Birmingham—1963*, showing us
through his child's perspective the mutual affection between parent and child. This
highly acclaimed and popular book is an excellent example of a trend in recent years
to weave parent characters into stories for children in ways that are important and
meaningful to the characterization of the protagonist and often to the story's plot. The
father in this novel is the traditional breadwinner of the 1960s setting, firm and
authoritative, but he is also shown to be a man with an abundant sense of humor, a
love of music, and a knack for communicating with his young sons. Likewise, the
mother functions as a nurturing woman who looks after the family's everyday needs,
but she is also strong and opinionated and respected by her husband and family. Both
characters emerge as interesting, multidimensional individuals, and their relationships
with each other and with their children embody a balance of gender attributes and

values. This represents a shift in how parents are being portrayed in children's novels. In the past, parent characters were generally "cookie-cutter" stereotypes who stayed in the story's background.

Parent characters in current children's novels are not always so loving and positive, however. They may also be important to the story in *negative* ways, abusing or abandoning their children and setting in motion stories of survival or healing (Apseloff 1992). These stories may be difficult to read and share because adults are often inclined to want to shelter young readers from pain and suffering. It is important to remember, however, that many children today experience such pain and suffering firsthand and may find comfort, release, and recognition through literature. And, for those children whose lives are more "comfortable," they may find that reading about characters who are experiencing extreme difficulties helps promote a deeper understanding and empathy. It may be painful to read about negative parent role models, but we are well aware that they exist in the real world.

In addition, "parent" characters in recent fiction are not just the child's birth parents anymore. Many novels for young people portray adult caregivers who are not the protagonist's parents but are important and pivotal story characters. Some stories weave together a variety of adult characters as supporting players in the child's growing-up experience. As the African proverb confirms, "It takes a village to raise a child." Mann (1999) found that different role models allow children to see that many kinds of people can serve this function. It can also be comforting to those students who are not part of a nuclear family because they realize that people other than parents can be role models; they show compassion and give comfort to the main characters of the stories but are never themselves the main characters. She continues, "The role models also convey a great deal of understanding for what the children are dealing with and never trivialize their issues or concerns. Students are able to see that someone does understand them and care about them . . . Students need relationships with adults to be able to tap into the wisdom and strength that is there" (Mann 1999).

This trend toward the inclusion of parent characters as essential to the narrative, and the depiction of a variety of types of parent characters in children's novels, is relatively recent (Taylor 1996). In the early part of the twentieth century, children's novels provided a "secure escape," according to Goforth, where "parents were not necessarily well-developed characters, but remained in the background providing safety and security if needed" (1998, 150). "In the past two decades, society and its norms have changed . . . In the Western world, one of the fastest changing social norms is that of the family in which father goes out to work and mother is at home. Though still in existence, this family no longer stands as the measure by which all other family styles are judged. The number of families in which both parents are in the labor force and the number of single-parent families is increasing" (Kinman and Henderson 1985, 885).

Harriet the Spy by Louise Fitzhugh (1964) signaled a turning point in novels for young people (Tomlinson and Lynch-Brown 1996; Jacobs and Tunnell 1996). Here was a girl protagonist who was sometimes unhappy and outcast, and whose well-to-do and busy parents seemed to neglect her. Many contemporary novels that followed, especially the "problem novels," reflected more complicated and challenging aspects of modern life, such as children coping with divorce, disease, death, and so on. Kortenhaus and Demarest (1993) also found a more even distribution of both genders in their analysis of child characters in central roles in books published after 1970. "Contemporary realistic fiction tends to serve as the bellwether for what is acceptable subject matter in children's books . . . changes in the content of children's literature typically appear first in this genre and then spread to others," claim Jacobs and Tunnell (1996, 92). This quality also makes the genre susceptible to censorship, as authors tackle taboos that adults who select books for children may find uncomfortable. "Today, children's literature reflects the variety of philosophies of childhood and child-raising techniques held by adults" (Goforth 1998, 152); some adults may yearn for books that reflect the pre-1960s era of a supposed safe and secure environment, with benign and homogeneous parent characters. A close examination of the Newbery award winners of the 1990s, however, will reveal that parent characters are nearly as varied as the child characters in children's literature, in general. In some cases, parent characters are given traditional gender roles, but still emerge as richly drawn individuals within the narrative. In other examples, the parent characters bend gender expectations in unique ways.

Newbery Award Novels of the 1990s and Beyond

Each year the Association for Library Service to Children Division of the American Library Association chooses one children's book to honor as the "most distinguished contribution to children's literature." It seems natural, therefore, to examine these titles closely as representative of the standards and ideals of their times. For example, Agee (1993) studied Newbery award winners from 1936 and 1981 and found deeply embedded assumptions about gender roles and relationships. Traditional roles for women (and daughters) within the family and in society at large were largely the norm in nearly fifty years of Newbery books. What do the Newbery titles of the nineties tell us about current perceptions of parent roles and gender expectations? In addition, what do we find in children's novels beyond the Newbery winners? In particular, as new authors appear on the publishing scene, with more diverse perspectives given a voice, how are parents and families represented in this writing? How does culture, sexual preference, and/or disability affect the depiction of gender in the newest novels for children?

Strong Parents

Number the Stars

On first examination, one can easily find parent characters in Newbery books who are strong individuals, perhaps traditional in their roles, but admirable in their strength and determination. In addition, they are also strong characters, vividly drawn and pivotal to the story's conflict. Consider *Number the Stars* by Lois Lowry (1989), a historical novel set during Hitler's occupation of Denmark. The protagonist is a ten-year-old girl whose Christian family has suffered the death of the oldest daughter. Still, they hide Annemarie's Jewish friend and participate in the Resistance. Annemarie's parents (as well as other adults) are important characters as the story evolves, interacting with the children as caring and protective parents but as also as coconspirators.

At the climactic point of the story, Annemarie's mother entrusts her with a life-or-death errand. "Annemarie, you understand how dangerous this is. If any soldiers see you, if they stop you, you must pretend to be nothing more than a little girl. A silly, empty-headed little girl, taking lunch to a fisherman, a foolish uncle who forgot his bread and cheese" (1989, 105). Speaking to her young daughter almost as an equal, she charges Annemarie with protecting herself by manipulating the feminine stereotype to her advantage. In doing so, she shows herself to be both the nurturing caregiver and the shrewd problem solver. Hardy claims that feminist novels may do just that: "Instead of the stereotypical rejecting of all that is feminine, these characters emphasize the positive aspects of the gender, including community and compassion" (1999, 2).

At the conclusion of the story, "Annemarie's parents told her the truth about Lise's death at the beginning of the war. 'She was part of the Resistance, too,' Papa had explained. 'Part of the group that fought for our country in whatever ways they could'" (1989, 129–30). These parent characters model strength, compassion, and courage. Though it may be wartime that forces them to become equals with each other and with their children, they clearly communicate the dignity of the individual and the connectedness of community.

Shiloh

Traditional roles also define the parent characters in the Newbery award-winning contemporary novel *Shiloh* by Phyllis Reynolds Naylor (1991). Ma manages the household, Dad manages the money. However, the characters are so vividly drawn that one also sees the strength of the mother, the compassion of the father, among other individual attributes. In fact, Naylor even includes conversations between husband and wife in the story narrative, revealing details about their relationship as well as their parenting. As Ma discovers Marty's hiding of Shiloh, she worries about telling her husband: "Marty, I've got to. He ever finds out about this dog and knows I knew but didn't tell him, how could he trust me? If I keep this one secret from him, he'll think maybe there are more" (1991, 83). In this exchange, she communicates again her strong moral stance, highlighting the quandary Marty has been struggling with in wanting to care for the dog, but having to lie about it. As the story comes to a climax, Marty's parents have clearly expressed their views on what is practical, right, and legal, through their words and their deeds. In the end, Marty himself must resolve the situation and make it right. "Now all we got to worry about is how we can afford to feed him as well as ourselves," Dad says finally. "But there's food for the body and food for the spirit. And Shiloh sure enough feeds our spirit" (1991, 132). In this conclusion, the father is willing to show he's changed his mind, and he supports his son and the rest of the family in their love for this animal. Marty himself has brought about this change.

Listening Fathers

Out of the Dust

Fathers seem to have emerged as the important caregiver in a number of recent Newbery books, often against their wills or in spite of themselves. Gallo (1997) reported an increase in the incidence of single-parent families in children's novels of the 80s and early 90s. These father characters quietly fulfill traditional male roles, but they also gradually take on more "feminine" attributes in the course of the story, such as empathy (and housework!). In *Out of the Dust* by Karen Hesse (1997) Billie Jo's mother is killed in a horrible accident for which she and her father share some responsibility. And, although her mother's stoicism is clearly communicated in the beginning of the story, she and her mother shared a close bond, so after her mother's death, Billie Jo struggles to feel at home with her father. In the end, she leaves. She realizes, however, "Getting away, it wasn't any better. Just different" (204), and she returns to what she now realizes is home. "I thought once to go through these boxes with Ma, but Daddy is sitting on the edge of my bed" (210). Her father listens and watches; he too has come to recognize their special connection. Billie Jo also comes to see that he has dug the pond that his wife had suggested, and he has learned to help out in the kitchen thanks to the influence of a new woman, Louise, his night-school teacher. Both women, as well as his daughter, have helped him learn how to change in order to grow and survive. "And I'm learning, watching Daddy, that you can stay in one place and still grow" (226).

Walk Two Moons

A similar story of the loss of a mother and the bonding of a father and daughter is told in *Walk Two Moons* by Sharon Creech (1994), although in a far different style and tone. Here there are far more characters, each with their own distinctive personalities. And it is a blending of their stories, with a special contribution from Gram and Gramps, that enables Salamanca (the protagonist) to begin to heal. "One day I realized that our whole trip out to Lewiston had been a gift from Gram and Gramps to me. They were giving me a chance to walk in my mother's moccasins—to see what she had seen and feel what she might have felt on her last trip. I also realized that there were lots of reasons why my father didn't take me to Idaho when he got the news of her death. He was too grief-stricken, and he was trying to spare me. Only later did he understand that I had to go and see for myself" (276). This father, too, comes to value his daughter and her love though he still doesn't express it directly. He and Sal return home together to Bybanks, coming full circle through a similar year of pain.

The Giver

Both parents are present in the Utopian fantasy *The Giver* (1993) by Lois Lowry; however, the traditional roles are reversed. The mother is a judge, the father a "Nurturer," or nursery worker. "His mother moved to her big desk and opened her briefcase; her work never seemed to end, even when she was at home in the evening" (19). Both parents are active participants in their children's lives, as mandated by the "perfect" society, but the father's role as a "professional parent" provides more opportunities for connections with children. "The newchild, Gabriel, stirred and whimpered, and Father spoke softly to Lily, explaining the feeding procedure as he opened the container that held the formula and equipment" (25). It is his dilemma in caring for the newborn baby Gabriel, in fact, that becomes the impetus for his son Jonas's daring and courageous act at the conclusion of the book. Neither of his parents, however, serves as the role model Jonas needs. Instead it is another man, the Giver, who genuinely nurtures and guides Jonas, helping Jonas discover his own unique path.

Surrogate Parents

Maniac Magee

In contrast, Jerry Spinelli's Newbery award-winning novel *Maniac Magee* (1990) features an absence of parents. Here the focus is on the child alone, making his way through the world oblivious to adult expectations. Several adult characters act as role models along the way, some in not-so-positive ways. It is independent Amanda Beale and her mother who emerge as a lifeline for Maniac as he searches for a place to call home. After their first encounter, Maniac tells Mr. Beale "he didn't really have a home, unless you counted the deer shed at the zoo. Mr. Beale made a U-turn right there and headed back. Only Mrs. Beale was still downstairs when they walked into the house. She listened to no more than ten seconds' worth of Mr. Beale's explanation before saying to Maniac, 'You're staying here'" (42–43). Both the Beale parents demonstrate a compassion for Maniac that crosses racial and economic boundaries. Maniac himself is nearly gender neutral and color-blind in his natural, almost naïve interaction with others from all segments of the community. "He played with the little ones and read them stories and taught them things . . . he did the dishes without anybody asking. . . . He carried out the trash, mowed the grass, cleaned up his own spills, turned out the lights, put the cap back on the toothpaste tube, flushed the toilet, and . . . kept his room neat" (45–46). Some view *Maniac Magee* as a fantasy or parable, an exaggeration of real life. If Spinelli has indeed created a moral tale, it is interesting to note that his protagonist possesses a balance of the best traits associated with both genders: male strength, independence, and courage; female endurance, compassion, and patience.

Missing May

A similar "adoption" takes place in *Missing May* by Cynthia Rylant (1992). Six-year-old Summer is passed around from one relation to another until her elderly Uncle Ob and Aunt May take her home with them, about whom Summer proclaims, "I never saw two people love each other so much" (3). Somewhat traditional in their roles—May keeps house, Ob creates whirligig sculptures—they are one in their union with Summer. May muses, "So the Lord let us get old so we'd have plenty cause to need you and you'd feel free to need us right back. We wanted a family so bad, all of us. And we just grabbed onto each another and made us one. Simple as that" (87). Both Ob and May are unafraid to express their love or to act on their impulses, and they teach Summer to be an individual. As Trites (1997) claims in *Waking Sleeping Beauty: Feminist Voices in Children's Novels*, "books which empower girls to recognize and claim their subject positions empower the entire culture, for our society can only grow stronger as we teach our children to be stronger" (137).

The Midwife's Apprentice

One final example of the role of the surrogate parent can be found in the 1995 Newbery award winner *The Midwife's Apprentice* by Karen Cushman. Here the protagonist is homeless and nameless at the beginning of the story. Although the era is medieval, the aloneness and rejection the girl experiences feel very contemporary. It is a sharp midwife who comes upon her and offers food for work. This is no loving and sensitive role model. The midwife is all business, with little thought for the girl beyond the work she can contribute. Over time, however, the girl (who names herself Alyce) impresses, even challenges the midwife with her ability to learn and grow. In time, in fact, she earns more than one offer of a home. Deciding her own fate is a brave first step for Alyce, one that takes her from passive village victim to valued contributor to the community. For, as Trites (1997) has stated, "The greatest distinguishing mark of the feminist children's novel is that the character who uses introspection to overcome her oppression almost always overcomes at least part of what is oppressing her" (3). The midwife's competence, her prestige, her special place in the lives of the people, are clearly etched. Interestingly enough, she does not exhibit the usual "feminine" virtues of a role model: patience, caring, and empathy. And yet, Alyce chooses her as mentor and companion. "Feminism's most obvious contribution to children's literature lies in the ways that female protagonists have been liberated from inevitably growing into passivity" (Trites 1997, 11).

Peers as Parents

One other trend in recent children's fiction is an emphasis on the power of the peer group to help or hurt each other. The protagonist(s) must struggle with issues of identity within a social, not familial, context. Parents and other adults may be present in the story, but they do not generally exert a significant influence on the story's outcome. Perhaps as Harris (1998) has recently hypothesized, the role of peers is more significant in a child's growing up than the role of parents. If that is true, it is definitely worth studying literary examples of "peers as parents" more closely.

Holes

In *Holes* by Louis Sachar (1998), Stanley's parents are loving, if largely ineffectual. "Stanley's father was an inventor. To be a successful inventor you need three things: intelligence, perseverance, and just a little bit of luck. Stanley's father was smart and had a lot of perseverance. Once he started a project he would work on it for years, often going days without sleep. He just never had any luck. . . . Despite their awful luck, they always remained hopeful. As Stanley's father liked to say, 'I learn from failure'" (8–9). His mother sends affectionate, if clueless, letters from home. Stanley easily deceives her about the true nature of the camp he is attending, out of a rather adult desire to protect her. "Dear Stanley, [his mother writes] It was wonderful to hear from you. Your letter made me feel like one of the other moms who can afford to send their kids to summer camp. I know it's not the same, but I am very proud of you for trying to make the best of a bad situation. Who knows? Maybe something good will come of this. . . . Love from both of us" (75). The other adults in the story are camp employees—Mr. Pendanski, Mr. Sir, and the Warden. They seem to embody evil itself; they taunt, belittle, and abuse the boys.

It is the boys at camp who "parent" Stanley, not in the usual way of nurturing the young, but in an almost tribal fashion with trials and tests of mental and physical challenge. The boys, Zero, X-Ray, Armpit, Zigzag, and Squid, create a collective that is not always pleasant, but is rather representative of the dynamics of the adult workplace. Stanley does grow up, and on his own terms. He returns to a more "normal" or balanced environment as stronger, clearer, freed from the family curse. Armpit offers him these parting words, "Now you be careful out in the real world. Not everybody is as nice as us" (221).

The View from Saturday

The View from Saturday by E. L. Konigsburg (1996), by contrast, is full of well-intentioned adult characters: the teacher and sponsor of the Academic Bowl team, Mrs. Olinski, several parents and grandparents, the principal, and other administrators. There are even connections among the grandparents of the four protagonists, Julian, Noah, Nadia, and Ethan, who float in and out of the story. It is these four children themselves, however, who develop a special bond that transcends the adults around them. Their points of view punctuate the narrative. Their interactions move the story actively forward. It is their relationship the reader follows amidst the exposition of adult perspectives and advice. Most of the major adult characters in the novel serve to empower the child protagonists, teaching them, introducing them to new people and new challenges. Though this might seem very didactic and manipulative, it becomes humorous and ironic when the adults themselves are characterized as quirky individuals. It is the four children themselves who offer each other stability. Their maturity builds through a series of encounters, as they pressure each other to open up, take risks, and stand up for themselves and each other. "They called themselves The Souls. They told Mrs. Olinski that they were The Souls long before they were a team, but she told them that they were a team as soon as they became The Souls" (1).

Parents of Color

Some of the most interesting parent characters in recent years can be found in multicultural children's literature. Many authors of color are writing fiction that incorporates parent and other family characters in integral ways. Not only do the parent characters serve as role models of experience and maturity, but they exhibit cultural pride, too, often preparing their children to face possible prejudice while lifting up their own unique heritage. This element of the family dynamic is a fairly new feature in children's novels and offers another avenue of exploration and discussion that feels fresh and real. Like Curtis's *The Watsons Go to Birmingham—1963*, the story of a lively and loving middle-class family who are also African American, many authors of color are writing family stories with multidimensional parent characters.

Baseball in April

For example, in "The Marble Champ" from Gary Soto's short story collection *Baseball in April* (1990), Lupe is a Latina girl whose strength is academics, not athletics, and she knows it. She challenges herself, however, to expand her repertoire by teaching herself how to play marbles, and how to play well. When it's time for a major tournament, her father begins to notice. "Her father looked at her mother and then back at his daughter. 'When is it, honey?' 'This Saturday. Can you come?' Her father had been planning to play racquetball with a friend Saturday, but he said he would be there. He knew his daughter thought she was no good at sports and he wanted to encourage her. He even rigged some lights in the backyard so she could practice after dark. He squatted with one knee on the ground, entranced by the sight of his daughter easily beating her brother" (93–94). She wins the tournament and is justifiably proud of herself, and she knows her family is, too.

In another story from the collection, "Growing Up," Maria and her father have a more adversarial relationship. He lectures her: " 'You have it so easy,' he continued. 'In Chihuahua, my town, we worked hard. You worked, even *los chavalos*! And you showed respect to your parents, something you haven't learned.' Here it comes, Maria thought, stories about his childhood in Mexico. She wanted to stuff her ears with wads of newspaper to keep from hearing him. She could recite his stories word-for-word. She couldn't wait until she was in college away from them" (1990, 99). She comes to miss her family when they're gone, however, and learns to appreciate their place in her life. In both stories, the fathers take an active role in their daughters' upbringing.

The Star Fisher

The mother is a pivotal character in Laurence Yep's novel *The Star Fisher* (1991). Teenage daughter Joan is trying hard to assimilate into her West Virginia community. Near the end of the novel, she walks with her mother, and they reflect on their experiences. "I tugged her along the path. Feeling ashamed for how I had acted over the pies, I promised. 'We may talk and dress and act like Americans, but in our hearts we'll always be Chinese.' 'You will if I have anything to say about it,' Mama said firmly" (146–47). Interestingly enough, it is in this Asian American novel that we encounter a model of a working mother. In Miller's recent review of children's books, she found relatively few (about eight per year) that depicted working mothers, and these were generally shown in a positive manner. The women were well adjusted and their children had positive attitudes about their mothers' working as well as good relationships with them (1994).

Habibi

Both parents are important and interesting characters in Naomi Shihab Nye's story of an Arab American family transplanted in Jerusalem and adjusting to their new home, *Habibi* (1997). The teenage protagonist is well aware of the special relationship she has with her parents and comments upon it. "'Habibi,' darling, or 'Habibti,' feminine for my darling. Poppy said it before bedtime or if they fell off their bikes—as a soothing syrup, to make them feel sweetened again. He said it as good morning or tucked in between sentences. . . . Whatever else happened, Liyana and Rafik were his darlings all day and they knew it. . . . Their mother called them 'precious'—her own English version of the word. She fed them, folded their clothes even when they could have done it themselves, and squeezed fresh orange juice instead of opening frozen cans. . . . They had a father who wrapped their mother in his arms. They had 'Habibi, be careful, Habibti, I love you,' trailing them like a long silken scarf. Liyana knew it didn't happen for everybody" (213–14). These adult characters are models of loving parents, romantic adults, and political activists. Liyana is clearly guided by their example in her evolving sense of self and of her place in the world.

These few examples of multicultural children's novels underscore the possibilities parents can play in the "coming of age" story. They ground the story in details of place and language and tradition that add richness to the relationship between parent and child and to the child's natural desire to establish him- or herself as separate from the parents.

Parents Who Are "Different"

Feeling separate or "other" is also a key element in novels that cast the parents as homosexual or disabled. Here the protagonist's struggle is not only in growing up, but in coping with societal expectations and misconceptions as well. Adult characters can play a pivotal role in these scenarios.

From the Notebooks of Melanin Sun

One recent example is *From the Notebooks of Melanin Sun* by Jacqueline Woodson (1995). The nearly fourteen-year-old protagonist, Mel, is dealing with his mother's revelation that she is a lesbian. " 'No, Mama,' I whispered, letting her pull me close. I couldn't stand having her touch me but if she wasn't holding me then who would I be? Where would I be? Alone. Almost fourteen and alone. No mother. No father. No nobody" (62). " 'Kristin's going to be around a while, so we might as well start dealing, Mel. I'm sorry if this hurts, if it's hard, but it is, and that's the jump-off point.' 'What, E. C.?' You want me to just say, 'Okay, my mama's a dyke and everything's perfect?' Mama raised her eyebrows. 'Yes. Basically, that's what I want' " (112–13).

E.C. (the mother) is an interesting role model of an effective and loving single parent who forges a strong bond with her only child. Her "coming out" creates a conflict between mother and son that rocks the relationship, but also causes them both to reevaluate their expectations in a very adult way. Mel reflects at the end of the book: "Had I written Mama off? She must have been afraid. Afraid that she'd lose me. And all the while I had been afraid, too. Of what everybody would think. And of losing her" (135). "We didn't know how any of this would end. But maybe it didn't matter. We had each other. We would always have each other" (140).

My Louisiana Sky

In contrast, *My Louisiana Sky* by Kimberley W. Holt (1998) features a girl whose parents are both mentally challenged, while she herself is not. It is a well-written and compelling story set in Louisiana in the late 1950s. Tiger Ann Parker's parents are slow—her mother due to a brain injury at six, her father simply learning disabled. They are models of love and affection, not expectation and ambition. Tiger Ann reveals, "I heard Granny's voice whisper to me: Your momma's love is simple. It flows from her like a quick, easy river. And for the first time in a long time I felt safe in my momma's arms" (188).

When Tiger Ann has an offer to move to the city with her sophisticated aunt, she struggles with the choice. "People are afraid of what's different. I guessed in some ways Momma and Daddy were like Otis and Magnolia and even that colored boy outside the drugstore. They were just too different to some folks" (164). Finally, a crisis reunites her with her parents and she sees their interdependence in a positive light. "Then Daddy drove up in the pickup, jumped out, and rushed to Momma's side. His face was wrinkled with worry, but Momma just kissed him on the lips like he was Marlon Brando. I ran up to them and joined their circle. . . . I felt my head and heart clear. I was home, and it was exactly where I wanted to be" (192). Tiger Ann knows she will bear more adult responsibilities in a home with her parents rather than her aunt, but she also recognizes what she needs from home: love and loyalty, a sense of place and self-acceptance.

These are important issues in the examination of parent roles in children's fiction. It is brave authors who are tackling these diverse perspectives and experiences.

As highly acclaimed Australian author Mem Fox states, "I care about what I write, in particular with regard to sexism, because I'm of the world, not suspended above it in a valueless, apolitical vacuum. From my point of view there's a great danger in writers being cooped up alone, cocooned from the prevailing movements of our time. . . . Writers and publishers should acknowledge society's fast-changing attitudes about women, people of color, the elderly, and minorities. Being unaware is dangerous and arrogant . . . Both genders have to be allowed to be as real in literature as they are in life" (1993, 87–88). Parent characters in recent children's novels are looking more and more like real people in real life: nurturing, neglectful, loving, lost, hardworking, hardly noticing—a mixed bag. They make for interesting reading.

Conclusion

When children read children's books they read to identify with protagonists their own age. Some authors weave adult characters into the story in a way that makes them integral to the narrative. Their interactions with the child characters help the reader to see the dynamic growth of the young hero or heroine. Many authors choose to focus the action and narration around the children themselves, even telling the story from the child's point of view. When successful, children respond with engagement and identification. "That character is just like me!" Children's responses are naturally different to adult characters, in that the child reader will not have the benefit of the author's life experience for interpreting the motives or behaviors of adult characters. The child reader is not generally inclined to respond to the parent characters with "That's just like me!" Thus the challenge is to incorporate adult characters in ways that seem real and believable to both children and adults. The temptation, of course, is to unconsciously (or even consciously) inject didactic elements into the characterization of adult characters, hoping to sneak in a message for growing up. These emerge as the weakest of literary characters, and children's responses are often negative or apathetic.

Fortunately, the best books avoid this trap. The men and women who are the parents in the best new novels sampled here are more often than ever before interesting literary characters in their own right. They may not always be the best parents or role models, but they are interesting book characters. They communicate a fascinating array of gender expectations, reflecting an increasing reality for most of America's children: a world of working parents, struggling single parents, caring adults who are surrogate parents, even peers as parents. And some of the most outstanding examples of these "meaty" grown-up characters come from authors of color who convey a complex blend of expectations for gender, culture, language, and status in thoughtful stories about growing up in diverse contexts. As adults who choose books for children, the challenge is to seek out good books for kids, no matter how good the parents in the stories are. Putting aside our own biases about gender, culture, or sexual orientation, for example, may be necessary in order to insure that young readers have access to all kinds of good stories. Perhaps we can learn from them both—the children and their stories.

References

AGEE, J. M. 1993. "Mothers and Daughters: Gender-Role Socialization in Two Newbery Award Books." *Children's Literature in Education* 24 (3): 165–83.

APSELOFF, M. F. 1992. "Abandonment: The New Realism of the Eighties." *Children's Literature in Education* 23 (2): 101–6.

FOX, M. 1993. "Men Who Weep, Boys Who Dance: The Gender Agenda Between the Lines in Children's Literature." *Language Arts* 70 (2): 84–88.

GALLO, E. M. 1997. "A Content Analysis of the Family Structure in Children's Literature for the Periods Between 1955–1970 and 1980–1995." ERIC document. ED 412556.

GOFORTH, F. 1998. *Literature and the Learner*. Belmont, CA: Wadsworth.

HARDY, H. 1999. "Defining Feminist Novels." Unpublished paper. University of Texas at Arlington.

HARRIS, J. R. 1998. *The Nurture Assumption: Why Children Turn Out the Way They Do; Parents Matter Less Than You Think and Peers Matter More*. New York: Free Press.

JACOBS, J., & M. TUNNELL, 1996. *Children's Literature, Briefly*. Columbus, OH: Merrill.

KINMAN, J. R., & D. L. HENDERSON, 1985. "An Analysis of Sexism in Newbery Medal Award Books from 1977–1984." *The Reading Teacher* 38 (9): 885–89.

KORTENHAUS, C. M., & J. DEMAREST, 1993. "Gender Role Stereotyping in Children's Literature: An Update." *Sex Roles* 28 (3&4): 219–32.

LANSKY, B., ed. 1994. *If We'd Wanted Quiet, We Would Have Raised Goldfish: Poems for Parents*. Minnetonka, MN: Meadowbrook Press.

MANN, K. 1999. "Role Models in Newbery Award Winning Books." child_lit@email.rutgers.edu. April 19.

MILLER, M. B. 1994. "We Don't Wear Aprons Anymore: An Annotated Bibliography of Working Mothers in Children's Literature." ERIC document. ED378977.

TAYLOR, A. 1996. "'Where Have All the Parents Gone?' The Place of Parents in Children's Literature." *Emergency Librarian* 24 (1): 20–22.

TOMLINSON, C., & C. LYNCH-BROWN, 1996. *Essentials of Children's Literature*. Boston: Allyn & Bacon.

TRITES, R. S. 1997. *Waking Sleeping Beauty: Feminist Voices in Children's Novels*. Iowa City, IA: University of Iowa Press.

Children's Literature

CREECH, S. 1994. *Walk Two Moons*. New York: HarperCollins.

CURTIS, C. P. 1995. *The Watsons Go to Birmingham—1963*. New York: Delacorte.

CUSHMAN, K. 1995. *The Midwife's Apprentice*. New York: Clarion.

FITZHUGH, L. 1964. *Harriet the Spy*. New York: HarperCollins.

HESSE, K. 1997. *Out of the Dust*. New York: Scholastic.

HOLT, K. W. 1998. *My Louisiana Sky*. New York: Henry Holt.

KONIGSBURG, E. L. 1996. *The View from Saturday*. New York: Atheneum.

LOWRY, L. 1989. *Number the Stars*. Boston: Houghton Mifflin.

———. 1993. *The Giver*. Boston: Houghton Mifflin.

NAYLOR, P. R. 1991. *Shiloh*. New York: Atheneum.

NYE, N. S. 1997. *Habibi*. New York: Simon & Schuster.

RYLANT, C. 1992. *Missing May*. New York: Orchard.

SACHar, L. 1998. *Holes*. New York: Farrar, Straus & Giroux.

SOTO, G. 1990. *Baseball in April*. San Diego: Harcourt Brace.

SPINELLI, J. 1990. *Maniac Magee*. New York: Little Brown.

WOODSON, J. 1995. *From the Notebooks of Melanin Sun*. New York: Blue Sky Press.

YEP, L. 1991. *The Star Fisher*. New York: Penguin Putnam.

12

Parallels, Polarities, and Intersections: Gender and Religion in Children's Books

ANN TROUSDALE

Religious values have permeated children's books from the days when children's lesson books were handwritten by monks. Following the invention of the printing press and well into the eighteenth century, literature for children tended to be heavily religious and didactic in nature. The publication in 1744 of *A Little Pretty Pocket-Book* marked a new direction; its title page announced that it was "Intended for the Instruction and Amusement of Little Master Tommy and Pretty Miss Polly . . . the Use of which will infallibly make Tommy a good Boy, and Polly a good Girl. . . ." To add an intent to amuse to the intent to instruct was a novel concept.

Following *A Little Pretty Pocket-Book*, literature for children moved away from overt pietism and didacticism, but it continued to be laden with implicit religious values, reflected in church attendance, daily prayer, and Bible reading. What it was that made Tommy a "good boy" and Polly a "good girl" was not questioned: obedience, fear of God, respect for authority, and a strong sense of duty. That there might be unstated but underlying differences in expectations for "Tommy" and "Polly" was not directly challenged until 1868, when Jo March, in Louisa May Alcott's *Little Women*, was to chafe under the restrictions placed upon females and long for the freedom and wider sphere of activity available to males.

Most children's books today altogether avoid the question of religion. In books that do address these issues, the questions have changed, as Werner and Riga (1989) have pointed out. Previously the questions that were asked were such questions as "What must I do to enter the kingdom of God?" Today the questions are more disquieting and more skeptical; the answers are more partial, less certain (2). And just as religious beliefs are being challenged in children's books, so are strictly prescribed gender roles. This chapter will address both these issues, and in particular what relations may be indicated between religion and gender.

I shall limit my discussion to books that deal specifically with the Christian tradition, first because of the limitations of space, but also because I shall take a critical look at representations of religious belief. I am neither qualified nor willing to criticize religious traditions other than my own; it is rather like criticism of one's own family. Permissible from the inside; a bit inappropriate and presumptuous when it comes from the outside. It is likely, however, that the issues that are raised can be raised across religious boundaries. Again, because of the limitations of space, the discussion will be limited in scope to works of fiction that are representative of trends that I see in the field. I have categorized these books under three headings, realizing that these are, to some extent, artificial boundaries.

Spiritual Quest

To an extent all of the protagonists in the books discussed in this chapter are on a spiritual quest of some kind. In several of the books, however, the central focus seems to be on this aspect of character development. The protagonists may find themselves on a quest almost involuntarily, a result of unexpected events or circumstances beyond their control.

The protagonist of Cynthia Rylant's *A Fine White Dust* (1986) is the one young person among the "quest" books who has a strong religious impulse. Pete, thirteen, "loved church from the start," though his "folks were never much interested" (4). Pete is drawn to Jesus. "I sat there that morning, looking at that picture of Jesus, and I liked him. I started liking him that morning and I've never stopped. I can't figure it out. Before I was ever taught heaven and hell with any understanding of it, I liked Jesus" (6). Then Preacher Man comes to town to lead a revival. Pete is infatuated with the spellbinding preacher and agrees to run away to join him in his itinerant life. When the Preacher Man misses their appointment, Pete's profound disappointment leads him into a crisis of faith. In the end, he is able to come to terms with his experience, get beyond it, and even to see the good that has come of it. Rylant seems to be saying that while one may be disillusioned by the failings of religious folk, it does not have to result in losing one's faith in God.

There are no interesting female characters in the book. Pete's major relationships are with his friend Rufus and Preacher Man. Both of Pete's parents are flat characters, and the young woman the Preacher Man runs off with is not given any dimension either. But it is in connection with her that a slight note of misogyny creeps in. Being left by the Preacher Man is bad enough, but what makes it harder for Pete is that "he left with a girl. He left with a girl and me waiting for him" (93).

In Rylant's *Missing May* (1992) the quest is communication with the dead. Summer is an orphan who had been passed from uncaring relative to uncaring relative until May and Ob took her in. It has been in May and Ob's eccentric home that Summer has come to know for the first time what being loved and wanted means. Now May has died and Ob misses her so terribly that Summer is afraid that he will give up and die to go and be with May.

Cletus, an unconventional classmate of Summer's, brings Ob a newspaper clipping about a "Spiritualist Church" whose pastor is able to communicate with the dead.

Ob, Summer, and Cletus set off on a pilgrimage, "traveling like wise men to Bethlehem," Summer says, "looking for that star in the sky that might point us to May" (56).

All four of the main characters operate on an assumption of God's presence in the world. May, Ob, and Cletus also believe in an afterlife. Indeed, Ob has already had fleeting impressions of May's spirit visiting him since her death. Despite their religious beliefs, however, May and Ob have not been churchgoers. In fact, there is an assumed but unexplained aversion to church attendance in the book. The Spiritualist Church is acceptable, however, apparently because of its unusual purpose—which happens to meet Ob's present desire. The pilgrims arrive, only to find out that the pastor has died and the church has folded since none of the members except the pastor had the ability to communicate with the dead. Despite this disappointment, Ob decides to go on living.

Missing May has been criticized for its portrayal of Summer as a "dependent, passive, fearful female," in contrast with Cletus, who is more active and resourceful (Ernst 1995, 73). It is true that Cletus functions as something of a savior for both Ob and Summer, but his resourcefulness and ability to take action seems not to result from his gender so much as from psychological dynamics that allow some children to grow up self-confident and others insecure. Summer herself recognizes how Cletus's self-assurance has developed from the kind of security he has known in the deep and stable love of his parents. Moreover, the differences between Summer and Cletus are, to a degree, counterbalanced by the relationship between May and Ob; May has been the strong, secure, and practical partner in that marriage; Ob is sweet but dependent on May, imaginative but impractical.

The world of Lois Lowry's *The Giver* (1993) is a world that denies a spiritual dimension in life. It is also devoid of color, of emotion, of imagination, of sexuality, of choice. Men's and women's roles are presented as gender neutral; people are chosen for their jobs strictly according to abilities which have little to do with their sex— except in the case of the birth mothers, who are used as breeding stock.

Jonas is chosen to be the Receiver of Memories, perhaps the most highly esteemed calling in the society. Ordinary rules are suspended for the Receiver, who, esteemed as he may be, is used rather as a scapegoat to carry memories that are denied the rest of the community. Included in the memories are experiences of love, of color and beauty, of pain, of suffering, of war—and of Christmas. The Receiver is chosen largely because he is able to "see beyond." His is a prophetic role among the elders. Jonas is being prepared to step into his role by working under the tutelage of the present Receiver, who now becomes the Giver. The transferring of memories takes place through the laying on of hands, a common religious ritual. It is an experience that takes Jonas beyond the immediate material realm into a reality that lies beyond.

There is considerable pressure for Jonas to be able to withstand the rigors of Receiving; the Giver is growing old and the last Receiver chosen proved to be unequal to the task. Her name was Rosemary. She was able to endure receiving the memories for only five weeks. Finally, after seeing a memory in which a child is taken from its parents, she asked to be Released—a euphemism for being injected with a lethal drug. Jonas, by contrast, has endured Receiving for almost a year. The Giver tells Jonas that he could not "bring [him]self to inflict physical pain" on Rosemary, though he was obliged to give her "anguish of many kinds" (142). This kind of patriarchal protectiveness, based on the odd assumption that women are not able to deal with psychological or physical pain, is also reflected in Jonas's protective impulses for his female friend Fiona; he realized that he "wouldn't want his gentle friend to suffer the way he had, taking on the memories" (139).

It appears that it was a mistake for a female to have been chosen to be the Receiver—and an aberration, despite the supposedly gender-free assignment of jobs. There seems to be an assumption that the high calling of Giver is, historically and properly, a masculine one. As the Giver explains to Jonas, "'They gave the burden [of the memories] to me. And to the previous Receiver. And the one before him.' 'And back and back and back,' Jonas said, knowing the phrase that always came" (105). This rather sexist perspective on spiritual authority leaves one wondering whether the gender-neutral assigning of work in this dystopia is not something of a blind for an underlying patriarchal worldview. Has the patriarchal tradition that has dominated the Judeo-Christian tradition so convinced us of the "natural" spiritual superiority of males? Is gender neutrality in societal roles one of the problems of this dystopia?

Louise Bradshaw's quest in Katherine Paterson's *Jacob Have I Loved* (1980) is not so much a quest for spiritual meaning as it is a quest for self-identity, which necessitates leaving behind the strict and dogmatic religion of her childhood. Louise is the elder of twin girls born to a fisherman and his wife on an island in the Chesapeake Bay. The younger twin, Caroline, almost dies at birth and is pampered by her parents through her childhood and into adolescence. She is also strikingly beautiful and talented. Louise grows up resentful of the preference she sees always being shown to Caroline. The church on the island presents a rigid and judgmental view of God. The household is further subject to a cruel and shaming use of the Bible by Louise's grandmother, a bitter and increasingly deranged woman who lives with the family.

Paterson takes the title of the book from the story in Genesis of the twins Jacob and Esau, the younger of whom "rules over" the elder—a parallel which Louise recognizes in her own life. But when she realizes that it is God who is quoted in the passage, "Jacob have I loved, but Esau have I hated" (Rom. 9:13), she interprets the passage to mean that God hates her as God hated Esau. She turns her back on God, on church, on religion.

Louise also suffers rejection because of her gender. She loves the water and would like to help her father on his fishing boat, but as a female such "men's work" is not permitted to her. Instead her father teaches her how to pole a skiff and net crabs in the shallow waters near the island. Ultimately Louise leaves the island. Her dream is to be a doctor, but she is told that, as a female, she has no chance of being admitted to medical school. Instead she becomes a nurse-midwife and takes a job in a town in a remote Appalachian valley. There she meets a man whom she subsequently marries. He wonders, in much the same way that Louise had wondered about her own mother, what had brought such a woman to such a remote place. He answers his own question: God had been preparing her all her life to come to that valley.

There Louise finds deep satisfaction both in her work and in her role as wife and mother. She achieves a comfortable distance from God. The book ends with a sense of closure on the issues that made her childhood and search for self-identity so painful. Yet there is a hint at the end of the story—if we are to give any credence to Joseph's insight about God's leading Louise to the valley—that there has been a merciful and caring God watching over her all along.

Religious and gender issues are not so much intertwined in *Jacob Have I Loved* as they are parallel, both springing from repressive patriarchal traditions. The book clearly portrays the strongly polarized roles permitted women and men in the mid-twentieth century, but it also presents women as capable of making choices and finding meaning in their lives. Men like Louise's father and her husband contribute to that process.

Conservative Religious Beliefs

Jacob Have I Love provides a nice segue into books that focus on the effects of religious beliefs. These books seem to fall at either pole of a continuum between conservative beliefs and liberal ones. At the extreme end of the conservative pole are books that deal with religious fundamentalism. Altemeyer and Hunsberger have provided a helpful definition of fundamentalism:

> the belief that there is one set of religious teachings that clearly contain the fundamental, basic, intrinsic, essential, inerrant truth about humanity and deity; that this essential truth is fundamentally opposed by forces of evil which must be vigorously fought; that this truth must be followed today according to the fundamental, unchangeable practices of the past; and that those who believe and follow these fundamental teachings have a special relationship with the deity. (cited in Hunsberger 1995, 118)

Two of the books in this category were written by Kathryn Lasky, both published in 1994. *Beyond the Burning Time* is a work of historical fiction set in Salem, Massachusetts, during the Salem witch trials. *Memoirs of a Book Bat* is a work of contemporary realistic fiction. In both books religious fundamentalism is presented as a threat to freedom of thought.

Beyond the Burning Time is told from the point of view of Mary Chase, a young girl the same age as the girls who were involved in the witch trials. The events are interpreted largely through the comments of Mary's mother, Virginia. Mary's father is dead, and her older brother Caleb is apprenticed to a ship's carpenter in Salem.

Lasky has written in her author's note that her "goal is to present young readers with a compelling story that will introduce them to the dynamics of the Salem witch trials, hopefully encouraging them to think about this fascinating but troubling time"

(267). The mass hysteria that led to the witch trials, fed by the self-aggrandizing town leaders and clergy, is chillingly presented. How a mob mentality, rooted in fear of those who are "other" or "different," can result in the accusation and conviction of innocent people rings very true. And yet the dynamics at work in the story come across, finally, as rather simplistic. It is very clear who is "right" and who is "wrong," who is "good" and who is "evil"—and these polarized positions are just the opposite of those held by the Salem villagers.

The book reflects the carefully defined gender roles of that historical period. Actually, it exaggerates them. Virginia stands out from the other women in Salem Village because she is educated and reasonable. Also she teaches her daughter to read, which, in Lasky's Puritan community, is not acceptable; only boys are taught to read. According to historical accounts both boys and girls were taught to read in Puritan communities (Holliday 1999; Smith 1934).

There is polarization in *Beyond the Burning Time*, but it tends not to be along gender lines. It occurs in contrasting the educated, intelligent, reasonable, and honest Chases, male and female, with the ignorant, superstitious, conniving women and the greedy, self-aggrandizing men of Salem Village. That Virginia emerges as the voice of reason has little to do with her gender; presumably her deceased husband would have taken the same stand. That she is a woman does, however, leave her more vulnerable to being accused herself of witchcraft. It is a curious thing that the misogyny that underlies male suspicion of women's spirituality is not so much as hinted at. In fact, there seems to be an implicit denial of a spiritual dimension in life at all, other than two ironically intended references to the magistrates themselves as the only ones who manifested the "Devil." Consequently any complexities involved in religious or spiritual matters are absent from the book. Belief in supernatural forces of evil is particularly presented as ignorant, superstitious, or born of self-righteousness. Reasonable, educated people know that there is no such thing as witches or witchcraft—something tens of thousands of practicing witches and warlocks today would be surprised to learn. The book tells a compelling story, but it does not so much encourage children to think about these events as tell them what to think about them, thus, ironically, returning to a didacticism that characterized overtly religious books of earlier centuries.

Lasky's *Memoirs of a Book Bat* also deals with the conflicts between religious fundamentalism and freedom of thought. Harper Jessup, the fifteen-year-old protagonist, is an avid reader. Her parents have come under the influence of Rev. LePage, a fundamentalist preacher of questionable sincerity, and his obedient flock. The people in this sect are mistrustful of the imagination; they organize efforts to censor books in the schools. Their mistrust of sexuality inhibits them from discussing sexuality with their children, even while they involve their very young children in picketing abortion clinics.

Harper is forced to hide her books from her family. She goes underground in many ways, trying to remain sane and true to herself while living in a household that is becoming increasingly repressive and close-minded. She finds a friend in Gray

Willette, also a "book bat." Gray introduces Harper to the works of Delores Macuccho, who writes horror stories. It turns out, in fact, that Delores Macuccho is a Christian whose books have been banned by fundamentalist groups. On the surface, then, religious beliefs and the capacity for intellect and imagination are not so polarized in *Book Bat* as in *Burning Time*. Delores Macuccho supposedly presents evidence that Christian belief and imagination can coexist in one person. Yet the way Lasky uses this fictional Christian writer is a bit troublesome. When Rev. LePage prays a long and manipulative prayer over Harper, she thinks, "I would . . . have rather been in a witches' coven in a Delores Macuccho book than here . . ." (158). Thus Lasky associates witchcraft with a laudable Christian writer, by implication giving it a stamp of Christian approval. At the same time its actual existence seems to be denied again, ascribed to the world of fantasy.

In many ways the admirable females in *Memoirs of a Book Bat* transcend conservative gender roles. Both Gray's mother and Delores Macuccho counter traditional stay-at-home prescriptions for women. Harper's grandmother is an independent free spirit. And Harper herself is a bright, curious, resourceful young woman. She longs to escape her parents' home and fantasizes about running away, but in the end she is not able to do it of her own volition. It is Gray who makes her escape possible, planning it for her and purchasing her bus ticket himself. Not only is Gray Harper's friend; he becomes her savior as well.

The third book that deals with religious fundamentalism is *Armageddon Summer* (1998) by Jane Yolen and Bruce Coville. This book has two protagonists—Marina, just turning fourteen, and Jed, about the same age. They tell the story in alternating first-person narratives.

Marina's mother and Jed's father have fallen under the influence of Rev. Beelson, who has convinced his followers that the world is about to end. He has led his flock to the top of a mountain to await Armageddon. It is from Marina and Jed's perspectives that the inconsistencies and the hypocrisies of this fundamentalist sect come into focus. Yet Yolen and Coville do not treat these issues in a simplistic way. They are seen as the result of personal disintegration, a consequence of people's so losing any sense of themselves that they desperately grasp at authority and meaning that they do not find in their own lives. When a person in such a state comes under the influence of a manipulative, ego-driven leader, the result is what occurs on that mountaintop.

Both Marina and Jed are put in the position of having to act as adults to compensate for their parents' inadequacies. Despite niggling doubts, Marina has decided to become a Believer herself. Jed, a skeptic, is able to see through the inconsistencies and hypocrisies of the group.

Marina is a strong but conflicted character. She has taken on the care of her younger siblings, her mother having abdicated those responsibilities. At times she sees through Rev. Beelson's preaching, but tries to blind herself to what she sees. It is Jed's clear-headedness that helps her regain perspective and, in the end, to separate herself from the madness around her. At the end of the story she becomes a hero, leading the children of the community out of the ultimate conflagration to safety. Her sphere of influence and strength, however, is limited to the maternal one. She achieves a degree of independence, yet it is Jed who acts as her enabler, in effect the savior of her sanity.

Liberal Religious Views

In Katherine Paterson's *Preacher's Boy* (1999) it is liberal religious views that the young protagonist struggles with. In this book gender and religion are more intricately related than in any of the foregoing books, but the gender norms under question are male norms. And in this book religion does not undergird societal gender norms but challenges them.

Robert Burns Hewitt is the ten-year-old son of a Congregationalist minister at the turn of the twentieth century. Robbie's older brother Elliot is mentally and physically handicapped. The female members of the family do not figure strongly in the story; they conform to the socially prescribed female gender roles of the day. Later in the story a spunky, more independent female is introduced, Violet Finch, who has the responsibility of caring for her vagrant, alcoholic father.

Robbie, a rough-and-tumble boy, has a hard time dealing with the townspeople's expectations of him as the "preacher's boy." But his central struggle has to do with his own love and admiration for his father and his father's failure to conform to Robbie's notions of manliness and the community's notions of a "successful" preacher. Rev. Hewitt is a pacifist. He humiliates Robbie by pulling him out of fights—even when he is fighting to defend Elliot from the taunts of other boys. He decries the United States' involvement in war, and, to Robbie's horror, actually prays for his country's "enemies." Second, Rev. Hewitt reads Darwin, which is a scandal among the townsfolk, who regard Darwin's work as coming from the Devil himself. But the final blow to Robbie's estimation of his father comes when he witnesses his father weeping in his wife's embrace. Elliot has wandered away and after a long search Rev. Hewitt has found him and brought him home. His relief is so great that he collapses, weeping, in his wife's arms. Robbie is appalled at his father's lack of manliness.

The congregation, longing for some "hellfire and damnation" preaching, calls their former preacher back for a "Revival Sunday." Robbie's spiritual conflicts come to a climax when he reflects that, if heaven is going to be populated by people like this preacher, he wants no part of it. He decides to give up trying to be a Christian at all and becomes a self-proclaimed "apeist."

Ultimately Robbie faces a moral crisis. He draws upon his father's example in making his decision and, following a "miracle" of sorts, gives up being an "apeist" and decides to "sign on as a true believer for all eternity" (156). There is a sense, as the story concludes, that Robbie will continue to negotiate his way between society's notions of manliness and the kind of integrity and compassion that mark his father's response to the Gospel.

Conclusions

When I began this research I expected to find much more pronounced patterns among these books than those that appeared. It turns out that my "conclusions" come more in the form of questions than answers—perhaps in keeping with the trends in the field of children's literature as a whole.

Most of the protagonists of these books are female, and I expected to see much stronger connections between religion and gendered expectations for girls, either subtle advocacy of a "submission theology" for females (Trousdale 1990) or angry reactions against such notions. I did not find either of those patterns, but a more conflicted one. In three of the books with a supposed "liberal" agenda—critique or rejection of conservative religious beliefs—a male functions as savior for the female protagonist. If in *Missing May* there are psychological reasons for that, in both *Book Bat* and *Armageddon Summer* the female protagonist is an otherwise "strong" female who nevertheless needs a male to rescue her. And in *The Giver* males seem to be granted both more spiritual authority and more psychological resilience than females. In Katherine Paterson's *Jacob Have I Loved*, by contrast, Louise Bradshaw fights her own battles and negotiates a satisfying life for herself despite patriarchal restrictions.

Neither did I expect to find books about religious issues in which a spiritual dimension of life is noticeably absent. Lasky tells a good story, and her two novels discussed in this chapter are about important issues, yet she seems to deny the presence of any spiritual reality.

Most surprising was the discovery that, among these books, the one with the most integral connections between religion and gender addresses male gender issues. Katherine Paterson's *Preacher's Boy* explores the often overlooked tension between the Gospel and societal expectations for males—certainly one that is healthy to address for the sake of boys who also are limited by narrow gender expectations.

There are other books that address religious or spiritual matters. Gary Paulsen's *The Island* (1988), while not about religious beliefs per se, does present an adolescent male on a type of spiritual quest. Stephanie Tolan's *Save Halloween!* (1993) presents a struggle between conservative and religious points of view regarding Halloween. *Is That You, Miss Blue?* by M. E. Kerr (1975) is a fine example of a youngster's confronting narrowness and hypocrisy amid people of liberal theological leanings. These books variously extend, complement, and qualify the conversation begun on these pages.

References

ERNST, S. B. 1995. "Gender Issues in Books for Children and Young Adults," *Battling Dragons: Issues and Controversy in Children's Literature*, Susan Lehr, ed. Portsmouth, NH: Heinemann.

HOLLIDAY, C. *Woman's Life in Colonial Days*. Mineola, NY: Dover Publications.

HUNSBERGER, B. 1995. "Religion and Prejudice: The Role of Religious Fundamentalism, Quest, and Right-Wing Authoritarianism." *Journal of Social Issues* 51 (2): 113–29.

SMITH, N. B. 1934. *History of Reading in America.* New York: Silver, Burdett and Ginn.

TROUSDALE, A. M. 1990. "A Submission Theology for Black Americans: Religion and Social Action in Prize-Winning Children's Books about the Black Experience in America." *Research in the Teaching of English* 24 (2): 117–40.

WERNER, C., & F. P. RIGA. 1989. "The Persistence of Religion in Children's Literature." *Children's Literature Association Quarterly* 14 (Spring): 2–3.

Children's Literature

ALCOTT, L. M. [1868] 1983. *Little Women.* New York: Bantam.

KERR, M. E. 1975. *Is That You, Miss Blue?* New York: HarperCollins.

LASKY, K. 1994a. *Beyond the Burning Time.* New York: Blue Sky Press.

———. 1994b. *Memoirs of a Book Bat.* San Diego: Harcourt Brace.

LOWRY, L. 1993. *The Giver.* New York: Bantam Doubleday Dell.

NEWBERY, J. [1744] 1967. A *Little Pretty Pocket-Book.* New York: Harcourt, Brace & World, Inc.

PATERSON, K. 1980. *Jacob Have I Loved.* New York: HarperCollins.

———. 1999. *Preacher's Boy.* New York: Clarion.

PAULSEN, G. 1988. *The Island.* New York: Orchard.

RYLANT, C. 1986. *A Fine White Dust.* New York: Bradbury Press.

———. 1992. *Missing May.* New York: Orchard.

TOLAN, S. S. 1993. *Save Halloween!* New York: Morrow Junior Books.

YOLEN, J., & B. Coville. 1998. *Armageddon Summer.* San Diego: Harcourt Brace.

13

Why Do Educators Need a Political Agenda on Gender?

KATHY G. SHORT

For many years, my response to suggestions that I needed a "political agenda" was a negative one—"It just wasn't my thing." I associated being political with writing letters to the editor and attending protest rallies, and while I was deeply committed to educational issues, there were other ways I acted on that commitment. Now I realize that this response was naïve, since everything I do as an educator reflects a political agenda. Silence or avoidance in response to bias and stereotypes *is* a political stance. The question I must face is whether I am willing to make that agenda a conscious one that *I* control instead of being controlled by the agendas that others impose.

There is no such thing as a politically innocent book for kids. Authors and readers bring their own life experiences and social views of the world to a book, and these shape the story that they construct through writing or reading. Whether or not the author or reader does that shaping consciously or unconsciously isn't the determining issue—reading and writing are *always* transactional experiences (Rosenblatt 1978), in which the understandings we create as we read or write are influenced by the beliefs and experiences we bring to a book and, in turn, our beliefs and experiences are changed by that transaction.

So it really does matter what kids read. While it's not the only factor in determining how children think about their gender identities, their transactions with books are influential. It also matters how we bring books and children together. Creating more gender-diverse collections in classrooms and libraries is a first step, but it isn't enough. In addition, we must find ways to challenge students to think about gender issues without imposing our perspectives onto students.

In other words, we need to teach. If teaching is always a political activity, then we need to consider what the nature of that activity will be. Gender can't simply be a special set of books or a theme unit. Sleeter and Grant (1987) argue that our goal should not be to develop multicultural education as an additive to the curriculum, but to create an education that *is* multicultural where multiculturalism is a perspective, an

186

orientation that students bring to all of their actions and thinking. An education that is multicultural in relation to gender will touch all aspects of children's lives in schools, but issues of book selection, reader preferences, and engagements for responding to and critiquing literature are particularly significant.

Selection of Literature

The authors of the chapters in this book have argued that the children's books currently being published still do not reflect diverse and equitable perspectives on gender. Clearly there are individual books that challenge gender stereotypes, and the publishing field as a whole reflects a more representative view now than in the past. However, there are still many inequities in depictions of adult females, the options available for female characters, and representative stories about boys and girls who are ethnically diverse. Given these biases, we will need to continue aggressively collecting literature that portrays females and males in nonstereotypical roles.

Given that children's books are not ideologically neutral and that the sociocultural values, beliefs, and attitudes conveyed in these books continue to reflect serious gender bias, book selection becomes a political decision-making process in which the selection of some books results in the exclusion of others. Literary quality, personal preferences, children's interests, and the curriculum remain essential criteria in book selection, but we also need explicit criteria related to gender issues. Luke, Cooke, and Luke (1986) and Jipson and Paley (1991) found that while teachers carefully select books based on personal preferences and the curriculum, their selections often reflect unconscious gender and racial bias. Selection is frequently a naïve, acritical process that perpetuates the diminishment, misrepresentation, and exclusion of the experiences of females. A political agenda on book selection is already in place and needs to be disrupted.

Heine and Inkster (1999) define a "good" gender book as one that, first of all, is high-quality literature and second, provides a positive role model for children. The criteria they developed for evaluation focuses on personal characteristics, issues, problem-solving methods, relationships, stereotypes, and underrepresented groups. Clearly no one book can ever reflect the entire range of gender images and roles, but a collection of books within a classroom, library, or unit of study should. The goal isn't to eliminate any book in which a girl cries or a woman's career is in the home, but to ensure that these are not the only books that children encounter.

Reading Preferences

One of the "truths" that serves as a basis for publishing and selection decisions is that "girls will read boys' books but boys won't read girls' books." Therefore as publishers make decisions on which manuscripts to publish, librarians decide what books to purchase on a limited budget, and teachers choose what to read aloud, it "makes sense" to choose a majority of books in which the main character is male.

Another "truth" about reading preferences is that girls prefer fiction and books about relationships while boys prefer nonfiction and books with lots of action. Since teachers and librarians almost exclusively highlight fiction, this research is typically used to encourage educators to provide more nonfiction to meet the reading interests of boys who are seen as the more reluctant readers in school contexts. Girls' lack of familiarity with nonfiction is viewed as problematic because competence in this genre has implications for social and political power (Luke and Freebody 1997). What's perplexing is that the boys' avoidance of books dealing with relationships isn't also seen as problematic in terms of social competence and self-growth.

While research has validated these "truths" about gender differences in reading preferences, these differences between the sexes are not inherent but are culturally determined behavior (Simpson 1996). Other research has pointed out that the differences between girls and boys are not greater than the differences among boys and among girls and that kindergarten and first-grade children show more flexibility in their reading choices than upper elementary students (Langerman 1990).

As educators, we find ourselves caught between the tension of providing whatever books will "hook" kids as readers and challenging them to broaden their reading. In many cases, teachers, librarians, and authors cater to students' interests based on the belief that the most important goal is to get them reading. While we do need to begin with students' interests, education should never stop at that point—our focus should be on learning and on how to help kids outgrow their current selves and understandings of the world. I believe that education is neither student-centered nor teacher-centered, but learning-centered. In an either/or choice, the teacher or the student "wins" but learning loses. We do need to support students and provide the materials that grow from their interests but never stop there.

Attempts to broaden students' reading preferences by simply providing a wider range of reading materials can lead to no change at all as students continue to choose only the books they're already comfortable with (Simpson 1996). A political agenda on reading preferences involves consciously expanding students' reading choices through invitations and demonstrations. Since read-aloud times play such a significant role in inviting students into new genres and types of books, educators need to make especially careful choices in what they read aloud to students. However, they can also influence students' reading preferences through book displays, the books used as the focus of literature discussions and guided reading groups, the authors and illustrators who are highlighted, and the book recommendations offered to students during reading conferences and informal conversations. If, for example, some students are not reading nonfiction, teachers can organize a class genre study on nonfiction that includes literature discussion groups on nonfiction, lessons that focus on strategies for reading nonfiction, and nonfiction author studies. Teachers can also integrate nonfiction into ongoing classroom studies so that nonfiction is always included as an option within book displays, text sets, read-aloud times, and literature discussion groups, no matter what the topic of study.

As we work to challenge students as readers, we also need to continue to provide the books that appeal to them. To expand reading choices does not mean that readers must abandon what they are already reading. Many educators have faced this dilemma with the horror and romance series books that are so popular with students. Banning these books only makes school seem less relevant to kids and creates an underground reading network. Another possibility is to acknowledge readers' interests but to offer other alternatives by providing series books and, at the same time, recommending high-quality literature that includes adventure or romance. The same response is pertinent to gender issues. If girls aren't reading nonfiction, we can provide nonfiction that relates to their interests. If boys aren't reading fiction, we can provide fiction that involves adventure stories with both boys and girls as main characters and then move to other fiction about relationships, first with boys as main characters and then with both males and females. Instead of opposing kids' interests, we need to act like educators and learn to both support and challenge students.

Reader Response and Critical Literacy

In reader response approaches, students are encouraged to talk and/or write about their personal connections to books. Rosenblatt's (1978) transactional theories are usually referenced as the basis for encouraging students to share "what's on their minds" as they talk with others, instead of answering lists of questions or writing book summaries. What many have forgotten, however, is that Rosenblatt considered personal response as necessary but not sufficient. She believed that readers need to share their personal connections and feelings with others in a setting where those connections are accepted as that person's experience with the book and not judged as "right" or "wrong." However, she also argued that readers need to move from sharing personal responses into critique, where they take intellectual responsibility for their views by reflecting on and analyzing their responses and by returning to the text for further critical examination (Pradl 1996).

Unfortunately, in most classrooms the teacher either retains control of the "correct" meaning of a book through teacher-directed discussions and written exercises or encourages students to talk about their personal connections but keeps the teacher's own perspectives silent. Calls for critical literacy and reading multiculturally encourage teachers to take on a political agenda and voice in these discussions. Many teachers respond negatively to this call because they see critical literacy as an attempt to impose a particular perspective onto students and to demand that students replace their opinions with the teacher's. So they choose to remain silent.

Hade (1997) points out that silence *is* a political position because educators imply through their silence that injustice, stereotypes, and inequity are acceptable. By not saying anything, educators send a message that is just as loud as if they were speaking openly in the classroom. If silence isn't an option, then our struggle is how to bring our voices into the classroom in ways that challenge but don't dictate.

Educators constantly talk about issues of choice and giving students a voice in the classroom. However, students can't make a choice for options they don't know exist or don't understand. Given the constant mass media messages students are bombarded with regarding inequity and stereotypes, it is no surprise that they do not attend to these same biases in books. A critical reading is usually not available as an option for students, so response engagements that focus only on personal response lead to the continuation and endorsement of these same stereotypes. Simpson (1996) argues that encouraging readers to identify and empathize with characters does not encourage alternative readings or the questioning of gendered practices in that text. She challenges us to educate ourselves and our students to read critically and talk about stories as *constructions* of the world and not merely as reflections of the world.

So how do teachers and librarians encourage critical literacy and reading multiculturally, but still provide space for students' voices and perspectives? One possibility is engagements that encourage students to make intertextual connections across books so that students confront more than one perspective of the world. Hade (1997) suggests having students read paired books that are in some type of opposition to each other regarding race or gender. He argues that books that appear cute, such as *The Giving Tree* (Silverstein 1964), take on new dimensions and encourage a critical reading when read alongside a book such as *Piggybook* (Browne 1986). Text sets of ten to fifteen conceptually related books that reflect diverse perspectives and genres on a particular theme or topic are another possibility (Short 1992). These text sets can be used within a literature circle or read gradually over time during the class read-aloud. Students can also be encouraged to compare books through charts, webs, and Venn diagrams. More important, as educators we can integrate intertextual connections into our talk about literature so that searching for connections across books becomes a natural part of book talk for kids.

We can also move beyond either silence or imposition by demonstrating "reading against the grain" through our talk about literature and through inviting critical conversations among students (Temple 1993). The read-aloud time is particularly significant as a time when teachers demonstrate ways of talking about books. Students constantly "read" the teacher to consider other ways of thinking and responding. If we raise issues through our own responses to books, even if students don't accept the invitation, at least they have had a demonstration of other possibilities for thinking about books. The first time I raised the issue of sexism in a discussion of Cinderella variants with second graders, they completely ignored my comment and went on talking about other issues. I didn't push my point, but I continued to make occasional comments about gender bias as we talked about other variants, and these issues gradually became part of their talk as well. I didn't ask a series of questions designed to lead the students to my point of view, but contributed my comments to the discussion through reflecting as a reader on my connections to the books.

Some educators have suggested broad questions or issues that can be raised within discussions in order to bring gender issues into the discussion without forcing the students to think in particular ways. For example, Temple (1993) suggests raising the issue of whether changing the gender of the main character will change the story.

Luke and Freebody (1997) suggest asking questions such as "Whose story is this?" "Who benefits from this story?" and "What voices are not being heard?" to invite students to interrogate the systems of meaning that operate consciously and unconsciously in text and in society.

Another issue is recognizing that talk itself is gendered. Cherland (1992) found that in unstructured literature discussions where students were not supported in knowing how to talk about books or deal with group dynamics, the groups broke down into gendered talk where girls talked about emotions and relationships and boys talked about action and plot. "Children do not freely choose to value action or to value feeling. They are led to choose on the basis of gender" (194). Evans (1996) found that these groups can go beyond gendered talk to boys harassing girls when the social context is unsafe.

While talk about action remains more highly valued in our society, the answer isn't moving everyone into talk about action but expanding the talk of all students. We also need to move beyond the stereotypes to recognize that talk about feeling and action are interdependent, not dichotomous. Eisner (1994) argues that cognition and affect are not distinct, separate processes, but are part of the same reality in human experience. In the same way, we need to consider the ways in which feeling talk is active and action talk is rooted in emotion.

Because boys' voices often dominate in these groups, it is helpful to organize groupings so that boys are in groups where girls are the majority and girls are either in all-girl groups or groups where they are not in the minority. Another possibility is having boys and girls work together as partners in engagements such as Say Something (Short and Harste 1996). These groupings can either develop competencies and place value on diversity or reinforce stereotypes. Building a sense of community among class members and establishing structures to support the talk in these groups is essential. Unless students are part of a classroom community where risk taking is encouraged and different perspectives are respected, those contexts will remain unsafe for critical conversations about books.

Conclusion

To teach is to have a political agenda. We don't have a choice about whether or not to be political. Our only real choice is whether to take control of that agenda so that we can support and challenge students as learners and as human beings. We don't need to be strident and stand on a soapbox preaching about gender to our students. They are experts at turning off adults who preach to them. However, silence is also not an alternative because it loudly communicates and perpetuates biases and inequities. Through silence, we actually restrict the options that students consider in how they think about themselves and others. Our goal is not to make decisions for students or impose our beliefs about gender onto students but to open up new possibilities in their lives.

References

Cherland, M. 1992. "Gendered Readings." *The New Advocate* 5 (3): 187–98.

Eisner, E. 1994. *Cognition and Curriculum Reconsidered.* New York: Teachers College Press.

Evans, K. 1996. "A Closer Look at Literature Discussion Groups: The Influence of Gender on Student Response and Discourse." *The New Advocate* 9 (3): 183–96.

Hade, D. 1997. "Reading Multiculturally." In *Multiethnic Literature in the K–8 Classroom*, ed. V. Harris. 233–56. Norwood, MA: Christopher-Gordon.

Heine, P., & C. Inkster. 1999. "Strong Female Characters in Recent Children's Literature." *Language Arts* 76 (5): 427–34.

Jipson, J., & N. Paley. 1991. "The Selective Tradition in Teachers' Choices of Children's Literature." *English Education* 23: 148–59.

Langerman, D. 1990. "Books & Boys: Gender Preferences and Book Selection." *School Library Journal* 36 (3): 132–36.

Luke, A., J. Cooke, & C. Luke. 1986. "The Selective Tradition in Action: Gender Bias in Student Teachers' Selections of Children's Literature." *English Education* 18: 209–18.

Luke, A., & P. Freebody. 1997. "Shaping the Social Practices of Reading." In *Constructing Critical Literacies*, ed. S. Muspratt, A. Luke, & P. Freebody, 185–225. Cresskill, NJ: Hampton Press.

Pradl, G. 1996. "Reading and Democracy." *The New Advocate* 9 (1): 9–22.

Rosenblatt, L. 1978. *The Reader, the Text and the Poem.* Carbondale, IL: Southern Illinois University Press.

Short, K. G. 1992. "Making Connections Across Literature and Life." In *Journeying: Children Responding to Literature*, ed. K. Holland, R. Hungerford, & S. Ernst, 284–301. Portsmouth, NH: Heinemann.

Short, K. G., & J. Harste with C. Burke. 1996. *Creating Classrooms for Authors and Inquirers.* Portsmouth, NH: Heinemann.

Simpson, A. 1996. "Fictions and Facts: An Investigation of the Reading Practices of Girls and Boys." *English Education* 28 (4): 268–79.

Sleeter, C., & C. Grant. 1987. "An Analysis of Multicultural Education in the United States." *Harvard Educational Review* 57: 421–44.

Temple, C. 1993. "'What if "Beauty" Had Been Ugly?' Reading Against the Grain of Gender Bias in Children's Books." *Language Arts* 70: 89–93.

Children's Literature

Browne, A. 1986. *Piggybook.* New York: Knopf.

Silverstein, S. 1964. *The Giving Tree.* New York: HarperCollins.

14

The Anomalous Female and the Ubiquitous Male

SUSAN LEHR

Modern Caricatures of Anomalous Female Children

"Many books make it clear that the strong willed, intelligent, self-managing, disobedient female heroes are anomalies. Some female heroes are extremely lonely and unhappy young women, despite their bravado" (Rudman 1995, 189). Why are these isolated female icons perpetuated in literature for children and young adults? Mem Fox's harsh observation in her author profile about the current status of many women is that women subsume their personalities under their husbands and their children and that by doing so they become unliberated, boring people who are too frightened to be interesting. The price of disobedience and free-spirited living may be too high for most women. Karen Cushman says that she writes about the girl that she was not through Birdy.

Tom Barron's plea that writers weave "bold new threads into our shared tapestry of story" is based on what he views as the debilitating and demeaning images of girls and women in contemporary culture. We must listen to the voices of women to know who they are. In his essay, he makes it clear that his search for the feminine voice in his writing has produced female characters who are not contaminated (Thorne 1993), nor are his male protagonists afraid to learn from women. He goes against the norm, however, because most female heroes are still pariahs.

In her chapter, Kathy Short states that there is no such thing as a politically innocent book for kids. She suggests that the transactions that children have with books are influential and that "consciously expanding students' reading choices through invitations and demonstrations" can challenge students' thinking. Since children's books are not ideologically neutral and can continue to reflect serious gender bias, Short concludes that book selection becomes a political decision-making process and that book selection frequently perpetuates gender and racial bias. When choosing books as part of the curriculum it becomes critical for teachers to make informed non-naïve choices with the understanding that children's books are not ideologically neutral.

Lloyd Alexander's *Gypsy Rizka* (1999) is illustrative of a recent book by a successful author in which the view of the female in society is not ideologically neutral and the character of the female protagonist is based on the symbolically tainted view of the female described by Thorne. Rizka is a young girl at the edge of puberty, when young girls are quite vulnerable psychologically and sexually. The majority of the women in the book fit the descriptions offered by Mem Fox and Masha Rudman, yet the book has been given high praise for offering children a strong female trickster tale. Gypsy Rizka has been described as "another strong heroine" by Carolyn Phelan writing a review in *Booklist* (1999). Kemie Nix writing for *Parents' Choice* (1999) hailed Rizka as a "consummate original . . . a girl fending alone in Greater Dunitsa." Kimberly Fakih in *Kirkus Reviews* (1999) refers to Rizka as a soothsayer, a matchmaker, and a healer who is quick-witted and can make grown men cluck, believe in ghosts, and stuff herring down their pants. The reviewer concludes that Alexander's power lies in his ability to use humor and the absurd to reveal truth about the human condition. The book was a 1999 Gold Award Winner. The lively, capable, cunning, intelligent, trickster heroine does everything that boys do, only better. I would suggest that these reviews are examples of naïve reading and that the book reflects troubling gender biases based on its embedded assumptions.

In the first page and a half of this fantasy, Rizka and eight characters, all male, are introduced. These men teach, blacksmith, own an inn, run a barbershop, and include the town mayor. Even Rizka's cat is a male. In the second chapter, five male characters from the town council are introduced, four of whom view Rizka as a threatening and contaminating female. Mr. Podskalny calls Rizka a "pestilential gypsy vixen." Synonyms for *vixen* include *tease*, *vamp*, *siren*, *wanton*, *seducer*. Alexander humorously pits one parentless female gypsy child against the male hierarchy of a small mythical village; Rizka remains an anomaly. Three of the females introduced in early chapters include a seamstress who is being bullied by one of the councilmen and threatened with a lawsuit, a servant who is fearful of her male employer and afraid to speak in court, and the town beauty, who is having a secret relationship with her father's archenemy. Her stunning accomplishment? She is the town beauty. The men hold the power, but the reader knows from the beginning that Rizka is obviously smarter than all of them and will win the day. The book is humorous and cleverly written, but it presents a worn cliché.

Rizka's role as a gypsy ensures her pariah status in this made-up patriarchal village. The attitude of the mayor is that Rizka contaminates his town. Interestingly, Thorne (1993) reports that this notion of women as contaminators or untouchables (what she calls pollution games) is often linked with an added stigma like being poor, overweight, or of a different ethnicity. Rizka is female, poor, and ethnically different. An embedded assumption of this tongue-in-cheek book is that there is no equality for men and women.

The women in this village represent Mem Fox's silent and subsumed wives, weak caricatures with little or no depth or dimension. A young girl, Sofiya, admires Rizka's spunk and clearly wants to be a "trickster" like her. How not? The females in this book are dismal models for children. Rizka's eventual success is assured; she does beat the men at their own twisted power games and she does find her place in the village. The fact that the book is a spoof does little to soften the male antipathy and name-calling directed at Rizka throughout most of the book.

Girls reading this book are reinforced in their perceptions that it is a man's world, but that by wits and cunning a girl might be able to become a whole person, find her place in society, and outsmart the male hierarchy. When Rizka stands up in court to defend her cat, the General spumes: "She's got no business here. A female at law? An ignorant girl! Disgraceful!" (30). Although Rizka battles hard and proves him wrong, the book's message is dismal and leaves little to celebrate in the lives of girls, because girls like Rizka are still anomalies. This fantasy world is the re-creation of a patriarchy offering no fresh visions of the potentials for males and females.

Juxtaposed against books about female anomalies are the most widely read books in the world, books chosen by children as being their favorites. These are the books that children pay millions of dollars to own. Jennifer Armstrong's essay offers some strong thoughts on series books and the notion of caricatures. Having penned approximately fifty Sweet Valley books she is in a position to know the mind of a series author. Her conjecture that series books have multiple purposes, are written by successful children's literature authors like herself, and contain positive gender images are not easily dismissed. If, however, feminist books offer girls and boys options and choices (Trites 1997), I would counter that series books continue to offer a limited palette of possibilities for girls, where beauty and brains are still at odds, where being aggressive is still linked with being a shrew or a temptress, where being attractive and getting the male is still the primary goal. Flat stereotypical characterizations and formulaic plots may give readers unlimited pleasure but they do so at some expense. They perpetuate myths of what it takes to be a successful male or female in contemporary society, and in a sense support the Cinderella version of living happily ever after. I read series books for years when I was a child, owned them all, and reread them with relish. The real question for me at the age of fifty is, how did reading all those endless romance novels, the Nancy Drew mysteries, the Cherry Ames and Sue Barton nurse stories, and the Trixie Belden series contribute to my sense of self, my vision of what a female was and is, and my view of the relationships and power structures between males and females? I wonder if I read those books resistantly as did the girls in Cherland's study. I wonder if I was encouraged to read to keep me safely tucked at home as were the girls in Cherland's study. I wonder if I resisted the notion that men were the dominant gender and that's just the way it was.

Who Are the Women in Children's Books?

"Women are rarely main characters in children's books, usually appearing incidentally as mothers, teachers, or adult foils for the plot" (Rudman 1995, 190). Rudman cites the one exception as being grandmothers, and older characters like Miss Rumphius, who is a picture book adventurer in a book bearing her name, *Miss Rumphius* (1982). Miss Rumphius is based on a real woman who traveled extensively and was much like Johnny Appleseed, in that she planted lupine seeds everywhere she went. In fact, most women in children's books do not have professional careers, nor do they receive salaries as illustrated in the chapters by Chatton and Vardell. Most, according to Rudman (1995), are housekeepers and cooks.

Chatton suggests that most picture book mothers are nurturers. She provides insight when she suggests that picture books for young children are not about parents or liberated career moms. Rather, the books take on the perspective of the young child who is most interested in having a nurturing, loving adult nearby. What doesn't work with this posit, however, is the image that Chatton says remains for young children when they refer to most active book characters as being male. Gender roles are learned at a very young age, so that by the age of three children are already socializing each other into prescribed gender roles in preschool settings. Research still supports the fact that most of the active roles and actions in books for children are held by males. Maybe background mothers merely support this embedded learning. This is a question for further research.

I'm not suggesting that all adult women in children's books must be nondomestic, high-profile lawyers and that plots should be contrived around a gender-oriented political correctness. Vera Williams offered a different perspective of working-class single parents in *A Chair for My Mother* (1982). Williams's poignant story about a family struggling to survive after an apartment fire burns all of their furnishings is illustrated in bold, expressionistic acrylic paintings depicting a weary mother who is a waitress in a diner, with no place to put up her feet at the end of the day. A bold rosy palette contrasts with deep velvety blues to support the emotional journey of this family. The tips she makes are all put in a large glass jar, savings for a new stuffed chair. The mother is a single parent supporting her mother and daughter, but somehow Williams manages to break the stereotype of poverty and gender by showing that this child living on the edge of poverty holds a special place and is loved by her family. This book focuses on the relationship between the child and her mother. The final illustrations of a rosy-flowered chair suggest that this family will do more than just survive.

What about the "bad" women in folklore, the evil witches and conniving mothers whose warty ugliness is only exceeded by their appalling acts of evil? Paul Zelinsky attempts to understand these folkloric stereotyped women in unique ways. He illustrated the mother in *Hansel and Gretel* (1984) as strong and unsympathetic, a woman who is concerned about herself. Zelinsky assumes she is a woman who takes care of her looks. He even suggests some sympathy for this mother who is faced with a terrible situation. Equally intriguing is his view of the sorceress in *Rapunzel* (1997) as the obsesive mother-figure who is losing her own youth and beauty. His illustrations do not equate evil or mental illness with physical ugliness, which is refreshing. By not equating physical ugliness with evil Zelinsky provides children with challenging images about what it means to be good or evil.

Jerry Pinkney describes his relationships with his mother, aunts, sisters, and his own children which are richly reflected in his young female characters. He depicts young Harriet Tubman, in *Minty* (Schroeder 1996), as proud and strong. Rebecca in *In for Winter, Out for Spring* (Adoff 1991) is a robust delight, active indoors and outdoors, strong and healthy and so very alive. Pinkney gives ebullient faces to girls who have healthy relationships with their fathers. His girls run, jump, fight, connive, climb trees, and cook in the kitchen. Not surprisingly, Jerry Pinkney is a family man inhabiting a world of loving connections with his own children and grandchildren. Ironically, his mothers remain in the background and are more traditional than are his girls. His young females form strong relationships with their fathers. The complex problem-solving relationship between the father and daughter in *Drylongso* (Hamilton, 1997) is a good example. Heads together, planning, calculating, deciding, both father and daughter are engaged in an active and healthy relationship. When Harriet Tubman is taken outside to learn her way to freedom in *Minty*, it is her father who is her patient and loving teacher. These depictions celebrate all that is good between fathers and daughters, but what are the mothers doing in the meantime? Where are they? Why are they so silent? I believe they are indoors waiting, waiting to hear what has happened, waiting to hear what has been decided. Implicitly that often becomes the adult woman's role.

Katherine Paterson offers insights about traditional mothers in children's literature when she talks about role models in her author profile. She does not consider herself a great role model for her own children, thinks she would not make a good character in a book, and reveals much when she writes that she was not allowed to go to seminary and become an ordained clergyperson. Paterson's novels follow the patterns Rudman describes and Paterson is well aware of those choices, saying that she writes about what she knows, yet she places high value on an emotional and intellectual range for her traditional women. Many are homemakers, while others are in a traditional female occupation as a teacher, nurse, social worker, writer, or mill worker. Paterson explores motherhood and what it means to be an adult through the eyes of her diverse characters. Ironically, Paterson's biological mothers are frequently absent, physically or emotionally. Paterson says she always offers her characters loving adults and supportive relationships. She never abandons her characters, although her adults are atypical and not always related biologically. She also puts in fully realized males who are capable of giving and receiving love.

Sylvia Vardell echoes Paterson's themes when she writes about the many 1990s book mothers who have not chosen career paths. Where are the adult women who work in laundromats, as waitresses, lawyers, doctors, store clerks, and senators? You will find them rarely in most chapter books and picture books for children. Literature for older children has little variety in terms of women's occupations as Vardell demonstrates when she examines recent Newbery winners. Her examination of these Newbery winners reflects mothers who stay at home, are dead, or are absent. Within those traditional frameworks, however, Vardell finds interesting real women who defy Mem Fox's finding of subsumed frightened status. Vardell maintains that these women are fully developed characters who are bright, articulate, and resourceful, but are still routinely homemakers. The exception is Lois Lowry's future world in *The Giver* (1993), in which emotions are tightly orchestrated and controlled; in this world Mother is a doctor, Father is a day-care worker. Ann Trousdale suggests that this world denies a spiritual dimension to life and that men's and women's roles are gender neutral, except for women who are used as breeding stock. And the one female chosen as a Giver is an aberration. In her chapter, Trousdale concludes that even in this future world there is an assumption that the "high calling of Giver is, historically and properly, a masculine one . . . males seem to be granted both more spiritual authority and more psychological resilience than females."

Since at least half of the women in the United States work outside the home and more than half of the college slots are filled by females, I find contemporary children's literature a poor reflection of reality. Can it be that the authors for children are nostalgic for a time when mothers stayed at home and nurtured their children full time? Even history doesn't support this premise. When have the majority of the world's women ever had the luxury of sitting at home with their children?

Establishing Voice for Women of Color

Patricia McKissack reminds the reader about celebrations of motherhood when she talks about her reasons for writing *Ma Dear's Apron* (1997). This book is a historical tribute to her great-grandmother, who was a laundress, sold pies, and raised three children, successfully and in poverty. Many types of mothers inhabit children's books in history, in fantasy, and in current times. McKissack gives tribute to this mother and her struggle as a working parent of color in the early 1900s.

Virginia Hamilton defines motherhood quite differently from Katherine Paterson, and builds on McKissack's view of the African American mother in *Ma Dear's Apron*. Hamilton's mothers range from the docile and frightened homemaker in *The House of Dies Drear* (1968), to the traveling entertainer in *Plain City* (1993) who loves her daughter but is frequently on the road, to the domestic worker in M.C. *Higgins the Great* (1974) who holds her family together at great cost, to the mother struggling to finish college in the Justice cycle. All of Hamilton's mothers reflect the range of constraints and opportunities afforded black women in the past four decades. The women may be absent at times, but love and support for their children are always apparent. Her range of mothers in the African American community is diverse, intelligent, loving, and resilient. The mothers often leave their children in search of employment because they are the primary breadwinners; at times they leave unemployed fathers at home; at times the children are on their own. Yet it is clear that Hamilton's moms are the suns around which the children and male characters orbit. Her characters learn to cope and they learn that they are loved.

Hamilton is quite clear that her characters don't have flaws. They simply are who they are, and her mothers are no exceptions. Hamilton wishes the propaganda about black families would end and says the key to the traditions and structure of the black community is apparent in the churches on Sunday. It is also apparent in the extended families that Hamilton writes about in her novels. This notion of motherhood in children's books is a complex issue. I think that Hamilton's mothers are book anomalies. They abound in real life but are rarely found in literature.

Debbie Reese describes how Native American women are also largely absent in books for children. Her recommended reading list is appallingly short. Reese is convincing when she writes about how European males had much to lose by accurately recording the independent status of Native women within the tribal culture. Depictions of independent working women who owned property, made decisions, selected male council members, and were able to divorce a husband were not likely to be recorded in the texts of European males who were committed to tightly controlling their women. These men had little motivation for observing and recording the anthropological complexities of Native women within tribal social structures.

Reese demonstrates how current books continue to misinterpret the roles of Native women. Rinaldi's book, *My Heart Is on the Ground: The Diary of Nannie Little Rose, a Sioux Girl* (1999), is an excellent example of the complexities and pitfalls of writing outside one's culture. Reese builds a convincing case outlining the difficulties Rinaldi has establishing a voice that resides within the Sioux culture. Katherine Paterson and Patricia McKissack both said that they were not comfortable writing outside their own cultures; both stated that they were not inclined to do so again. Reese demonstrates how Rinaldi misrepresents the characterization of Nannie and her interactions with her Sioux elders. Rinaldi apparently does not understand the complexities of male and female relationships within the Sioux culture, nor does she grasp the child's place in the tribe and the relationship between children and their elders. Children's books portraying Native women continue to be few in number, with the majority of the books being folktales, books presenting a European point of view, and, I would add, well-intentioned books that distort the Native American experience. Clearly, there is a need for more books written about Native American women and their experiences in history and in contemporary society.

Pat Mora extends this theme rather eloquently in her essay when she writes about the importance of having books by Latinos in libraries, bookstores and schools. More important, however, she hopes that her books and characters will find a place in people's hearts; that's the home she wants for her books. "I want the books to live long lives deep inside the reader."

Writing About Women on the Margin

Karen Cushman has met with much resistance to her strong medieval women because critics perceive her strong female protagonists as anachronisms who provide distorted views of history. There is a suggestion that strong, intelligent women are not realistic icons from history, because they were anomalies. Does Cushman offer realistic images of females, or is she writing about women who did not exist? In her author profile she suggests that the midwife's apprentice, Matilda and Catherine are authentic types of women who did exist in history. Strong women were burned at the stake, were considered the property of men, and could not generally own property; the laws of the patriarchy contrived to tightly control them. Assertive, intelligent women were targets of male political structures in the Europe that Cushman presents, but so were other minorities. Jews were frequently expelled from countries, forced to become baptized Christians, murdered, but that did not stop Jews from practicing their religion. Native Americans were paraded as savage oddities in European courts and were systematically murdered in North and South America, but many held their culture and values close and fought to survive genocide. Africans were captured, sold, and enslaved, but many dreamed of freedom and some were able to attain it. There is a strong folklore that suggests that dreams of freedom were always a part of the African American identity. Oppressed people in history were always unwilling victims.

Is it illogical to assume that women did not have similar dreams, coupled with strategies for maintaining a sense of self, a sense of freedom, a sense of voice, a sense of opposition? History simply does not support a totally passive view of women. Authors should not invent or reinvent history, but there is adequate primary documentation to suggest that some women did not submit willingly to male hierarchies throughout history, perhaps more than a few.

Janet Hickman writes about the complexities of reconstructing the lives of famous men in history even though their lives have been recorded in public documents. How much harder it is to find the voices and deeds of women in history, common people whose records may not have survived. The voices of children are the most difficult to find. Hickman conjectures, therefore, that the female child's voice may be the hardest to document, but that this perspective can be teased out in letters, journals, cookbooks, paintings, and photographs. Their voices are in the margins of men's texts. When Hickman wrote *Susannah* (1998), she made this female character as spirited as the times would allow, but wanted to be historically accurate by depicting what may have been true for a young female character.

Margaret Chang worries that those who advance feminist causes and wish to leave children a "better world" recoil from telling children the truth about "outmoded customs and beliefs." Serious writers try to understand and portray women who lived under other traditions as Lensey Namioka did in *Ties That Bind, Ties That Break*. Namioka's Chinese protagonist escapes rather than experiences the bound foot. Is it possible that even the authors who bridle at feminist depictions of women in history prefer to write about those who lived in the margins? As both Belinda Louie and Chang point out, Mu Lan is hardly the norm for a woman living in Imperial China, even if the folklorist manages to tell her tale with cultural accuracy. Why is it that the anomalous female in history has so much appeal?

The McKissacks write of African Americans in history, the heroes, both male and female, who became doctors, started newspapers, led dozens of men and women to freedom, started the Negro Baseball League, became the first union members for railroad porters. Sojourner Truth's passionate speeches about women's rights are documented in primary sources, a matter of public record, which the McKissacks wrote about as a biography for children. History is rich with women who risked their lives by living oppositionally; the escape for some was insanity (cf. *The Mad Woman in the Attic* by Gilbert and Gubart [1988]).

Karen Cushman passionately suggests that throughout history there have always been women who have lived on society's margins. These are the stories that she chooses to bring to children. Her feminist interpretations of history have caused quite a fuss in literary criticism because these women are the exceptions rather than the rule, but I believe that they offer readers new interpretations and insights about women's roles in history. And if one looks closely at Birdy one sees a fate rather similar to Caddie Woodlawn's or Laura Ingalls Wilder's at books' ends. All three female characters cannot ultimately escape historical constraints. It is actually the midwife's apprentice who is able to shape her own future, until medicine historically became a male domain and midwives were ultimately blocked from that career choice.

Perhaps reading about women who have lived on the historical margins can begin to show children how women in history have always had the option to live as "oppositional" conformists in order to survive, although large numbers of these non-conformists were probably stoned to death or burned at the stake, depending on the cultural conventions of the time.

Who Are the Male Protagonists in Children's Books?

Research and the authors in this book suggest collectively that boys still get the best parts in children's books. Minimally they get the most time on the *New York Times* bestseller list. Harry Potter is everyone's dream character, but Deborah Thompson wishes he could have been a girl. His friend Hermione is bright and resourceful, but it seems to me that she has so much more to prove as a gifted female child, a bit like Gypsy Rizka, but cast in a smaller role. Hermione is the bookworm. She participates in some of the action, but the center stage belongs to Harry and his male friends. Harry is the best athlete, the wittiest student, the ultimate detective, the chosen one. The fact that the first four Harry Potter books have been on the *New York Times* bestseller list beyond several hundred weeks shows the public's love of a good yarn about a feisty male wizard, punctuated by the fact that the *New York Times* created a new bestseller list exclusively for children's books. Harry has alienated the religious right with his wizardry, but has turned many nonreaders into strong advocates. Harry is capturing the hearts of male and female readers, adults and children, and will probably continue to do so through the seven books of the series. Could Harry have been as successful as a girl? I don't think so, at least not at the beginning of the twenty-first century.

Gary Paulsen most often presents strong male protagonists who are lonely survivors. Paulsen writes from his experiences as a male who learned to cope with abusive, alcoholic parents by escaping outdoors. He says: "I am a function of the wilderness." His passions for dogsledding, hunting, fishing, trapping, surviving in the wilderness, and now sailing the Pacific for the past seven years are pulsing themes in his books. Paulsen lives his books and says that books became powerful friends when he turned fourteen or fifteen. He read about all of the male characters who survived against great odds, from the classics to the pulp fictions of his day. Not surprisingly, he did not mention one book with a female protagonist. One of his messages to his readers is that no matter how bad things are it is temporary and it will pass. Would he have read Harry Potter if Harry were a girl? I don't think so. His protagonists are primarily males. Many are looking for roots, trying to find their voices, and some are literally set adrift as they search for inner peace. Paulsen's books are raw with emotion, muddling, mistakes, and yearning. His males are no less lost than their female counterparts in Paterson's books. Their struggles are real, and they have the depth to experience a range of emotions. Brian in *Hatchet* (1987) is a sniveling whiner who makes so many mistakes that the reader may be surprised when he finally survives. Paulsen's males are typically alone and must find strength through inexperience and the will to survive. But Paulsen suggests that there is no substitute for sailing your own boat across the ocean!

Male Rites of Passage in History

Male characters coming of age in historical fiction are frequently isolated, without their parents, orphaned, and struggling to assume adult roles as they become participants in wars, struggles, and political upheavals. Dan Woolsey convincingly writes about how male protagonists in current historical fiction are experiencing Arnold van Gennep's and Joseph Campbell's rites of passage as found in anthropology and the mythologies of the world. Like Paulsen with his isolated male struggling against nature, Woolsey describes stories in which emerging adolescent boys are forced toward adult roles. The arguments from contemporary commentators that modern-day males go through similar ceremonies by obtaining driver's licenses, high school diplomas, and/or draft cards, joining a gang, or attending college, however, are not convincing. Woolsey writes: "Once separated from home and the support of their families, all of these male characters engage in a time of intense experience and learning, a time of initiation whereby they gradually learn and grow into more mature ideas, actions, and attitudes." The modern male does not typically go through this separation unless he enlists in the army or goes off to attend college. The former supports this view of passage to manhood, whereas the latter is more like an extension of childhood if parents are still paying the bills. The detrimental effects of joining a gang make that type of movement into adulthood sinister and precarious as evidenced by the continued violence in high schools.

The self-discovery and self-acceptance that Woolsey describes for the male protagonists in historical fiction also means finding the balance between independence and interdependence and ultimately finding that one is not alone. Joseph Campbell writes about the male hero returning triumphantly. Part of that successful reentry involves assuming a mature role in the family and in the community, all of which can be true for both male and female characters.

Expect the Best from Girls and Boys

Elementary-age females and males have the same capacity to succeed and have similar physical development until puberty, and parents are still more influential than peers on influencing the lives and choices of their young daughters (Women's College Coalition 2000). According to the WCC the expectations and experiences from the family and community are more likely to influence their daughter's decisions than their actual abilities. If there are differing expectations based on gender there will be differences in achievement.

The Women's College Coalition (2000) reports the following about the achievement of females and males in the elementary classroom:

1. Developmentally girls talk earlier, read earlier, and count earlier.
2. In preschool girls score higher on IQ tests than their male peers.
3. Girls usually receive better grades in elementary school than boys.
4. By the fifth grade more gifted boys are identified than gifted girls.
5. Between the fifth and ninth grades girls tend to go underground with their talents and abilities.
6. Traditional teacher training has focused on boys' interests and behaviors.
7. Boys express their frustration in the classroom typically by "acting out."
8. Girls typically express their frustration by "acting in," becoming silent, withdrawn, and nonparticipative.
9. Boys are more willing to accept success and take credit for accomplishments than are girls.

Adapting the Elementary Curricula

How can teachers adapt their curricula to more fairly represent both females and males? The Women's College Coalition (2000) suggests the following:

1. Teachers can check out the textbooks that they are using to determine whether women are represented in the content that they teach. Are there women represented in history, science, the arts, literature?
2. Providing girls as well as boys with a variety of career options is essential, beginning in the elementary classroom. Literature showing a wide range of career choices and options can be included in the curriculum.

3. Females and males should be supported as they study science and math. Expectations should be high for both males and females.

4. Are children comfortable speaking in the classroom? Do boys dominate conversations? Are girls encouraged to speak up, to share their views, to be as assertive as their male counterparts?

5. Do boys get more resources and remedial support than girls?

6. Are there activities in the classroom and on the playground that are traditionally reserved based on gender? Encourage children to explore nontraditional areas of interest and be willing to praise their acts of daring and curiosity.

7. Focus on what girls do rather than how they look.

8. Resist rescuing girls or providing answers. This type of help undermines girls' confidence in their abilities.

9. Encourage nontraditional thinking and ways of solving problems. Send the message that it's OK for a girl to get dirty while working on a project or pursuing a goal. Boys do it all the time.

10. Encourage children to become media critics. Discuss portrayals of females in books, in texts, on television, in songs, in movies, in magazines. Are the images positive or negative? Explore the embedded assumptions that are present in media.

11. Words are powerful and can influence the attitudes of boys and girls in the classroom.

12. Find ways to build girls' computer and technology mastery and competence.

13. Don't assume that girls are not interested in technical things or that nonfiction will not be read and enjoyed.

14. Encourage girls to ask questions and take risks.

15. Encourage girls to speak up and speak out.

16. Encourage girls to try again. Mistakes are a part of the learning curve.

17. Encourage girls to take leadership positions.

Research has found that education is pivotal in improving the lives of women. Ninety-five percent of the college graduates report that their lives are going fairly well, compared to only three percent of the women who did not complete high school (Women's College Coalition 2000).

Bridges from Childhood

Children in modern society have never been more disconnected. Children need stories with characters to guide them through the startling, wild, and joyous experiences to places they never expected to find themselves, as Alice Mead writes. Mead also suggests that these journeys will help children develop a broad capacity for empathy. Books are places where children can grow emotionally to find their places in family and in society; however, Mead's caution that children are disconnected is based on the view that rampant consumerism has replaced bravery and sacrifice with objects to achieve personal status and self-worth. Thoughtful books can offer children alternative models of what it means to become a successful female or male.

Belinda Louie posits that although there are now more female characters in children's books, boys still are shown as powerful, independent, problem solvers, while girls are still portrayed as demure, weak, dependent, problem causers. Louie suggests that authors have a responsibility to create gender balance but cannot be expected to write with gender restrictions placed on them. Katherine Paterson's words provide insight from one of the most successful international authors for children. "When an adult writes for children, she's spanning a gap of experience and perception. A children's book is really a bridge between a child and a wider world, not only between child and author, but between other places, other times. Also a bridge from childhood to adolescence." Children need thoughtfully constructed bridges showing what it means to be male and what it means to be female. For example, the picture book biographies written by Andrea Pinkney and illustrated by her husband, Brian, provide children with powerful images of African American males who were able to triumphantly cross bridges from childhood to adolescence to adulthood. Mirroring Louie's suggestion about gender balance, I would add that the paucity of books about children of color goes beyond gender boundaries, although versatile authors like Andrea Pinkney, who also writes about African American females coming of age, are reducing that gap.

Cultural expectations for girls and boys continue to be different. Gilligan's (1990) "knotted dilemma" faced by young adolescent girls continues to place girls in the position of listening to their voices and traditions while learning to care for self and for others. The teacher's role cannot be one of silence or acquiescence, because that silence is debilitating both for young girls and for young boys.

Girls' and boys' literacy experiences can be strikingly different if they have access to a wider variety of books with active female protagonists, not sporadically, but consistently, and if there are opportunities for honest critical dialogue in a safely structured group. Girls can perceive themselves differently if teachers explicitly include female content across the curriculum. Boys' attitudes toward females can change if females are equitably represented in literature, history, science, and the arts. Children need to read critically, and as Short suggests, they need to read books as constructions of the world, not mere reflections of the world. Reading "oppositionally" or "against the grain" is one way that young girls have found their own voices in male-oriented classrooms, but it is a survival strategy that has often left girls in a gender vacuum; most won't navigate that gender gap without intervention and without strong, capable adult models. It is imperative that girls be given voice in the classroom, not as anomalies or aberrations but as equal participants. Teachers addressing gender equity will offer girls and boys options and choices within a curriculum that reflects the potentials of both sexes.

References

CAMPBELL, J. 1949. *The Hero with a Thousand Faces.* New Jersey: Princeton University Press.

CHERLAND, M. R. 1994. *Private Practices: Girls Reading Fiction and Constructing Identity.* London: Taylor & Francis.

FAKIH, K. 1999. Review of *Gypsy Rizka.* http://www.kirkusrev@kirkusreviews.com

GILLIGAN, C., N. P. LYONS, & T. J. HANMER. 1990. *Making Connections: The Relational Worlds of Adolescent Girls at Emma Willard School.* Cambridge, MA: Harvard University Press.

NIX, K. 1999. Review of *Gypsy Rizka.* http://www.parents-choice.org

PHELAN, C. 1999. Review of *Gypsy Rizka. Booklist* 95 (14): 1327

RUDMAN, M.K. 1995. *Children's Literature: An Issues Approach.* White Plains, NY: Longman.

THORNE, B. 1993. *Gender Play: Girls and Boys in School.* New Brunswick, NJ: Rutgers University Press.

TRITES, R. S. 1997. *Waking Sleeping Beauty: Feminist Voices in Children's Novels.* Iowa City: University of Iowa Press.

VAN GENNEP, A. [1908] 1960. *Les Rites de Passage,* trans. M. B. Vizedom & G. L Chafee. Introduction by S. T. Kimball. Chicago: University of Chicago Press.

WASON-ELLAM, L. 1997. "If Only I Was like Barbie." *Language Arts* 74 (6): 430–37.

Women's College Coalition Website. 2000. *Expect the Best from a Girl.* http://www.academic.org/organizations.html.

Children's Literature

ADOFF, A. 1991. *In for Winter, Out for Spring.* Illustrated by J. Pinkney. New York: Dial.

ALEXANDER, L. 1999. *Gypsy Rizka.* New York: Dutton.

COONEY, B. 1982. *Miss Rumphius.* New York: Viking Kestrel.

CUSHMAN, K. 1994. *Catherine, Called Birdy.* New York: Clarion.

———. 1995. *The Midwife's Apprentice.* New York: Clarion.

———. 2000. *Matilda Bones.* New York: Clarion.

HAMILTON, V. 1968. *The House of Dies Drear.* New York: Simon & Schuster.

———. 1974. *M. C. Higgins, the Great.* New York: Aladdin.

———. 1993. *Plain City.* New York: Scholastic.

———. 1997. *Drylongso.* Illustrated by J. Pinkney. New York: Harcourt Brace.

HICKMAN, J. 1998. *Susannah.* New York: Greenwillow.

LESSER, R. 1984. *Hansel and Gretel.* Illustrated by P. Zelinsky. New York: Dodd, Mead, and Company.

LOWRY, L. 1993. *The Giver.* Boston: Houghton Mifflin.

McKISSACK, P. 1997. *Ma Dear's Apron.* Illustrated by F. Cooper. New York: Simon & Schuster.

McKissack, P. & F. McKissack, 1992. *Sojourner Truth: Ain't I a Woman?* New York: Scholastic.

——. 1996. Rebels Against Slavery. New York: Scholastic.

Namioka, L. 1999. *Ties That Bind, Ties That Break.* New York: Delacorte.

Paulsen, G. 1987. *Hatchet.* New York: Bradbury Press.

Rinaldi, A. 1999. *My Heart Is on the Ground: The Diary of Nannie Little Rose, a Sioux Girl.* New York: Scholastic.

Rowling, J. K. 1997. *Harry Potter and the Philosopher's Stone.* London: Bloomsbury.

Schroeder, A. 1996. *Minty.* Illustrated by J. Pinkney. New York: Dial.

Williams, V. 1982. *A Chair for My Mother.* New York: Greenwillow.

Zelinsky, P. 1997. *Rapunzel.* New York: Dutton.

Resources

Echevarria, P. 2000. *For All Our Daughters: How Mentoring Helps Young Women and Girls Master the Art of Growing Up.* Worcester, MA: Chandler House Press.

New Moon Magazine and New Moon Network. 2000. New Moon: P.O. Box 3587, Duluth, MN 55803-3587 (phone: 218/728-5507) or e-mail: newmoon@newmoon.duluth.mn.us.

Take Action for Girls (TAG) Newsletter. 2000. TAG, UMWHC-TAG, Crossroads Center, 749 Simpson Street, St. Paul, MN 55014-1284 (phone: 612/644-1727) or e-mail: umwhc@ibm.net.

Bolden, T., ed. 1998. *33 Things Every Girl Should Know: Stories, Songs, Poems, and Smart Talk by 33 Extraordinary Women.* New York: Random House.

Contributors

Jennifer Armstrong has written dozens of books for children and young adults, including picture books, chapter books, nonfiction, historical novels, and easy readers. She is the recipient of numerous literary awards, including the Orbis Pictus Award, the Golden Kite, and the Boston Globe/Horn Book Award. She lives in Saratoga Springs, New York. You can find more details about her books online at www.jennifer-armstrong.com.

T. A. Barron is the author of many novels including *The Lost Years of Merlin* and *The Ancient One*, the picture book *Where Is Grandpa?*, and nature books about the Colorado wilderness. His books portray young heroes, the wonders of nature, and the power of imagination to create new worlds. Readers can visit his website at www.tabarron.com.

Margaret Chang teaches children's literature at Massachusetts College of Liberal Arts in North Adams. With her Chinese-born husband, Raymond, she has coauthored *Speaking of Chinese*, a popular introduction to the Chinese language, *In the Eye of War*, a children's novel set in Shanghai during World War II, and three picture book adaptations of Chinese folk tales.

Barbara Chatton earned a Ph.D. in children's literature from The Ohio State University in 1982. She is a professor of children's and young adult literature in the Department of Elementary and Early Childhood Education at the University of Wyoming. She has written *Using Poetry Across the Curriculum: A Whole Language Approach* (Oryx, 1993) and *Blurring the Edges: Integrated Curriculum Through Writing and Children's Literature* (with Lynne Collins, Heinemann, 1999). She is currently working on a book on literary structures.

Karen Cushman was born in Chicago. She received an M.A. in Human Behavior and another in Museum Studies and served as Assistant Director of the Museum Studies Department at John F. Kennedy University in the San Francisco Bay area before quitting to write full time. She and her husband share their Oakland, California, home with two cats and a dog. They have a daughter, Leah. Ms. Cushman has a long-standing interest in history. She says, "I grew tired of hearing about kings, princes, generals, presidents. I wanted to know what life was like for ordinary young people in other times." Her third novel was inspired by a historian's observation that 90 percent of the people who came to California during the Gold Rush were men. Ms. Cushman wondered about the other 10 percent and went on to write *The Ballad of Lucy Whipple*.

Mem Fox is the internationally known author of many bestselling, award-winning books for young children. She taught for twenty-four years in the Department of Literacy Education at Flinders University in South Australia and has since become a highly regarded international consultant in literacy. She is the recipient of prestigious Australian awards for her contributions to the cultural life of her country.

Virginia Hamilton is the award-winning author of *M. C. Higgins, the Great*, *The House of Dies Drear*, *Anthony Burns*, and *Zeely*. *Cousins* has now sold over one million copies. Her *Stories: African American Folktales, Fairy Tales, and True Tales*, introduces readers to seventeen feisty female characters in the African American tradition; this book won the 1996 Coretta Scott King Award. Ms. Hamilton lives in Ohio.

Janet Hickman teaches graduate courses in children's literature at The Ohio State University in Columbus. A coauthor of *Children's Literature in the Elementary School*, she has written widely about children's responses to literature and about books in the classroom. She is also the author of several novels for young readers, including *Jericho* (Greenwillow, 1994) and *Susannah* (Greenwillow, 1998).

Charlotte Huck is the coauthor of the well-known text *Children's Literature in the Elementary School*. She was a professor at The Ohio State University for thirty years. Her honors include The Ohio State University's Distinguished Teaching Award, The Reading Hall of Fame, NCTE's Outstanding Educator in the Language Arts, and the establishment in her name, at Ohio State, of the first endowed professorship in children's literature in the United States. She has written five books for children, including *Princess Furball*, *Toads and Diamonds*, and *The Black Bull of Norroway*, all illustrated by Anita Lobel.

Susan Lehr earned a Ph.D from The Ohio State University in 1985 and is currently a professor of children's literature and reading at Skidmore College in Saratoga Springs, New York. She is the editor of *Battling Dragons* (Heinemann, 1995) and author of *The Child's Developing Sense of Theme* (Teachers College, 1991), and numerous chapters in books about literacy and children's literature, including *Extending Charlotte's Web* and *Journeying*. She has had articles published in *The Reading Teacher*, *The New Advocate*, *Reading Research Quarterly*, *The Journal of Children's Literature*, and *The Journal of Research in Childhood Education*. Her research continues to focus on children's rich and dynamic responses to literature. She has been active in NCTE's Children's Literature Assembly as past president and chair of the Notable Children's Books in the Language Arts Committee. She is married and has two fabulous children.

Belinda Y. Louie is an associate professor at the University of Washington at Tacoma, where she teaches courses in integrated curriculum, literacy instruction, and children's literature. Her research interests focus on students' response to multicultural literature and literature instruction in content areas. She has published articles in *The Reading Teacher*, *English Journal*, and other journals.

Patricia and Fredrick McKissack are the award-winning authors of dozens of books about famous African Americans, including Sojourner Truth, Ida B. Wells, and

Booker T. Washington. They are respected for their meticulous research of African American history for books such as *Christmas in the Big House, Christmas in the Quarters* and *African American Inventors: A Proud Heritage*. Patricia is author of several well-known picture books, including *Ma Dear's Apron, Mirandy and Brother Wind,* and *Flossie and the Fox*. Her novel *A Picture of Freedom: The Diary of Clotee, a Slave Girl* is a compelling historical fiction about slavery. The McKissacks live in Missouri.

Alice Mead lives on the Maine coast with her husband. Born in 1952, she received a B.A. from Bryn Mawr College and received an M.S. in education plus a second B.A. in art. She taught art for many years in grades K–8. Since 1994, she has visited Kosovo many times. Her books include: *Crossing the Starlight Bridge, Adem's Cross,* the Junebug books, *Soldier Mom,* and, in 2001, *Girl of Kosovo*. She has two adult sons.

Pat Mora, a native of El Paso, Texas, is the author of more than fifteen children's books as well as adult poetry and nonfiction. Her memoir, *House of Houses*, reveals her interest in family, Mexican American culture, and the desert. Pat is a frequent speaker at conferences and campuses on creative writing, leadership, and multicultural education. For more information visit www.patmora.com.

Katherine Paterson is the author of more than twenty-five books, including thirteen novels for young people, and has twice won both the Newbery Medal and the National Book Award. She is the 1998 recipient of the most distinguished international award for children's literature, the Hans Christian Andersen Medal. The Patersons have four children and five grandchildren.

Andrea Davis Pinkney is the author of more than a dozen books for children, including *Duke Ellington*, which won the Caldecott Honor Medal in 1999. Her works range from picture books to young adult novels. Her novel *Silent Thunder: A Civil War Story* was named a Best Book for the Teenage by the New York Public Library. Ms. Pinkney is Executive Editor for Jump at the Sun, a Hyperion Books for Children imprint that celebrates the rich cultural diversity of African Americans. Ms. Pinkney lives in New York City with her husband, Brian Pinkney, and their two children.

Jerry Pinkney, a native of Philadelphia, studied at the Philadelphia College of Art. Jerry has been illustrating children's books since 1964, illustrating over eighty titles, and has been the recipient of four Caldecott Honor Medals, four Coretta Scott King Awards, and two Coretta Scott King Honor Awards. Jerry has had over twenty one-person retrospectives and has illustrated for a wide variety of clients, including the U.S. Postal Service, U.S. Park Service, and *National Geographic*. He lives with his wife, author Gloria Jean Pinkney, in Westchester County, New York.

Gary Paulsen is the author of over two hundred books for young people. He has also published fiction and nonfiction for adults as well as picture books created with his wife, the painter Ruth Wright Paulsen. The Paulsens live in New Mexico and on a sailboat in the Pacific Ocean. Gary is currently making preparations for a solo journey around Cape Horn.

Debbie Reese, Nambe Pueblo Indian, Ph.D., teaches and conducts research at the University of Illinois at Champaign-Urbana. The focus of her research is representations of Native Americans in children's literature. She is interested in the ways children's literature can be used to enhance understanding of social justice issues and is exploring critical race theory as a way of rethinking multicultural teacher education.

Kathy G. Short is a professor in the Department of Language, Reading and Culture at the University of Arizona and has coauthored a number of books, including *Talking About Books* (Heinemann, 1998), *Literature as a Way of Knowing* (Stenhouse, 1997), *Creating Classrooms for Authors and Inquirers* (Heinemann, 1996), and *Research and Professional Resources in Children's Literature* (IRA, 1995). She is coeditor of *Language Arts*.

Deborah L. Thompson is on the faculty at The College of New Jersey in Ewing, New Jersey. She teaches reading, education, and developmental psychology courses. Her writing and research areas include children's responses to literature, teachers' uses of multicultural literature in their daily curriculum, and the effects of whole-school reform on preservice teacher education.

Ann M. Trousdale is an associate professor at Louisiana State University in Baton Rouge. She has written on multiculturalism, gender, and religion in children's literature and is coeditor of *Give a Listen: Stories of Storytelling in School*. She is also a Master of Divinity student at Perkins School of Theology in Dallas, Texas.

Sylvia M. Vardell is associate professor at the University of Texas at Arlington where she teaches courses in children's literature. Her research has focused on literature-based teaching and is published in *Language Arts*, *English Journal*, *The Reading Teacher*, *The New Advocate*, *Young Children*, and *Horn Book*. She served on the NCTE Orbis Pictus committee.

Daniel Woolsey is a professor of children's literature, reading, and social studies education at Houghton College, Houghton, New York. A past president of the Children's Literature Assembly, he has authored articles in *Language Arts*, *Children's Literature in Education*, and *The Journal of Children's Literature*. His essays are included in *Parents, Teachers and Literacy* and *Children's Literature in the Classroom: Weaving Charlotte's Web*.

Paul Zelinsky's *Rapunzel* won the Caldecott Medal in 1998. His two other illustrated versions of the Grimms' tales, *Rumpelstiltskin* and *Hansel and Gretel*, were both Caldecott Honor Books. Known for the versatility of his style, Zelinsky's books range from the whimsical mechanical book *The Wheels on the Bus* to the folk imagery of Anne Isaac's *Swamp Angel* (also a Caldecott Honor winner). His illustrations for older children include Beverly Cleary's Newbery-winning *Dear Mr. Henshaw*, her popular *Ralph S. Mouse*, and several novels by E. Nesbit. He lives in Brooklyn with his wife and their two daughters.

Editor's Note:

The following authors and illustrators were interviewed by Susan Lehr for nine of the Author Profiles in this book: Karen Cushman, Mem Fox, Virginia Hamilton, Patricia and Fredrick McKissack, Katherine Paterson, Andrea Pinkney, Jerry Pinkney, Gary Paulsen, and Paul Zelinsky.